The Dialect of the English Gypsies

Bath Charles Smart, Henry Thomas Crofton

BIBLIOBAZAAR

THE DIALECT

OF THE

ENGLISH GYPSIES.

BY

B. C. SMART, M.D., & H. T. CROFTON.

SECOND EDITION.

REVISED AND GREATLY ENLARGED.

LONDON:

ASHER AND CO.,

13, BEDFORD STREET, COVENT GARDEN.

1875.

TO

DR. ALEXANDRE G. PASPATI,

OF CONSTANTINOPLE, AUTHOR OF

"ÉTUDES SUR LES TCHINGHIANÉS DE L'EMPIRE OTTOMAN,"

IN TOKEN OF THEIR HIGH APPRECIATION

OF HIS VALUABLE WORK,

AND IN ACKNOWLEDGMENT OF THE GREAT ASSISTANCE

THEY HAVE DERIVED THEREFROM

IN PROSECUTING KINDRED RESEARCHES,

THIS MONOGRAPH,

ON THE DIALECT OF THE ENGLISH GYPSIES,

IS WITH HIS KIND PERMISSION,

INSCRIBED BY

THE AUTHORS.

NOTE ON ERRATA.

The critical reader is particularly referred to the list of " Corrigenda " at the end of this volume, to rectify various typographical and other inaccuracies which have been inadvertently overlooked in revising the proofs.

PREFACE.

LITTLE requires to be said by way of preface to the present work, unless it be in reference to its conjoint authorship. Although termed a Second Edition, and so far as one of its authors is concerned being but an extension of his previously published researches, yet it is far from being a *réchauffé* of a prior publication. It has received such additions to its material, and undergone such changes in its arrangement, that we think it may fairly be described, in the prevalent language of the day, as having passed through a process of evolution from a lower to a higher stage of development. The infusion into the work of fresh blood, and the contact with younger enthusiasm, have stirred a somewhat stagnating interest, and awakened a zymotic activity, which have led to combined and successful efforts to obtain further facts to fill former vacancies.

From a critical point of view, a book is apt to suffer from the confusion of style and want of unity which are the almost necessary features of literary partnership. Such considerations, however, are of little moment in connection with a scientific treatise which depends for its value, not upon manner, but upon matter. There are even in questions of fact positive advantages to be gained by collaboration, and notably the increased authority which a statement derives from the corroboration of a second observer. Accordingly, we have in most instances carefully tested each other's results before adopting them as our own.

In the following pages we have endeavoured accurately to record facts as we found them, and to present them to our readers untinctured by the personal medium through which they are transmitted. Whatever be the merits or defects of our undertaking, we claim an equal share of the praise or blame which may be bestowed upon it.

BATH C. SMART.
HENRY THOMAS CROFTON.

MANCHESTER,
    June 15th, 1874.

INTRODUCTION.

———◆———

IN the year 1861 a short paper on the "Language of
the English Gypsies" was read by one of the authors
of the present work before the Ethnological Section of
the British Association, then holding its annual meeting
at Manchester. This paper was chiefly based upon a
vocabulary which was submitted to the inspection of the
members of the Section, and which the author, at that
time a very young man engaged in the study of medicine, had himself collected in the tents of various Gypsy
tribes. Subsequently this vocabulary was presented to the
London Philological Society, in conjunction with some
remarks upon Grammar, and is to be found printed in its
Transactions for the year 1863, where it is entitled "The
Dialect of the English Gypsies, by Bath C. Smart, M.D."
Since the publication of this contribution towards a fuller
knowledge of English Romanes, little has been written
on the subject in this country of any scientific preten-
sion, until the recent works of Borrow and Leland issued
from the press. Both these writers have dealt with Gypsy
topics in their own peculiar way. The picturesque man-
nerism of Mr. Borrow's well-known style, his roving experience, and evident sympathy with Bohemian life and
character, impart a charm to all his works quite inde-
pendent of their linguistic value. The latest production

of his pen is the first systematic treatise he has written on the English Gypsy dialect, which is only referred to casually in his previous publications. Whatever be the judgment passed upon his labours from a philological point of view, to him must be conceded the crown as the *facile princeps* of English Gypsy writers. His infectious enthusiasm awakens in the hearts of even staid, respectable readers a dangerous longing for the freedom of the wilds; and disposes them to admire, if not to emulate, the example of the Oxford scholar, whose romantic story Mr. Matthew Arnold has commemorated in elegant verse. He, chafing within the "studious walls" of his college, sick of the culture "which gives no bliss," at length broke through the restrictions and conventional proprieties of his stately Alma Mater, and, yielding to the "free onward impulse" of a nomadic nature,

> " One summer morn forsook
> His friends, and went to learn the Gypsy lore,
> And roamed the world with that wild brotherhood,
> And came, as most men deemed, to little good."

Mr. Leland in his work has subordinated the scientific to the popular element; and in so doing has evoked, as he probably intended, a wider interest in his subject than if he had confined his remarks within severer limits.

The books of both these authors will well repay the perusal of those interested in Gypsy literature, but still neither of them has exhausted the material to be obtained by a diligent investigator in the same field of research. Much good grain yet remains to be gathered in before the harvest be completed, and the record of this remarkable race be written in its full entirety. Here lies the *raison d'être* of our own little treatise. We believe we have new matter to place before our readers, having collected sufficient data to warrant us in attempting, what has not been done before in this country, a tolerably complete exposition of the grammatical forms and construction of the 'deepest' extant English Romanes, namely, that spoken by the oldest members of the families most renowned among the Gypsies themselves for a knowledge of their ancient tongue.

These 'fathers in Israel,' the 'jinomeskros' or pundits of their tribe, are well acquainted with words and idioms which are unfamiliar to their sons, and will be almost unintelligible to the generation which shall come after them. Little else than bare root-words are to be obtained from the modernized Gypsy of the period; but in conversing with his patriarchal sire,

> " Whose spirit is a chronicle
> Of strange and occult and forgotten things,"

we have often been rewarded by hearing archaic terms and obsolete inflexions which, like the bones and eggs of the Great Auk, or the mummified fragments of a Dodo, are the sole relics of extinct forms. These need to be eagerly listened for and carefully treasured as the broken utterances of an expiring language.

Among these conservators of ancient ways, we have met with no Gypsy anywhere who can be compared with our friend Sylvester Boswell, for purity of speech and idiomatic style. No 'posh-and-posh' mumper is he, but a genuine specimen of a fine old 'Romani chal'—a regular blue-blooded hidalgo—his father a Boswell, his mother a Herne—his pedigree unstained by base 'gaujo' admixture. We have been especially indebted to him both for his willingness to impart information and for the intelligence which has enabled him satisfactorily to elucidate several doubtful points in the language. We mention his

name here with emphasis, because he himself wishes for
some public acknowledgment of his services, and because
we have pleasure in claiming for him a 'double first' in
classical honours, as a Romanes scholar of the 'deepest'
dye. Sylvester habitually uses in his conversation what
he calls the "double (*i.e.*, inflected) words," and prides
himself on so doing. He declares that he speaks just
like his father and mother did before him, but that many
of the younger folk around him do not understand him
when he uses the old forms current in his early days.
According to him, these degenerate scions of an ancient
stock only speak the "dead (*i.e.*, uninflected) words," and
say, when at a loss for an expression, "Go to Wester,—
he speaks dictionary." He affirms that none can use the
double words like some of the Hernes and Boswells; that
most of the old-fashioned 'Romani chals' are either dead
or have left England for America or elsewhere; but that
nevertheless some few remain scattered over the country,
though even they have lost and forgotten a great deal
through constant intercourse with other Gypsies who only
speak the broken dialect. To tell the truth, Wester himself occasionally lapses from his lofty pedestal, and we
have noted from his lips examples of very dog-Romanes.
He would, however, often recover himself from these slips,
and arrest our reporting pencil in mid-career with "Stop,
don't put that down!" and, after thinking for a moment,
would tell us the same thing in 'deep' Romanes, or even
find on further reflection "in the lowest deep a deeper
still."

There are several dialects of the Anglo-Romanes.
Sylvester Boswell recounts six: 1st, that spoken by the
New Forest Gypsies, having Hampshire for its head-
quarters; 2nd, the South-Eastern, including Kent and the

neighbourhood; 3rd, the Metropolitan, that of London and its environs; 4th, the East Anglian, extending over Norfolk, Suffolk, Cambs, Lincolnshire, Northampton, and Leicestershire; 5th, that spoken in the 'Korlo-tem,' or Black Country, having Birmingham for its capital; 6th, the Northern. We do not altogether agree with this classification, but it is interesting as a Gypsy's own, and we give it for what it is worth.

In addition, there is the Kirk Yetholm or Scotch Gypsy dialect, which is very corrupt, and anything but copious. Lastly, there is the Welsh Gypsy dialect spoken by the Woods, Williamses, Joneses, etc., who have a reputation for speaking 'deep,' but who mix Romani words with 'Lavenes,' *i.e.*, the language of the Principality.

For practical purposes, the English Gypsy tongue may be conveniently considered as consisting of two great divisions, viz.,—

1st. The Common wide-spread corrupt dialect, "quod semper, quod ubique, quod ab omnibus," containing but few inflexions, and mixed to a greater or less extent with English, and conforming to the English method in the arrangement of the sentences. This is the vulgar tongue in every-day use by ordinary Gypsies.

2nd. The 'Deep' or old dialect, known only to a few aged Gypsies, which contains many inflexions and idioms; which has its own 'ordo verborum;' which closely resembles the principal Continental Gypsy dialects, *e.g.*, the German, Turkish, etc.; and which contains a minimum admixture of English words. This last, which will soon cease to exist, is *par excellence* the Gypsy language, of which the first is merely the corruption.

Dialectical variations, whether local or tribal, undoubtedly exist, and may perhaps help to explain the discrepancies to be found in the writings of the different authors who have treated on the language of the English Gypsies. We think there is now sufficient evidence to enable us to estimate the nature and extent of topographical peculiarities. The materials most available for this purpose are: 1st, Dr. Richard Bright's imperfect and scanty, but at the same time valuable, examples of the dialect of the Norwood Gypsies, published in 1818; 2nd, Colonel Harriot's very excellent vocabulary obtained from the New Forest Gypsies, published in 1830; 3rd, our own vocabulary, principally collected in the North of England, but partly in the Eastern Counties, first published in 1863; 4th, the recent work of Mr. Leland, who appears to have conducted his researches principally in and around London, which may be taken to illustrate the peculiarities of the Metropolitan district, published in 1873 ; lastly, the "Lavo-lil" of Mr. Borrow, published in 1874, who, being an old resident in Norfolk, might be regarded as the exponent of the East Anglian dialect, were it not for the intrinsic evidence in his writings that many of his words have been procured from various and wide-spread sources. A comparative examination of the data furnished by these works, and our own additional experience, strongly incline us to the opinion that mere locality has very little influence in the formation or limitation of a genuine Gypsy dialect. The 'deeper' (i.e., purer) Romanes a Gypsy speaks, irrespective of his whereabouts, the nearer he approximates to one common standard. The language of Dr. Bright's Norwood Gypsies in 1818 closely resembles that of our Lancashire Boswells in 1874.

Posh-Romanes, the corrupt broken dialect, is of course intermixed with provincialisms, and this varies in different parts of England. If an infusion of broad Yorkshire be the excipient, the resultant mixture is not the same as when the vehicle is East Anglian. Seeing that Gypsies speak English like that of the surrounding population, it must happen that in turning English colloquialisms into Romanes, they follow the prevailing idiom of the district they frequent, and thus may arise special modes of expression. Romanes melts into the shape of the mould into which it is cast; or, to change the metaphor, its stream may be said to take the course of the channel, and to become impregnated with the soil of the country, through which it flows.

Our conclusion, then, is this: that local colouring does not affect Romanes proper, but only the medium in which it is conveyed.

But if we attach little importance to territorial variation, we are inclined to admit the probability of there being tribal differences of dialect. Whether these depend on the greater or less time which has elapsed since the separation of particular tribes from their Continental brethren, or whether on original and longer-standing peculiarities, are only matters for conjecture. It is likely that the Gypsies did not invade this island in a body, but landed in successive detachments, and thus a straggling immigration may have extended over a considerable period, and in that case the latest arrivals might be expected to speak the deepest Romanes. At all events, it is now a fact that certain Gypsy families speak their own language better than others; and words and idiomatic expressions habitually used in one tent may never be heard in another.

Dr. Paspati, in his "Memoir on the Tchingianés of the Ottoman Empire," minutely discriminates between the idioms spoken respectively by the 'Sédentaires' and the 'Nomades.' The words in these two dialects, as he gives

them, are sometimes so unlike as apparently to constitute
separate branches of a common stock. In England, the
distinction between the sedentary or settled Gypsies and
their wandering brethren has not the significance which
it has in Turkey, where, especially in the Danubian provinces, there are many villages inhabited by Gypsies alone.
Kirk-Yetholm is the only place in Great Britain where
there is a Gypsy colony of any magnitude, although
'kairengros,' or house-dwellers, are to be found scattered
over the whole country. No general dialectical distinction, however, can be drawn between English Gypsies on
these grounds. Our Gypsy settlers assimilate their speech
more or less closely to that of their neighbours, according
as the rust of disuse, and the forgetful lapse of time,
gradually obliterate their primitive language, until in a
generation or two there are left but few and imperfect
traces of their original mother-tongue. In spite of all that
has been said by Mr. Simson, in his "History of the
Gypsies," our own experience supports the conclusion
that a settled life is not favourable to the preservation
of the language, but that those who use it with greater
average purity are those who travel about the most, and
have therefore greatest need for a secret language, and
more frequent opportunities for its exercise and cultiva-
tion with others of their confraternity across whom they
may come in the course of their wanderings.

Most of our Gypsies cease their roving habits during
the colder months of the year, and take up their abode in
or near our larger towns. The houses they temporarily
occupy there present the same empty appearance as is
seen in the homes of the sedentary Gypsies in the East.
The whole household will be found squatting on the floor,
and dispensing with all unaccustomed articles of furniture.

Many families also resort to towns for shelter and con-
venience during the winter, without abandoning their tent
life. These encamp in unused yards, or on waste plots
left for building purposes, for which they often pay a small
ground-rent. The Gypsies' inveterate attachment to the
tent in preference to a house is indicated, as Paspati points
out, in their very language: thus, he says, the Turkish
Gypsies have twenty words applicable to a tent and its
appurtenances, but only two referring to a house.

But the dignity of a town residence has few attractions
even for the half-domesticated 'kairengro.' The nomadic
instinct underlies his assumed character of a householder,
and reappears as certainly as the traditional Tartar on
scratching a Russian. With the first spring sunshine
comes the old longing to be off; and soon is seen, issuing
from his winter quarters, a little calvacade, tilted cart,
bag and baggage, donkeys and dogs, 'rom, romni, and
tickni chavis,' and the happy family is once more under
weigh for the open country. With dark restless eye and
coarse black hair fluttered by the fresh breeze, he slouches
along, singing as he goes, in heart, if not in precise words,

> " I loiter down by thorpe and town ;
> For any job I'm willing;
> Take here and there a dusty brown,
> And here and there a shilling."

No carpet can please him like the soft green turf, and
no curtains compare with the snow-white blossoming
hedgerow thorn. A child of Nature, he loves to repose
on the bare breast of the great mother. As the smoke
of his evening fire goes up to heaven, and the savoury
odour of roast 'hotchi-witchi' or of 'canengri' soup salutes
his nostrils, he sits in the deepening twilight drinking
in with unconscious delight all the sights and sounds

which the country affords. With his keen senses alive to
every external impression, he feels that

> " 'Tis sweet to see the evening star appear ;
>   'Tis sweet to listen as the night winds creep
>   From leaf to leaf ; "

he dreamily hears the distant bark of the prowling fox
and the melancholy hootings of the wood-owls; he marks
the shriek of the "night-wandering weasel," and the rustle
of the bushes, as some startled forest-creature plunges into
deeper coverts; or perchance the faint sounds from a se-
questered hamlet reach his ears, or the still more remote
hum of a great city. Cradled from his infancy in such
haunts as these, "places of nestling green for poets made,"
and surely for Gypsies too, no wonder if, after the fitful
fever of his town-life, he sleeps well, with the unforgotten
and dearly-loved lullabies of his childhood soothing him
to rest,—

> " Beatus ille, qui procul negotiis,
>   Ut prisca gens mortalium."

Gypsies are the Arabs of pastoral England—the Bedouins
of our commons and woodlands. In these days of material
progress and much false refinement, they present the
singular spectacle of a race in our midst who regard
with philosophic indifference the much-prized comforts of
modern civilization, and object to forego their simple life
in close contact with Nature, in order to engage in the
struggle after wealth and personal aggrandizement. These
people, be it remembered, are not the outcasts of society;
they voluntarily hold aloof from its crushing organization,
and refuse to wear the bonds it imposes. The sameness
and restraints of civil life; the routine of business and
labour; "the dull mechanic pacings to and fro;" the dim
skies, confined air, and circumscribed space of towns; the
want of freshness and natural beauty ;—these conditions of

existence are for them intolerable, and they escape from them whenever they can. As in the present so in past time, their history for centuries may be written in the words of the Psalmist: "They wandered in the wilderness in a solitary way; they found no city to dwell in."

If we extend our survey beyond mere provincial limits, and examine the English Gypsy dialect in relation to geographical variation, we find that it has been influenced by the languages of different countries in a similar way to that described as operating over district areas.

Dr. Franz Miklosich of Vienna, the well-known Slavonic scholar, has made a comparative study of the great geographical varieties of the Gypsy dialect in Europe. In the vocabulary of the Anglo-Scottish Gypsies, he finds Greek, Slavonic, Roumanian, Magyar, German, and French ingredients. He specifies thirty Slavonic and about an equal number of Greek words, which constitute the most important foreign elements in Anglo-Romanes; and concludes that the Gypsies entered England after they had sojourned among Greeks, Slaves, Magyars, Germans, and French.

But if the Anglo-Gypsies be regarded as travellers who arrived at their destination stained with the dust of the road along which their journey had lain, a special interest has since attached to them on account of their more complete insulation in this sea-girt land than elsewhere, and their long separation from the cognate tribes of the Continent. It is curious to note in Anglo-Romanes the rarity or absence of certain words which seem to be in common use in other countries; and, conversely, to find that our Gypsies have retained some words which are not met with in any other European Gypsy dialect. These will be especially referred to in a subsequent page.

b

A detailed analysis of the English Gypsy Vocabulary
shows that the number of roots is comparatively small.
But it is interesting to observe, as illustrating the natural
growth of all languages, how in these few elements resides
a potentiality which renders the language equal to express
the simple wants and ideas of a nomadic people. A
Gypsy knows how to make the best use of his limited
stock of words, and is rarely at a loss for an expression.
He is an adept at extemporary word-building. When
requisite, he compounds and coins new names and phrases
with great facility; and not in an altogether arbitrary
fashion, but according to established usage, so that the
fresh word sounds natural, and conveys a meaning to the
ears of his fellows, hearing it perhaps for the first time.
His comrades sit in judgment on the production, and after
a critical examination, "welcome the little stranger," and
commend it as 'a good lav,' or crush it in its birth, and
pronounce it to be 'not tatcho,' if it doesn't come up to
average excellence. Language is plastic in the Gypsy's
mouth, and allows itself to be easily moulded into new
forms. In this readiness of speech he presents a striking
contrast to the slowness and poverty of utterance which
characterizes the ordinary English rustic. If a Gypsy
cannot find or frame a word to express a particular sense,
he often accomplishes his end by means of a paraphrase.
However fluent a 'rokeromengro,' or conversationalist, an
outsider may be, the tongue of the alien is apt to stumble
over the blanks which abound in the language and bar
his progress, and he is forced to throw in English words
to fill up the vacuities; but a knowing old 'Romani chal'
adroitly doubles, and circumvents most such difficulties in
a periphrasis, without extraneous aid or breaking the con-
tinuity of his 'rokeropen.' In these linguistic predica-

ments the 'gaujo's' extremity is the Gypsy's opportunity. The superior power of the skilful craftsman is best shown in the way he overcomes a defect in his tools. Like Paganini playing on one string, the Gypsy elicits from his imperfect instrument notes and phrases which a 'gaujo' in vain attempts to extract.

Place an English dictionary alongside of the Gypsy vocabulary, and on comparison many of our words will be found to have no corresponding Romani ones to express their meaning; but let it not be too hastily assumed that in such a case a Gypsy is unable to obviate the deficiency. "There is always a way of saying everything in Romanes, sir," a Gypsy once remarked to us, "if you can only find it out."

For example: the Gypsy has no single word answering to the English verb 'to untie.' If he wishes to give the direction, 'Untie the string,' he says, 'Mook o dori peero,' *i.e.*, Let the string loose.

There is no word for 'nephew'; but a Gypsy expresses the relationship 'He is my nephew' by reversing the order of ideas, and saying 'Lesko koko shom,' *i.e.*, I am his uncle.

In further illustration of this usage, we append a series of questions and the Romanes answers :—

Q. How would you say you were faint?
Ans. Mandi shom naflo pensa jawin' to sooto,—*i.e.*, I am ill like going to sleep (becoming unconscious).
Q. How would you say 'I humbled myself'?
Ans. Kairdóm mi kokkero choorokonó,—*i.e.*, I made myself poor (or lowly).
Q How do you say 'Divide it'?
Ans. Del mandi posh ta too lel posh,—*i.e.*, Give me half, and do you take half.
Q. How can you ask for a spade?

Ans. Lel the kovva to chin a hev adré o poov,—*i.e.*, Get the thing
for cutting a hole in the ground (for delving).

Q. What is 'to pray to God'?

Ans. To del kooshto lavaw kater mi Doovel,—*i.e.*, To give good
words to God.

Q. What is 'to answer him'?

Ans. To del lav lesti, *i.e.*,—to give word to him.—(Comp. with
Germ. ant-worten.)

Some of the descriptive definitions which take the place
of a substantive designation are fanciful and poetical.
Stars are 'Doods adré mi Doovelesko keri,' *i.e.*, Lights in
my God's home. Thunder is 'Mi Doovelesko Godli,' *i.e.*,
My God's noise (or voice). Lightning is 'Mi Doovelesko
yog,' *i.e.*, My God's fire. A Gypsy never mentions the
name of God without prefixing 'mi,' after the manner of
the opening invocation in Our Lord's Prayer.

The Gypsy word for a dog is 'jookel,' which becomes
a generic term in constructing names for allied species
which have no proper Romani designation. The Gypsy
unwittingly adopts a strictly scientific nomenclature not
unlike the binomial system of Linnæus. Thus:—

Jookel ... ... = Canis familiaris (the dog).

Lolo-veshkeno jookel—the } = Canis vulpes (the fox).
   red wood-dog ... ... }

Boro hollomengro jookel— }
   the great rapacious (or } = Canis lupus (the wolf).
   devouring) dog ... }

Naturalists have given the jackal (Canis aureus) a specific
name referring to its colour, which is analogous to the
Gypsy term for a fox, expressing both colour and habitat.

Another instance of the Gypsy's perception of analogy
(whether scientific or culinary) may be taken from the
vegetable kingdom. The Romani word for cabbage is

'shok,' but this is also applied as a generic name to the watercress, which is called 'panengri-shok,' *i.e.*, water-cabbage or water-wort. This appellation is quite correct, seeing that cabbages and cresses are closely related botanically, both belonging to the same natural order of plants—the Cruciferæ.

It is sometimes difficult to discover from its etymology how a particular word originated. We were puzzled to understand why 'lilengro,' from 'lil,' a book, should come to mean a star, until a Gypsy suggested the reason. It has an astrological significance, and refers to the practice of fortune-tellers and nativity-casters, who profess to read the heavens, to decipher the book of fate, in which the secrets of the unknown future are written in the language of the stars.

There are a few words, of which 'beshopen' may be taken as a good sample, which are singularly appropriate translations from other languages. Our word 'sessions,' from Lat. 'sedo,' to sit, is represented in Romanes by 'beshopen,' from 'besh,' to sit. We can hardly suppose that uneducated men like Gypsies were acquainted with the primary meaning, much less the Latin derivation, of 'sessions,' and yet its analogy to 'beshopen' is so exact that it can scarcely be attributed to chance.

Again, 'policeman,' from πόλις, a city, is turned by Gipsy tongues into 'gavengro,' from 'gav,' a town. So too 'potatoes' become 'poovengries' from 'poov,' earth, which recalls to mind the German 'erdbirne,' and the French 'pomme de terre.'

The foregoing examples will suffice to convey a general notion of the Gypsies' various methods of procedure in manipulating their mother-tongue to meet the exigencies of circumstances.

Slang and cant words peculiar to each country have become incorporated in the different Gypsy dialects, sometimes probably through a want of discrimination on the part of the reporter, who hearing them used has confounded them with the genuine Gypsy tongue. Most English Gypsies distinguish with great nicety between ·Romanes and the Cant tongue, in the use of which latter the greater part of them are likewise proficient. "That's not a 'tatcho lav,'" is a frequent Gypsy comment on hearing a canting phrase imported into a conversation which is being professedly carried on in their own proper dialect. Cant words are intermixed with Gypsy in the same way, and on exactly the same principle, as ordinary or provincial English, but to nothing like the same extent. Possibly some words of this class may have inadvertently found their way into our vocabulary; but if so, they do not occur in Hotten's Slang Dictionary (London, 1864), and we leave them to be relegated to their proper place by those who may detect their real character.

Before concluding these introductory remarks, it might be expected of us to say something on the Ethnology of the Gypsy race, but to expatiate on this subject would be beyond the scope of a strictly linguistic treatise. The Gypsy language is a member of the great Aryan family, and has long ago been ascertained to be closely allied to the Sanskrit. It is for scholars better versed than ourselves in the intricacies of comparative philology to determine to which of the Indian dialects in particular the Gypsy tongue is most nearly related. Pott, Ascoli, Paspati, and others, have severally helped to solve 'the Eastern question' by tracing the homologies and affinities of the Romani vocabulary. Our first list of words, already referred to as published in the Transactions of the London

Philological Society, had the advantage of being over-looked by the Rev. George Small, for many years a resident in India, who corrected and added to the column of Oriental derivations. We have not attempted anything of the kind in the present work, which aims at being nothing more than a succinct exposition of the English dialect of the Gypsy language, as we have actually heard it spoken.

GYPSY GRAMMAR.

BIBLIOGRAPHY OF THE DIALECT.

THE presence of Gypsies in Scotland can be traced as far back as 1506, (Simson's "History of the Gypsies," p. 98,) and in England as far back as 1512 ("Notes and Queries," 1st Series, vol. xi., p. 326).* Down to 1784, various statutes and authors mention that these foreigners spoke a language of their own, but we have not been able to learn that any examples are extant of earlier date than 1780.

About the year 1783, greater interest in the race and their language seems to have been aroused in this country, partly by the repeal (23 George III., c. 51,) of the statutes, rigorous in words, but obsolete in practice, against them, and partly by the publication in that year of the well-known German work of Grellman (translated into English by Raper, 1787).

Dating from 1780, we have several collections and speci-mens of this dialect, of more or less value, which we have arranged chronologically as follows :—

1780.—A collection taken down from the mouths of Gypsies in Somersetshire, by a clergyman resident there in 1780— Edited, with notes, by W. Pinkerton, Esq., F.L.S. London, Hotten, 1865. (Advertised, but never published.)

---

* On the authority of "The Art of Juggling," etc., by S. R. ; see also Bright's Travels (*post*), pp. 537, 538, and the authorities there cited.

1784.—MARSDEN, WILLIAM—"Archæologia," vol. vii., London, 1785, pp. 382—386. Twenty-eight words, and the numerals from 1 to 10, are given, and are stated to have been collected several years before 1784.

1784.—BRYANT, JACOB—"Archæologia," vol. vii., pp. 387—391. A considerable vocabulary arranged in the alphabetical order of the English words, and also stated to have been collected several years before 1784.

1784.—"The Annual Register," p. 83, Antiquities.—Bryant's vocabulary repeated.

1784.—RICHARDSON, Capt. DAVID—"Asiatic Researches," vol. vii., p. 474.—Twenty-seven of the words are taken from Bryant's vocabulary.

1812-13.—"Christian Guardian,"—A conversation by a Clergyman with a Gypsy named Boswell. See HOYLAND (next), p. 189.

1816.—HOYLAND, JOHN—"Historical Survey of the Customs, etc., of the Gypsies,"—York. Predari mentions an edition of 1832. Page 142, Comparative vocab. of several words and numerals, apparently taken from Marsden; p. 188, Specimens of their words, procured by friends.

1818.—BRIGHT, Dr. RICHARD—"Travels from Vienna through Hungary,"—Edinburgh. The Appendix (p. lxxix) contains a comparative vocab. of the English, Spanish, and Hungarian Gypsy dialects, as well as sentences in each of those dialects. A very valuable collection.

1819.—IRVINE, ——,—"On the Similitude between the Gypsy and Hindi Languages."—Transactions of the Literary Society of Bombay, 1819.

1819.—HARRIOT, Col. JOHN STAPLES—"Observations on the Oriental Origin of the Romnichal."—Roy. Asiatic Soc. of Great Britain, vol. ii., London, 1830, pp. 518—588, read 5th Dec., 1829, and 2nd Jan., 1830; Predari, pp. 213, 258, says that the paper was read before the Society of Calcutta, 12th April, 1822; Harriot, p. 520, says he collected his vocabulary in the north of Hampshire, 1819-1820. The vocab. is arranged in the alphabetical order of the English words, and is an important addition to all preceding it.

1832.—CRABB, JAMES—"The Gypsies' Advocate,"—London, Nisbet Westley. 3rd edit., sm. 8vo, price 3s. 6d. Page 14, Vocab. of 26 words besides numerals 1—10, and 20, taken from Grellman, Hoyland, and Richardson ; p. 27, *pizharris*, in debt ; *artmee devillesty*, God bless you.

1835.—JAMES, G. P. R.—"The Gipsy," 3 vols., London. Vol. 1, p. 36, *gazo*, peasant ; *raye*, gentleman.

1836.—ROBERTS, SAMUEL—"The Gypsies, their Origin, etc." London. 4th edit. (1839), 12mo ; 5th edit. (1842), post 8vo, Longman, price 10s. 6d.; pp. 97—100. List of words collected by his daughters from Clara Hearn.

1841.—BORROW, GEORGE—"The Zincali, or Gypsies in Spain," vol. i., pp. 16—28, gives an account of the English Gypsies. The vocabulary (vol. ii.) gives one or two words ; and the Appendix to vol. ii. of *subsequent* editions (1843, 1846, 1861,) gives a short dialogue with a Gypsy, and translation of the Lord's Prayer and Creed, in English Romanes, varying almost with each edition.

1841.—BAIRD, Rev. JOHN—"Report to the Scottish Church Society," printed 1841 ; collected 1817—1831.

1844.—POTT, Dr. A. F.—"Die Zigeuner in Europa und Asien," 2 vols. Halle. This profoundly learned work incorporates almost all the foregoing vocabularies.

1851.—BORROW, GEORGE—"Lavengro," etc., 3 vols., containing many words scattered throughout.

1851.—"Illustrated London News,"—Gypsy Experiences by a Roumany Rei : 13th Dec., pp. 655, 715, 777.

1856.—"Illustrated London News,"—"The Roumany-chi, or Gypsies ;" 20th Sept., p. 304 ; apparently by the same writer as the last. This article was reprinted separately at Bath, in 1870, by J. and J. Keene.

1857.—BORROW, GEORGE—"Romany Rye," a Sequel to "Lavengro," 2 vols., containing many words scattered throughout.

1858.—NORWOOD, Rev. T. W.—"On the Race and Language of the Gypsies"—Report of the British Association, etc., Leeds, p. 195 of Transactions of the Sections.

1860.—Smart, Dr. B. C.—" The Dialect of the English Gypsies."
Published for the English Philological Society, by Asher and
Co., Berlin, 1863, in the Society's Transactions, and separately. The vocab. was begun in 1860, and some remarks on
the dialect were printed in the British Association Transactions, 1861, and Trans. Ethnolog. Soc., vol. ii.

1862.—Borrow, George—" Wild Wales," 3 vols. ; chapter xcviii.
contains a conversation with an English Gypsy. From this
and Mr. Borrow's preceding works, nearly 300 words (including
varieties of spelling) may be collected. From passages in
chapters xiv. and xcviii., and on p. 233 of his " Lavo-lil,"
(post), it would seem that the author considered Wales without
a Gypsy inhabitant, which is by no means the case.

1865.—Simson, Walter—" A History of the Gypsies, with speci-
mens of their Language,"—London, Sampson, Lowe, and Co.
From a passage on p. 466, the work seems to have been in
MS. before 1840. Most of the Gypsy words were republished
in " The Adventures of Bampfylde Moore Carew," London,
W. Tegg, 1873; and several of them are quoted by Dr.
Paspati.

1872.—" The Times " (newspaper), Oct. 11—17, 2nd column, p. 1,
an advertisement in English Romanes, copied as a curiosity
into other papers; translated in " Notes and Queries," 4th
Series, vol. xi., p. 462, also in " Leland's English Gypsies,"
p. 184.

1873.—" Zelda's Fortune,"—" Cornhill Magazine," vols. 27, 28, 29.
There are several words and sentences used in the course
of the tale, the earlier ones resembling Hungarian rather
than English Gypsy, but of these *questo*, p. 127, resembles
Marsden's *questo*, good = *kooshto*.

1873.—Smith, Hubert—" Tent-life with English Gypsies in
Norway,"—London, H. S. King and Co., price 21s. Several
words, etc., are scattered throughout, and on pp. 527—529
is a comparative vocab. of the English dialect, and that of
Norway as given by Sundt.

1873.—Miklosich, F.—" Uber die Mundarten und die Wanderungen der Zigeuner Europas," iii., Wien, Gerold's Sohn, con-

tains remarks on this dialect grounded on some of the fore-going works.

1873.—LELAND, CHARLES G.—" The English Gipsies and their Language." London, Trübner and Co., price 7*s*. 6*d*. Very valuable, both as respects vocab., and a knowledge of customs, etc.

1874.—BORROW, GEORGE—" Romano Lavo-lil, Wordbook of the Romany, or English Gypsy Language,"—London, Murray, price 10*s*. 6*d*., pp. 11—101 ; vocab. not, however, exhaustive of the words used in this, or of those used in his other works.

1874.—" The Athenæum " (newspaper), No. 2426, April 25—A Review of Borrow's " Romano Lavo-lil."

1874.—" The Academy" (newspaper), No. 101 (new issue), June 13 —A Review of Miklosich, Leland, and Borrow's " Lavo-lil."

In addition to the above, may be added " Notes and Queries," 2nd Series, vol. xi., p. 129 ; p. 196, on Scotch Gypsies ; 4th Series, vol. xi., p. 443 ; p. 462, and elsewhere.

ETYMOLOGY, ETC.

As far as possible, to each root-word is annexed the corre-sponding one in the Turkish, or Asiatic, Gypsy dialects, as given by Dr. Paspati in his "Études sur les Tchinghianés," published in French, at Constantinople, in 1870. Where Dr. Paspati has afforded no comparison, we have had recourse to the German Gypsy dialect as given by Dr. Liebich in his " Die Zigeuner," etc., published in German, at Leipzig, in 1863. Further than this, we have in few instances deemed it advisable to attempt anything that can be more strictly called Etymology, as we could add nothing original in this respect to the labours of Dr. Pott, Dr. Paspati, and Sr. Ascoli, who have appended to almost every word the oriental word or words akin to it.

The comparisons thus made will, it is hoped, add an additional interest to our work, as showing the resemblance and difference in the two dialects, Turkish and English, after so long a separation as four centuries. We say four centuries, for Mr. Borrow in his "Lavo-lil," p. 212, asserts that the Gypsies first made their appearance in England in 1480, though we are not aware of his authority.

To those who, like M. Bataillard ("Les derniers travaux relatifs aux Bohémiens dans l'Europe orientale," Paris, 1872, pp. 47—53), lean to the theory of a long residence of the race in Turkey prior to a westerly drifting of these nomads, this comparison has, we venture to think, much to commend itself.

ORTHOGRAPHY.

To assist the pronunciation, we have endeavoured to adhere to a phonetic orthography, based on the Glossic system invented by Mr. A. J. Ellis, and used by the English Dialect Society and others.

In it the vowel sounds are expressed and pronounced as follows :—

Ai ·	as in	*Bait.*	*i*	as in	*Knit.*
a	„	*Gnat.*	*ŏ*	„	*Coal.*
aa	„	*Baa.*	*o*	„	*Not.*
au, aw,	as in	*Caul, caw.*	*eu*	„	*Feud.*
Final *é,*	as *ai* in	*Bait.*	*u*	„	*Nut.*
ee	as in	*Beet.*	*oo*	„	*Cool,* or *foot.*
e	„	*Net.*	*oi*	„	*Foil.*
ei	„	*Height.*	*ou*	„	*Foul.*

It must be borne in mind, however, that these sounds, and more especially the *u* sounds, vary according to the county or district of which the individual is a native.

As to the consonants, the majority are pronounced as in English. We have discarded altogether the ambiguous *c*, and substituted *k* or *s*, according as *c* would take the hard or soft sound. Throughout the book

Ch is to be pronounced as in *Church*.
Sh „ „ „ *Shirt*.
G, gh „ „ „ *Go* (never soft, as in *gin*).
F „ „ „ *For* (never dull, as in *of*).
Dj, dg „ „ „ *Fudge*.

Besides these, there is a deep guttural sound, which we have represented by χ, the sound being nearly that of *ch* in German.

ACCENT.

In the Turkish dialect, the accent is usually on the last syllable; but if the word is inflected, or liable to inflection, the accent is placed on the first syllable of the inflection, *e.g.*,

Bar-ó, great. Gen. *bar-éskoro;* pl. *bar-é.*
Besháva, I sit; *besh-éla*, He sits.

Relics of this system are found in the old dialect of this country, *e.g.*,

Bauró, great; pl., *bauré.*
Besh-óva, I sit; *besh-éla*, He sits.

Words too ending in *-éngro, -éskro*, (elsewhere shown to be inflections,) invariably take the accent on the first syllable of those terminations, in both the old and new dialects.

In the new dialect, dissyllables and trisyllables take an accent on the first syllable, and words of four or five syllables take an accent on the first and third, *e.g.*,

Baúro, great	*Béshto*, saddle
Béngalo, diabolic	*Brísheno*, rainy

Béroméngro, **sailor**   *Sóvlohóloben*, oath
Bóshoméngro, fiddler   *Tásserméngri*, frying-pan

The above are only general rules. There are several exceptions.

LETTER CHANGES, ELISIONS, ETC.

Interchanges of certain letters, initial or otherwise, frequently occur in Gypsy words, but always according to established rules, and this must be remembered in tracing their derivations.

Interchanges take place between the following letters: K and H, K and P, K and T, K and F, K and χ, χ and F, F and S, Sh and Dj, Sh and Ch, J and Y, D and B, B and V, V and W, L M N and R.

Examples.

K and H.

Kol, Hol, eat.   *Kátcher, Hótcher,* burn.

K and P.

Chúkni, Chúpni, whip.

K and T.

Kúshni, Túshni, basket.   *Kam, Tam,* sun.
Koóshko, Koóshto, good.

K and F.

Járifa, Járika, apron.

K and χ.

Yárduka, Jorjóχa, apron.

χ and F.

Jorjóχa, Jorjófa, apron.

F and S.

Wáfedo, Wásedo, bad.   *Násfelo, Náfelo,* ill.

Sh and Dj.

Kaish, Kaidj, silk.   ***Minsh, Mindj,*** pudendum muliebre.

Sh and Ch.
Choom, Shoon, moon.　　*Chárdoka, Shárdoka*, apron.

J and Y.
Joókel, Yákel, dog.　　*Jorjóχa, Yárduχa*, apron.

D and B.
Loódni, Loóbni, harlot.

B and V.
Bókocho, Vákasho, lamb.　　*Lívena, Líbena*, beer.

V and W.
Várdo, Wárdo, cart.　　*Vast, Wast*, hand.

L, M, N, R.
Shírilo, Shílino, cold.　　*Dínilo, Dínvero*, fool.
Soom, Soon, smell.　　*Vániso, Váriso*, any.

The English Gypsies are in the frequent habit of confounding the liquids; and Mr. Borrow has remarked the same of the Spanish Gitanos ("Zincali," vol. ii., p. 4, preceding vocab.) According to Gilchrist ("Hind. Dict." vol. ii., 1790, p. 489), the natives of Hindustan so confuse the use of the liquids L, N, and R, that it is often difficult to say which of those letters ought to be adopted in spelling.

Besides this interchange of consonants, the Gypsies occasionally transpose them.

Examples.
Sóvlohol, Súlverkon, to swear.
Dooméksno, for *Doomésk'no*, broken-backed.
Sheréksno, for *Sherésk'no*, lawyer.

The dialect is also remarkable for its systematic elision of the letter *n* in certain words.

Examples.

English.	Turkish.	Meaning.
Adré	*André*	Into
Aglál	*Anglál*	Before

English.	Turkish.	Meaning.
Haúro	*K'hanró*	Sword
Máuro	*Manró*	Bread
Márikli	*Manriklı*	Cake
Mcéro	*Minró*	My
Teéro	*Tinró*	Thy
Yóra	*Anró*	Egg
etc.	etc.	etc.

Of the full forms, Mr. Borrow, in his " Lavo-lil," supplies us with *ando, anglo, manro, manreckly,* etc.

Similar instances of this elision could be adduced in other dialects, but, so far as we are aware, not to the same extent as in this.

ARTICLE.

DEFINITE.

Dr. Paspati ("Tchinghianés," 1870, p. 39) says the Turkish Gypsies have borrowed their article from the Greeks, and the Asiatic Gypsies have none; and further states that among the wandering tribes in Turkey the use of the article is less frequent than among the Christian (settled) Gypsies. Amongst the Turkish Gypsies, the article is—masculine *o*, feminine *i* in the nominative, and *e* masculine and feminine in all other cases, of the singular; and *o* masculine and feminine in the nominative, and *e* masculine and feminine in all other cases, of the plural.

The English Gypsies have a masculine definite article *o*, and feminine *i*, but now hardly ever employ any other than the English word *the*, which they, like other foreigners, often pronounce *de*. Their own article, however, is preserved in certain phrases which have been retained in common use, *e.g.,*

Paúdel i padni, Over the water (transportation).

Dr. Bright, in his "Travels in Hungary," Edinburgh, 1818, Appendix, affords the following examples, obtained from a family of Gypsies residing at Norwood :—

Pre si o kam, The sun is up.
Le o gri, Catch the horse.
O tascho wast, The right hand.
Dalo o giv, Gives the snow (it snows).

In some families, from analogy to English, *o* is indeclinable, being used wherever *the* occurs, and irrespective of gender or case.

The Definite article is frequently omitted altogether, *e.g.,*

Boshéla jóokel, Barks (the) dog, for The dog barks.
Rίserέla gάiro, Trembles (the) man, for The man trembles.
Choom see oprέ, (The) Moon is up.

INDEFINITE.

The English Gypsies invariably use the English word *a* for the indefinite article, and say, *e.g., Mάndi diks a gάiro,* not *Mandi diks yek gairo,* which would mean I see one man. In the old.dialect this article is very frequently omitted entirely. Example, *Dikόva gάiro,* I see a man.

NOUN.

GENDER.

Some of the nouns have a masculine termination in *-o,* and a feminine in *-i.* There are also masculine nouns and feminine nouns which end in a variety of consonants and vowels, but usually the gender is determined by that of the corresponding English word, *e.g.,*

Masculines in *-o,* with corresponding feminines in *-i.*

Chάvo, boy	*Cha(v)i, Chei,* girl
Chίriklo, bird	*Chίrikli,* bird

Gaíro, man
Gaújo, male Gentile
Ptrino, male sweetheart
Ráklo, boy
        etc.

Gdiri, woman
Gaúji, female Gentile
Ptrini, female sweetheart
Ráklí, girl
        etc.

Masculines in -o.

Bairéngro, sailor
Baréngro, stallion
Bókroméngro, shepherd
Boóko, liver
Góno, sack
Kóko, uncle
        etc.

Feminines in -i.

Beébi, aunt
Bóoti, work
Chóori, knife
Kánni, hen
Kekávvi, kettle
Múmbli, candle
        etc.

Masculine.

Chóovikón, wizard
Grei, horse
Grŏv, bull
Joókel, dog
Krális, king
Manoósh, man
Rom, husband
        etc.

Feminine.

Chóofihóni, witch
Grásni, mare
Grŏvˊni, cow
Joókli, bitch
Kralíssi, queen
Manoóshni, woman
Rómni, wife
        etc.

Irregular.

Dad, father
Pal, brother
Rei, gentleman

Dei, mother
Pen, sister
Ráuni, lady.

DECLENSION.

To illustrate the declension, examples, from pp. 50, 51, of Dr. Paspati's " Tchinghianés," are subjoined.

SINGULAR.

Nom.	*O raklŏ*, the boy	*I raklí*, the girl	*Rái*, lord
Gen.	*e rakléskoro*, of the boy	*e rakliákoro*, of the girl	*raiéskoro*
Acc.	*e raklés*, the boy	*e rakliá*, the girl	*raiés*
1st Dat.	*e rakléste*, to the boy	*e rakliáte*, to the girl	*raiéste*
2nd „	*e rakléske*, in the boy	*e rakliáke*, in the girl	*raiéske*
Instr.	*e raklésa*, with the boy	*e rakliása*, with the girl	*raiésa*
Abl.	*e rakléstar*, from the boy	*e rakliátar*, from the girl	*raiéstar*
Voc.	*e rakléya*, Boy !	*e rakliá*, Girl !	*ráia*

PLURAL.

Nom.	*Raklé*, boys	*Rakliá*, girls	*Raiá*, lords
Gen.	*rakléngoro*	*rakliéngoro*	*raiéngoro*
Acc.	*raklén*	*raklién*	*raién*
1st Dat.	*raklénde*	*rakliénde*	*raiénde*
2nd „	*raklénghe*	*rakliénghe*	*raiénghe*
Instr.	*rakléndja*	*rakliéndja*	*raiéndja*
Abl.	*rakléndar*	*rakliéndar*	*raiéndar*
Voc.	*raklále*	*raklále*	*raiále*

The inflections preserved in the English Gypsy dialect may be classed as follows :—

SINGULAR.

Genitive, *-éskoro* (plural, *-éngoro*).

A great peculiarity of this dialect is the large number of words ending in *-éskro, -méskro, -oméskro ; -éngro, -méngro, -oméngro*. These endings were originally genitive forms, as will be gathered from the above declensions, but are now added to verbs and adjectives, as well as nouns, and thus form nouns denoting an agent, or possessor, the termination *-o* being masculine, and *-i* feminine or neuter, though these rules of gender are honoured more perhaps in the breach than the observance.

Examples.

-éskro.

Baréskro-grei, stallion,   from *bar*, stone; *grei*, horse.

-méskro.

Pógerméskri, hammer,   from *póger*, to break.
Sásterméskro, blacksmith,   „ *sáster*, iron.

-oméskro.

Chínoméskro, chopper,   from *chin*, to cut.
Pórnoméskro, miller,   „ *pórno*, flour.
Yógoméskro, fire-range, gun,   „ *yog*, fire.

-éngro.

Baréngro, stallion,   from *bar*, stone.

-méngro.

Tátterméngro, fryingpan,   from *tátter*, to heat.
Bókoroméngro, shepherd,   „ *bókoro*, sheep.

-oméngro.

Chínoméngro, hatchet,   from *chin*, to cut.

Sometimes the forms *-éndri* and *-imóngeri* occur, *e.g.*,

Kótoréndri, fragment,   from *kótor*, piece.
Múter-imóngeri, tea,   „   *múter*, urine.

Dr. Paspati remarks, in a letter to Dr. Smart, "your *-engro*, or *-méngro*, is our (Turkish Gypsy) *-koro*, rendered *-ngoro* by the nasal *n*. Your *bokoromengro*, a shepherd, is here (Constantinople) *bakréskoro;* pl. *bakréngoro*, a shepherd of many sheep, *bakrénghere*, shepherds of many sheep."

From the above examples, and others to be found in the vocabulary, it would appear that the *m* is euphonic, and was originally added to nouns ending in vowels; and that the termination *-méngro*, which was thus formed, was sometimes with and sometimes without, the preceding vowel, attached to other roots as a termination denoting an agent, or possessor, and equivalent to the English termination *-er*.

Besides *-éskro*, etc., there are, in the English Gypsy dialect, the terminations *-ésko* and *-ésto*, in common use, both as genitives singular and adjectival terminations.

These may have arisen from a gradual confusion of the inflections for the genitive masculine (*éskoro*), and first and second Datives masculine (*éste* and *éske*) in the singular (see declension above), due to the influence of the idiom for possession " *Dóova stárdi see lésti,*" That hat is to him, = That hat is his, or That is his hat.

Examples.

-éskro.

Baréskro-grei, stallion,   from *bar*, stone; *grei*, horse.

-ésko.

Béngesko-tem, hell,   from *beng*, devil; *tem*, country.
Mi-dóovelésko-dood, moon,   „   *Mi-dóovel*, God; *dood*, light.
Dásko tan, mother's tent,   „   *Dei*, mother; *tan*, tent.
Réiesko-kair, gentleman's house,   „   *Rei*, gentleman; *kair*, house.
(Bright) *O tascho wasteskee wangesto*, The finger of the right hand.

-ésto.

Chíriklésto kair, birdcage,	from *chíriklo*, bird; *kair*, house.
Gádesto-bei, shirt-sleeve,	„ *gad*, shirt; *bei*, sleeve.
Gréiesto-kóppa, horserug,	„ *grei*, horse; *kóppa*, blanket.
etc.	etc.

Sometimes the forms *-mésto* and *-omésto* occur, from analogy to the forms *-méskro, -oméskro*, e.g.,

Pórnomésto, miller,	from *pórno*, flour.
Pógeromésto, hammer,	„ *póger*, to break.

The genitive is, however, usually formed by adding 's to the nominative, as in English, *e.g.*,

Mi-doóvel's-dívvus, Christmas; lit. my god's day.

We have not been able to meet with any example of the feminine genitive form *-ákoro*.

Accusative : *-és*.

The only example we have heard is *pálla kookéss*, after Sunday.

Dr. Pott, vol. i., p. 232, conjectures that " *Res*, nobleman," given by Col. Harriot (" R. Asiatic Society Transactions," 1830), is the accusative of *rei*, gentleman, (see declension above).

Mr. Borrow, in "Lavengro," vol. iii., pp. 53, 172, edit. 1851, has put " *Hir mi devlis*," and in " Romany Rye," vol. i., p. 230, edit. 1857, has put " *Hir mi diblis*" into the mouths of English Gypsies. *Devlis* and *diblis* appear to be accusative forms. The same expression, " *Heri devlis*," occurs on p. 126 of his " Lavo-lil," at the foot of the Lord's Prayer the Gypsy dialect of Transylvania.

Datives : 1st, *-éste*; 2nd, *éske*.

Dr. Bright gives the following example: " *Deh acove a gresti giv chi*," Give to this horse corn, girl. See also remarks on the terminations *-ésko*, and *ésto*, under the head of genitive.

Instrumental : *-ésa*.

According to Pott, vol. i., p. 192, the instrumental case of *dewel*, god, is *deweleha*, with god—the -*eha* representing -*esa* (*h = s* in some continental Gypsy dialects). Mr. Borrow, in "Lavengro," vol. i., p. 186, edit. 1851, has put " *Chal devlehi*," Go with God = good-bye, into the mouth of an English Gypsy. We have ourselves met with no examples of this inflection amongst nouns, though examples will be observed amongst the pronouns.

Vocative : -*eya*, -*a*, -*e*.

The only instances apparently extant in this dialect are *Déia*, Mother ! and *Réia*, Sir !

PLURAL.

Nominative : -*é*.

1. The few who still retain a knowledge of the old dialect, sound the nominative plural of nouns ending in -*o* in the singular, with an accent on the final syllable, which they pronounce -*é*.

The most ordinary instances are the plurals of the common words *gaíro*, man, and *chóorodo*, mumper or tramp ; plural *gairé*, men ; *chóorodé*, mumpers or tramps.

Many other instances will be found in the vocabulary, *e.g.*,

> *Bókro*, sheep ; plural, *bokré*, sheep.   Pasp. *bakré*.
>
> *Petro*, foot ;   „   *peeré*, feet   „   *piré*.
>
>   „   *Pelé*, q.v.   „   *pelé*.

2, 3. The plurals of other nouns end in -*aw*, or -*yaw*, equivalent respectively to -*á* and -*iá*, of the Turkish Gypsy dialect, and less correctly represented by -*or* and -*yor*, there being no true *r* sound in the syllable. The difference, however, between -*aw* and -*or*, -*yaw* and -*yor*, in ordinary English, is almost, if not quite, imperceptible.

Examples.

ENGLISH GYPSY.		TURKISH GYPSY.
SINGULAR.	PLURAL.	PLURAL.
Grei, horse	*Gréiaw*	*Graiá*
Hev, hole	*Hévyaw*	*Kheviá*

ENGLISH GYPSY.		TURKISH GYPSY.
SINGULAR.	PLURAL.	PLURAL.
Nei, nail	*Néiaw*	*Naid*
Pen, sister	*Pényaw*	*Penid*
Vast, hand	*Vástaw*	*Vastá*
Yok, eye	*Yókaw*	*Yaká*

4. More frequently, however,—and this is becoming the general rule,—the nominative plural is formed by the addition of *s*, as in English, *e.g.*,

> *Pen*, sister ; *Pens*, sisters.
> *Vast*, hand ; *Vasts*, hands.
> *Yok*, eye ; *Yoks*, eyes.

5. Sometimes two forms are combined, *e.g.*,

> *Bar*, stone ; *Báryaws*, stones.
> *Poov*, field ; *Póovyaws*, fields.
> *Ran*, rod ; *Rányaws*, rods.

Genitive : *-éngoro*.

See remarks on the genitive singular.

Examples.

Rookénghi, or *Rookéngri Chóχas* (Wester), The coats of trees,—*i.e.*, leaves. *Shushénghi hévyaw*, Rabbit-burrows.

Accusative : *-én*.

We have not met with any examples.

Dative : 1st, *-énde;* 2nd, *-énghe.*

The only instance that has occurred to us is, "*You see tárderin' shélo kotoréndi,*" He is pulling rope to pieces, *i.e.*, He is picking oakum.

Instrumental : *-éndja;* Ablative : *-éndar.*

These cases are apparently obsolete, unless *gáver* in the following sentence may be regarded as an ablative *: Méndi jal yek gáver káter wáver*, We go from one town to another.

Vocative : *-ále.*

This inflection is, so far as we know, only retained in the word *choovále*, mates; a word which has a variety of modifications of sound, and is by no means uncommon.

Locative.

Dr. Paspati (p. 57) says, "Sometimes one hears the locative case, which probably existed formerly in the tongue," and quotes from p. 108 of Burns' Essay : "The termination of the locative *e* is the same in the two tongues," *i.e.* in Sanscrit and Pali, and amongst other examples mentions *keré* (*djal keré*, he goes home), which in the English Gypsy dialect would be, *e.g., yov jals kéri*, he goes home, or, *yov see ghílo keré*, he is (has) gone home. Dr. Paspati adds that the abverbs *andré*, inwardly, *opré*, above, *telé*, below, are in the locative case. These forms are preserved in the English *adré*, in, *opré*, upon, *talé*, down.

Sometimes nouns appear to have been formed from the past participles of verbs, *e.g.,*

ENGLISH DIALECT.		TURKISH DIALECT.		
Béshto, saddle,	from *besh,* to sit.	*Beshāva,*	p. part.	*beshtó.*
Bóshno, cock,	„ *bosh,* to crow.	*Bashāva,*	„	*bashnó.*
Díklo, handkerchief,	„ *dik,* to see.	*Dikāva,*	„	*diklό.*
Moólo, ghost,	„ *mer,* to die.	*Merāva,*	„	*mulό.*

DIMINUTIVES.

Dr. Paspati (p. 45) states that the Turkish Gypsies form, from almost all nouns, in imitation of the Turks and Greeks, diminutives in *-oró,* as well as some in *-tchó,* a form borrowed from the Bulgarian language.

The English Gypsy dialect has one example at least of the latter form, viz., *bókocho,* lamb, from *bókoro,* sheep.

Perhaps Dr. Bright's "*chaori,* female children," and our *chavorí,* chicken, are examples of the other form.

ABSTRACT NOUNS.

Dr. Paspati (p. 47) says, "Abstract nouns are formed from verbs, adjectives, and nouns" (p. 46) ; "they are very numerous, and always end in *be* or *pe.*" He gives, amongst other examples,—

TURKISH GYPSY.

From verbs,	*Astaribé*, prize,	from *astardva*, I seize.
	Djibé, life,	„ *djivdva*, I live.
	Meribé, death,	„ *merdva*, I die.
From adjectives,	*Mattipé*, drunkenness,	„ *mattó*, drunk.
	Barvalipé, wealth,	„ *barvaló*, rich.
	Kalipé, blackness,	„ *kaló*, black.
	Nasfalibé, illness,	„ *nasfaló*, ill.
	Tchatchipé, truth,	„ *tchatchó*, true.
From nouns,	*Benghipé*, devilry,	„ *beng*, devil.
	Rupuibé, silversmith trade,	„ *rup*, silver.
	Trushuibé, thirst,	„ *trush*, thirst.

He adds that inflections of these nouns are rare, but that the instrumental case shows that primitively they ended in *pen*.

In the English dialect, also, abstract nouns are formed from verbs, adjectives, and nouns, and retain the primitive endings of *pen* or *ben*, e.g.,

From verbs,	*Stáriben*, prison,	from *astardva* (obsolete in Eng. dialect), I seize.
	Jivoben, life,	„ *jiv*, to live.
	Mériben, death,	„ *mer*, to die.
From adjectives,	*Móttoben*, drunkenness,	„ *mótto*, drunk.
	Bárvalipen, wealth,	„ *bárvalo*, rich.
	Kaúlopen, blackness,	„ *kaúlo*, black.
	Náflopen, illness,	„ *náflo*, ill.
	Tátchipen, truth,	„ *tátcho*, true.
From nouns,	*Choómaben*, kissing,	„ *choóma*, kiss, n. and v.
	Bréedopen, breed,	„ *breed* (Eng.), n. and v.

COMPOUND NOUNS.

The English Gypsy dialect has, in analogy to the English language, many compound nouns formed by the union of nouns with verbs, adjectives, and nouns, e.g.,

Kanéngri-moosh, gamekeeper,	from *kanéngri*, hare; *moosh*, man.
Kaúli-raúni, turkey,	„ *kaúli*, black; *raúni*, lady.
Lólo-mátcho, herring,	„ *lólo*, red; *mátcho*, fish.
Meéasto-bar, milestone,	„ *meéa*, mile; *bar*, stone.
Moosh-chávi, boy,	„ *moosh*, man; *chávi*, child.
Poókering-kosht, signpost,	„ *poókering*, telling; *kosht*, post.

Pórni-raúni, swan,	from *pórni*, white ; *raúni*, lady.
Símmering-boódega, pawnshop,	„ *símmering*, pawning ; *boódega*, shop.
Táíto-padni, spirits,	„ *táíto*, hot ; *padni*, water.
etc.	etc.

PUNNING APPELLATIVES.

The English Gypsies have manufactured and adopted a class of words which are essentially of the nature of puns. They consist of words in which a fancied resemblance of sound in English has suggested their translation into *Rómanes*.

The German Gypsies have done the same, as will be seen on referring to p. 91 of Dr. Liebich's " Die Zigeuner," Leipzig, 1863, where amongst other instances he mentions —Vienna, *gwinakro foro* (honey town),—German *Wien*, Vienna, sounding like the German Gypsy word *gwin*, honey.

The following are examples of this practice by English Gypsies :—

Béngesko-mel, Devil's Die, for Devil's Dyke, Cambridgeshire.

Boóko-padni-gav, Liver-water-town, for Liverpool.

Kálesko-tem, Cheese-country, for Cheshire.

Kaúlo-padni, Black-water, for Blackpool, Lancashire.

Lálo-gav, Red-town, for Reading.

Lálo-peéro, Red-foot, for Redford.

Méilesto-gav, Donkey's-town, for Doncaster.

Moóshkeni-gav, Man-town, for Manchester.

Póbesko-gav, }
Póbomuski-gav, } A-norange-town, for Norwich.

Woódrus-gav-tem, Bed-town-country, for Bedfordshire.

DESCRIPTIVE APPELLATIVES.

They have also invented another class of words, nearly related to the last, and descriptive of some actual or fancied peculiarity.

Examples.

Choóresto-gav, knife-town, for Sheffield.

Chórkeno-tem, Grassy-country,
Bárvalo-tem, Rich-country, } Yorkshire.
Kaúlo-gav, Black-town, Birmingham.
Lávines-tem, Wordy-country, Wales.
Peéro-délin'-tem, Foot-kicking-country, Lancashire.
Póbesko-peeméskri-tem, Apple-drink-country, Hereford-
　　shire.
Póχtan-gav, Cloth-town, Manchester.
Távesto-gav, Cotton (thread)-town, Manchester.
Túlo-mas-tem, Fat-meat-country, Lincolnshire.
　　etc.　　　　etc.　　　　etc.

The following tribes have punning appellatives in *Ró-
manes* :—

　　　　Cooper—*Wardéngro*.
　　　　Gray—*Bal.*
　　　　Herne—*Mátcho.*
　　　　Lee—*Poórum.*
　　　　Lovell—*Kómomeskro, Kómelo*, pl. *Kómyaws.*
　　　　Pinfold—*Pándoméngro.*
　　　　Smith—*Petaléngro.*
　　　　Stanley—*Baréngro.*
　　　　Taylor—*Sivoméngro.*
　　　　Young—*Tárno.*

To these Mr. Borrow, in his "Lavo-lil," adds *Rossarmescro,
Herne* (*Duck*, for *Heron*), and *Choóma-místo*, Buss (*i.e.*, kiss)-
well, *Choómoméngro*, Busser (*i.e.*, kisser), for *Boswell*. Both
of these terms are, so far as we can find, unknown in the
North, which is the more remarkable as the Hernes and
Boswells are the chief tribes in the northern counties.

NOUNS PECULIAR TO THIS DIALECT.

Of these, the following appear to be the most remarkable
and in commonest use :—

1. *Bángheri*, n., Waistcoat. Bryant, *bringaree ;* Bright,
　　bangeri ; Borrow ("Lavo-lil," p. 22), *bengree.*

2. *Bor*, n., Friend, mate.   Irvine, *mă bă*, don't, sir ; Smith
   ("Tent Life in Norway," p. 22), *baugh ;* Borrow
   ("Lavo-lil," p. 21), *baw, bau.*

3. *Bóuri*, n., Snail.   Borrow ("Zincali," 1861 ed., p. 58),
   boror, snails ; Lld. (Engl. Gs., p. 32ⁿ, 33, 34ⁿ, 223,) *bawris.*

4. *Gáiro*, n., Man ; *Gáiri*, Woman.   Bright, *purugero*, old
   man ; Borrow ("Zincali," 1843 ed., vol. ii., p. 145*),
   geiro, gairy ; ("Zincali," 1861 ed., p. 17,) *geiro ;* Simson
   ("History of the Gypsies," 1865, pp. 295, 331), *gourie ;*
   Leland ("English Gipsies," pp. 146, 254), *geero ;* (p. 221,
   241, 254,) *geeros,* pl. ; 57, *geeri's,* gen. ; 256, *geeris,* pl. ;
   Borrow ("Lavo-lil," p. 48), *guero, gueri.*

5. *Jorjóχa*, n., Apron.   Almost every family pronounces
   this word differently.   We have heard *chárdoka,*
   járifa, járika, jorjóffa, shárdoka, yárdooka, and *yar-*
   duχa.   Simson ("History of the Gypsies," pp. 315,
   332), *jair dah ;* Leland ("English Gipsies," p. 66),
   iellico ; Borrow ("Lavo-lil," p. 54), *joddakaye ;* Roberts,
   shaducca.

6. *Meila*, n., Ass.   Bryant, *millan,* ass ; *milo,* mule ; Hoyland (Survey, etc., p. 188), *moila ;* Bright, *mila, meila ;*
   Harriot, *maila,* ass, donkey ; *tane mail,* young donkey ;
   Irvine, *myla ;* Borrow ("Lavengro," 1851 ed., vol. iii.,
   p. 228), *mailla ;* Smith ("Tent Life in Norway," pp.
   105, 106, 345, etc.), *merle ;* Leland ("English Gipsies,"
   pp. 29, 30, 90, 107, etc.), *myla ;* Borrow ("Lavo-lil,"
   p. 63), *mailla.*

7. *Swágler, swégler,* n., Pipe, tobacco-pipe.   Bright, *swegli ;*
   Smith (p. 152), *swagler ;* Leland ("English Gipsies,"
   pp. 35, 113), *swägler ;* Borrow ("Lavo-lil," p. 93),
   swegler, swingle.

VARIOUS TERMINATIONS.

Class 1. *-ama, -amus, -imus, -omus.*
   Bítchama, sentence ; *Rókamus,* speech ; *Kérimus,*
   battle ; *Tárnomus,* youth.

Class 2. *-árus, -crus, -ero.*
> *Monkárus,* monkey ; *Rushárus,* rush ; *Westárus,* Sylvester; *Bósherus,* cough ; *Bóshero,* fiddler.

Class 3. *-ári, -i.*
> *Besomári,* besom-makers ; *Burk-ári,* breasts ; *Foozh-ári,* fern ; *Rushári,* rushes; *Bluelegi,* bluelegs ; *Nuti,* nuts.

Class 4. *-er.*
> *Bár-er,* stone ; *Gád-er,* shirt; *Róok-er,* trce.

Class 5. *-us, -os.*
> *Bostárdus,* bastard ; *Fáirus,* a fair ; *Hánikos,* a well.

Class 6. *-um.*
> *Goóshum,* throat.

Of these terminations, *-mus* (1) appears in many words to be equivalent to the termination *-pen,* or *-ben ; -dri* (3) is probably the plural form of *-árus* (2), and the two forms *-árus, -ári,* may owe their origin perhaps to the termination *-oro* (see DIMINUTIVES) ; *-us, mus,* etc., are apparently cant terminations.

ADJECTIVE.

Adjectives, in the singular, almost invariably end in *-o* or *-i,* which are respectively masculine and feminine terminations, *e.g.,*

Masculine.	Feminine.	Meaning.
Baúro	*Baúri*	Great
Chíklo	*Chíkli*	Dirty
Chobro	*Chobri*	Poor
Rínkeno	*Rínkeni*	Pretty
Roópno	*Roópni*	Silver

These terminations are even added to English adjectives, *e.g.,*
> *Déar-i dei,* dear mother.
> *Fíne-o péios,* fine fun.

The Gypsies in Germany do the same, as is shown in the following example taken from Pott :

Bunto bakro, ein buntes Schaf, a spotted sheep.

An instance in which a German word, with the normal Gypsy adjectival termination, appears prefixed to a Gypsy noun, occurs in the English Gypsy dialect, viz.,

Stíffo-pal, brother-in-law (*stief-bruder*).
Stíffi-pen, sister-in-law (*stief-schwester*).

We have also in this dialect what seems to be an example of a French word similarly treated, viz.,—

Bítti chei, little girl (*petite fille*).

For the plural, those who speak the ordinary dialect apparently prefer the termination -*i*, and the very few who speak the old dialect make use of -*é*.

SINGULAR.	PLURAL.
Chíklo drom, dirty road	*Chíkli drómaw*, dirty roads (ordinary dialect).
Chóoro gaíro, poor man	*Chooré gairé*, poor men ⎫
Poóro gaíro, old man	*Pooré gairé*, old men ⎬ (old dialect).
Wáver bókro, another sheep	*Waveré bokré*, other sheep ⎭

The following examples will illustrate the agreement between adjectives and nouns. The rule is, however, constantly violated by every Gypsy.

SINGULAR.	PLURAL.
Baúro rei, great gentleman	*Poóri dei*, old mother
Baúro padní, great water	*Rínkeni rákli*, pretty girl
Káisheno díklo, silk handherchief	*Roópni roi*, silver spoon

Many of the adjectives in common use are almost pure Hindostani, Sanscrit, or Persian (*vide* Paspati, p. 59), *e.g.*,

English Gypsy Adjective.	Oriental representative.	Meaning.
Baúro	*Bura*, Hind.	Great
Bókolo	*Bhookha*, Hind.	Hungry
Kaúlo	*Kala*, Hind.	Black
Koóshko	*Khoosh*, Pers.	Good
Lólo	*Lal*, Pers.	Red

English Gypsy Adjective.	Oriental representative.	Meaning.
Lóngo	{ *Lung*, Pers. } { *Lungra*, Hind. }	Lame
Moólo	*Mooa*, Hind.	Dead
Mótto	*Muttu*, Sans.	Drunk
Nevo	*Nuvu*, Sans.	New
Nóngo	*Nunga*, Hind.	Naked
Poóro	*Boorha*, Hind.	Old
Shírilo	*Seera*, Hind.	Cold
Shoóko	*Sookha*, Hind.	Dry
Tátto	*Tutta*, Hind.	Hot
etc.	etc.	etc.

Some adjectives are formed from Gypsy nouns by adding *-no* or *-lo*, *e.g.*,

NOUN.	ADJECTIVE.
Chik, dirt.	*Chík-lo*, dirty.
Kaish, silk.	*Kaíshno*, silken.
Roop, silver.	*Roópno*, silver.

Dr. Paspati, p. 60, says, "The greater number of Turkish Gypsy adjectives end in *-lo*." More than half the adjectives in the English Gypsy dialect end in *-lo* or *-no*, *e.g.*,

-lo, m.; *-li*, f.

Bálli, hairy	*Joóvli*, lousy	*Peévlo*, widowed
Bárvalo, rich	*Kaúlo*, black	*Rátvalo*, bloody
Béngalo, wicked	*Kómelo*, loving	*Shírilo*, cold
Bókolo, hungry	*Moólo*, dead	*Shoóbli*, pregnant
Choóralo, bearded	*Násfalo*, ill	*Túllo*, fat
Goódlo, sweet	*Peédlo*, drunk	*Túvlo*, smoky

-no, m.; *-ni*, f.

Hŏïno, angry	*Kóshno*, wooden	*Rínkeno*, pretty
Joóvni, female	*Moóshkeno*, male	*Roópno*, silver
Káishno, silken	*Párno*, cloth	*Tárno*, young
Kíno, tired	*Paúno*, white	*Tíkno*, little

Some few end in *-do*, *e.g.*,

Kíndo, wet	*Kórodo*, blind	*Pórdo*, full, etc.

These last in general have meanings akin to past participles; though the division between adjectives in *-lo*, *-no*, *-do*, and past participles with the same terminations, is by no means distinct.

Others have various terminations.

We have also adjectives in *-sko*, *-sto*, formed from the genitive singular, *e.g.*,

> *Králisko*, royal, from *krális*, king.
>
> *Vénesto,* } relating to winter, from *ven*, winter.
> *Vénesko,* }

[See remarks on the declensions of nouns, p. 14.]

We have several adjectives, in the very commonest use, which seem to be almost peculiar to the English Gypsy dialect, *e.g.*,

> *Koóshko*, good (Persian, *koosh*).

The word occurs in Dr. Pott's work, but is taken from English sources. M. Böhtlingk, in "Mélanges Asiatiques," tome ii., 2me livraison, 1854, has *känsto*, good. Dr. Paspati says, in a letter to Dr. Smart, "This word (*koóshko*) is unknown to me."

The word *Latscho*, or *Laczo*, takes its place in most dialects,—*e.g.*, instead of *Koóshko dívvus*, Good day, one would say *Latscho dives*.

Almost all English Gypsy vocabularies contain the word :—

> Bright—*Coshko, kosliko* (? *li* for *h*).
> Harriot—*Kashto, kashko*.
> Irvine—*Kooshka*.
> Borrow—*Kosgo, kosko, koshto, kushto*.
> "Illustrated London News," 13th Dec., 1851—*Cushgar, kushgar*.
> Hubert Smith—*Cushty*.
> Leland—*Kushto*, etc.

Another adjective which appears peculiar to this dialect is

> *Rínkeno*, pretty.

Mr. Hubert Smith, in his "Tent Life with English Gypsies in Norway," London, 1873, p. 332, says, "In the Italian Gypsy, it (*rankny*) is pronounced *rincano.*" This assertion may perhaps be accounted for on referring to Predari, "Origine e Vicende dei Zingari," etc., 8vo, Milan, 1841 (see "Tent Life," etc., p. 165), for Predari has taken words from Kogalnitschan's "Esquisse sur l'hist., et la langue des Cigains," 8vo, Berlin, 1837 (see Pott, i. 25), and Kog. contains many English Gypsy words and phrases taken from Roberts.*

The word for *pretty*, on the Continent, is,—Liebich, *Schukker ;* Paspati, *Sukár, Shukár ;* Pott, *Schakker, Szukar,* etc., which is represented in this dialect by *Shookár,* an adverb meaning *gently, nicely, easily.*

Rínkeno is represented in most of the English Gypsy vocabularies :—

> Bright—*Richini.*
> Harriot—*Rickeno.*
> Borrow—*Rinkeno, rikkeni.*
> "Illustrated London News," 13th Dec., 1851—*Rinckne;*
>   ditto, 20th Sept., 1856—*Rinkni.*
> Hubert Smith—*Rankny.*
> Leland—*Rikkeno, rinkeni, rinkni.*

Another of these adjectives is

> *Vásavo,* bad, evil.

The pronunciation varies slightly with individuals. The word may be spelt *wásedo, wáfedo,* or *wáfro.*

The only word resembling these is Borrow's Spanish Gypsy *basto,* adj., evil, which is apparently connected with his *bastardo,* s.a., affliction, evil, prison.

Most of the English vocabularies represent this word, *e.g.,*

---

* This theory of the origin of *rincano* viâ Kogal is strengthened by the statement ("Tent Life," p. 479,) that "the French Gypsies use *wuddress* for bed," whereas there is no *w* in the French alphabet, but "*wuddress, lit*" occurs in Kogal., who wrote his book in French, and *rincana,* and *wuddress,* both occur in Roberts.

Bright—*Waffro.*
Harriot—*Vasavo, vesavo.*
Borrow—*Vassavo, vassavy, vassavie, wafudo, wafodu,
    wafudupénes* (sins).
"Illustrated London News," 13th Dec., 1851—*Va-
    fardes.*
Leland—*Vessavo, wafro, wafri, wafrodearer* (worse).

A fourth peculiar adjective is

Bítto, little.

Mr. Hubert Smith, p. 527, quotes *bittan* as Norwegian
Gypsy for *little,* according to M. Sundt.

It probably owes its origin to the French *petit.* The
English *bit,* though corresponding with this adjective in
sound, is never synonymous with *small.* The English say
indifferently "a *bit* of bread" and "a little bread"; and
English Gypsies may perhaps have confused these two
phrases, from the assonance of a *bitto* = a small, and a
bit o' = a bit, or small piece, of.

The following forms occur in former collections :—

Bryant—*Bittu, bottoo.*
Bright—*Bitta, bitto.*
Harriot—*Bitta, biti, bite, beti, bete.*
Borrow—*Biti, beti.*
Leland—*Bitti.*

COMPARISON.

The comparative degree is formed by adding *-dair, -dár,*
or *-dáiro,* to the positive. There seems to be no form for
the superlative beyond the English methods of adding *-est,*
or prefixing *most,* to either the positive or comparative,—
in the former of which cases the feminine termination *-i*
seems preferred to the masculine. At times the comparative is used as a superlative.

Examples.

POSITIVE.	COMPARATIVE.	SUPERLATIVE.
Baúro, great	*Baúrodár*	*Baúriest, baurodárest*, most *baúrodar*
Choóro, poor	*Choórodár*	*Choóriest, choorodárest*
Poóro, old	*Poórodár*	*Pooriest*, most *poórodar*
Tárno, young	*Tárnoddír*	*Tárniest*, most *tarni*

So boótoder too koméssa ? What do you want most ?
O kolé so komóva feterdaír. The things I want most.

These forms for the comparative are fast dying out, and giving way to English formations; they are, however, still in ordinary use in several families.

The Turkish Gypsies use a similar termination. Dr. Paspati, p. 56, gives

Baró, great ; *Baredér.*
Kaló, black ; *Kaledér.*
Tiknó, young ; *Tiknedér.*

The comparative degree in Persian is formed by adding *-tur* or *-tar*, e.g.,

Door ; Doortur.

Sometimes this degree in the English Gypsy dialect is formed irregularly, *e.g.*,

Koóshko, good ; *Fétterdáir*, better.

ADVERB.

Adverbs are formed from adjectives by adding *-nes* or *-es*, e.g.,

Bóngo, lame ; *Bónges*, lamely.
Choóro, poor ; *Choórones*, poorly.
Rómano, gypsy ; *Rómanes*, gypsily.
Tátcho, true ; *Táchenes*, truly.

Some are formed irregularly, e.g., *Koóshko*, good; *míshto*, well. *Míshto* they use occasionally as an adjective, and say *míshto dívvus*, good day.

The following examples are from Continental Gypsy vocabularies :—

Baro, great ; *Bares*.
Latcho, good ; *Latches*.
Tchulo, fat ; *Tchules*.

SOME ABSTRACT NOUNS

Are formed from adjectives, by adding *-pen* or *-ben*. [See remarks on the noun, p. 19.]

AUXILIARY VERB.

Dr. Paspati (p. 80) gives the following, as the inflection of the verb *to be*, in the Turkish Gypsy dialect :—

PRESENT.		IMPERFECT.	
SINGULAR.	PLURAL.	SINGULAR.	PLURAL.
Me *isóm*, I am	Amen *isám*, We are	*Isómas*	*Isámas*
Tu *isán*, Thou art	Tumen *isán*, Ye are	*Isánas*	*Isánas*
Ov *isí*, He is	Ol *isí*, They are	*Isás*	*Isás*

In the English Gypsy dialect, parts of this verb are not unfrequently employed in conversation, *e.g.*,

PRESENT.		IMPERFECT.	
SINGULAR.	PLURAL.	SINGULAR.	PLURAL.
Shom	*Shom, shem*	*Shö'mas, sas*	*Shúmas*
Shan	*Shan*	*Shánas*	*Shánas*
See	*See*	*Sas*	*Sas*

A few examples will serve to show the use now made of this verb.

PRESENT.

Kinó shom, I am tired.
Sar shan, pal, How art thou, brother ?
Sar shan, choováli, How are ye, mates ?
So see, What is it ?
Jinéla méndi shem akéi, He knows we are here.
Doósta Rómani-chálaw see akéi, Many Gypsies are here.

IMPERFECT.

Mándi sas kéker kobrdno 'dré mi mérripen, I was never beaten in my life.

Beéno shó'mas, I was born (Wester Bos.)

Too shánas náflo, Thou wast ill.

Yov sas beéno aglál mándi, He was born before me.

Méndi shúmas wáfedo, We were bad.

Wáveré sas wélling, Others were coming.

It is also used in the sense of *must*, e.g.,

So shom te keráw, What must I do? What am I to do?

It occasionally takes the meaning of *have*, a usage derived from the form *Mándi see*, To me there is, = I have (*est mihi*), e.g.,

Yov see a pórno stárdi, He has a white hat.

Too shanas trin gréiaw, Thou hadst three horses.

To be able, can (*posse*).

Mr. Borrow ("Romano Lavo-lil," London, Murray, 1874, p. 18,) gives * *astis mangué*, I can.

Wester Boswell uses the following forms, viz.: *Sastís*, or *Sustís* (can); *Nastís*, or *Nastíssa* (cannot); *Tastís*, or *Tustís* (If I can). Liebich has *Sasti* (can), *Nasti* (cannot); but does not represent our third form. Paspati has the second form only, viz., *Nasti* and *Nastik* (cannot).

Examples.

Sar sastís te yek moosh del? How can one man give?

Pobkeróva toot, Rei, tastís, I will tell you, sir, if I can.

Yov'll kair toot tátcho, tastís, He will cure you, if he can.

Nastís wantasóva, I cannot want.

"*Hol doóva.*" "*Nastíssa.*"—"Eat that." "I cannot."

---

* *cf.* Pasp., p. 48 : ASTI (As) it is.

VERB.

According to various authorities, the German, Hungarian, and Turkish Gypsies have a peculiar conjugation of their own. The Gitanos of ·Spain assimilate their verbs to the Spanish conjugation. In this country the Gypsy dialect exhibits only remnants of the ancient mode of conjugating the verb, which now generally conforms to the English method in preference.

To elucidate the few remarks to be made on this point, specimens of the conjugation of the Turkish Gypsy verb, taken from pp. 87 and 89 of Dr. Paspati's recent work, are subjoined.

Láva, to take.　*Keráva*, to make.

Participle.

Linó, f. *liní*, pl. *liné.*　*Kerdó*, f. *kerdí*, pl. *kerdé.*

Gerund.—*Kerindós.*

INDICATIVE.

Present.

SINGULAR.	PLURAL.	SINGULAR.	PLURAL.
1 *Láva*, or *lav*	*Lása, las*	*Keráva, -ráv*	*Kerása, -rás*
2 *Lása*, „ *las*	*Léna, len*	*Kerésa, -rés*	*Keréna, -rén*
Lísa, „ *les*		*Keréla, -rél*	*Keréna, -rén*
3 *Lála*, „ *lal*	*Léna, len*		
Léla, „ *lel*			

Imperfect.

Lávas	*Lásas*	*Kerávas*	*Kerásas*
Lásas	*Lénas*	*Kerásas*	*Kerénas*
Lélas	*Lénas*	*Kerélas*	*Kerénas*

First Aorist.

According to the Settled Gypsies.

SINGULAR.	PLURAL.	SINGULAR.	PLURAL.
Linióm, lióm	*Liniám*	*Kerghióm*	˙*Kerghiám*
Linián, lián	*Linián*	*Kerghián*	*Kerghián*
Liniás, liás	*Liniás*	*Kerghiás*	*Kerghiás*

According to the Wandering Gypsies.

Linóm	*Linám*	*Kerdóm*	*Kerdám*
Linán	*Linán*	*Kerdán*	*Kerdán*
Linás	*Linás*	*Kerdás*	*Kerdás*

Second Aorist.

According to the Settled Gypsies.

Liniómas	*Liniámas*	*Kerghiómas*	*Kerghiámas*
Liniánas	*Liniánas*	*Kerghiánas*	*Kerghiánas*
Liniás	*Liniás*	*Kerghiás*	*Kerghiás*

According to the Wandering Gyysies.

Linómas	*Linámas*	*Kerdómas*	*Kerdámas*
Linánas	*Linánas*	*Kerdánas*	*Kerdánas*
Linás	*Linás*	*Kerdás*	*Kerdás*

Future.

Kamalául, -láv	*Kamalása, -lás*	*Kamakeráva*	*Kamakerása*
Kamalésa, -lés	*Kamaléna,-lén*	*Kamakerása*	*Kamakeréna*
Kamaléla, -lél	*Kamaléna, -lén*	*Kamakeréla*	*Kamakeréna*

IMPERATIVE.

2 *Le, lo*	*Len*	*Ker*	*Kerén*
3 *Me lel*	*Me len*	*Me kerél*	*Me kerén*

SUBJUNCTIVE.

Present.

Te láva, -lav	*Te lása, -las*	*Te keráva*	*Te kerása*
Te lésa, -les	*Te léna, -len*	*Te kerésa*	*Te keréna*
Te léla, -lel	*Te léna, -len*	*Te keréla*	*Te keréna*

In most instances the English Gypsy verb consists of the bare root, *e.g.*,

3

English Gypsy.	1st Pers. Sing., Pres., Turkish Gypsy.	Meaning.
Chin	*Tchin-áva*	Cut
Jin	*Djan-áva*	Know
Kair	*Ker-áva*	Make
Kin	*Kin-áva*	Buy
Koor	*Kur-áva*	Fight
Mor	*Mar-áva*	Kill
Pen	*Pen-áva*	Say
etc.	etc.	etc.

The few inflections still extant may be grouped as follows :—

INDICATIVE.

Present.

1st pers., sing., *-ov, -óva.*

In deep Rómanes this termination is still used, not only for the present tense, but the future also, *e.g.*,

Andóva, I bring   *Dóva,* } I give   *Jinóva*, I know
Chinóva, I cut   *Delóva,* }   *Jóva,* } I go
Chivóva, I put   *Hóva*, I eat   *Jalóva,* }
Dikóva, I see   *Hótcheróva*, I burn   *Kairóva*, I make
etc.   etc.   etc.

The same termination is occasionally added to English verbs, *e.g.*,

Think*asóva*, I think ; Want*asóva*, I want.

This form of *-óva*, or *-áwva*, is often contracted in rapid conversation, *e.g.*,

Parikráw, or *Páriko toot*, Thank you.
Jináw, I know.
Law, I take.

As comparisons of the old with the ordinary dialect, the following examples will serve :—

Jóva mé, I am going   *Mándi's jálin'*
Jinóva mé, I know   *Mándi jins*

A '*v*,' which appears to be the remains of -*áva*, or rather of the lengthened form -*avdva*, is found in the English dialect annexed to the root of many of the commonest verbs :—

Hindustani.	Root.	Turkish Gypsy.	English Gypsy.	Meaning.
A-na	*A*-	*A*-v-áva	*A*-v	Come
Ro-na	*Ro*-	*Ro*-v-áva	*Ro*-v	Cry
See-na	*See*-	*Si*-v-áva	*Si*-v	Sew
So-na	*So*-	*So*-v-áva	*So*-v	Sheep
Dho-na	*Dho*-	*To*-v-áva	*To*-v	Wash
etc.	etc.	etc.	etc.	etc.

2nd pers., sing., -*ása*, -*ésa*.

A few of the old Gypsies still use this form, pronouncing it -*ássa*, -*éssa*, and frequently contracting it to -*ás*, -*és*, e.g.,

Too jinésa, thou knowest ; *jása*, goest ; *dikésa*, seest ; *jivésa*, livest ; *kairésa*, or *késa*, doest ; *komésa*, or *komés*, lovest ; *shoonésa*, hearest.

Too rókerása, or *rókerás*, thou speakest ; *pookerás*, tellest.

Examples.

Jinésa too Westárus? Do you know Sylvester?

Komés too bálovás? Do you like bacon?

Jinóva, pal, sorkón kobvaw too pookerás mándi see tátcho, I know, brother, everything thou tellest me is true.

3rd pers., sing., -*éla*, -*él*.

This termination is also in use at the present time, *e.g.*,

Boshéla, barks.	*Kairéla*, makes.
Brishinéla (brishin-déla), rains.	*Nasheréla*, loses.
Chivéla, puts.	*Rokeréla*, talks.
Jála, goes.	*Trashéla*, fears.
Kanéla, stinks.	*Yivéla (yiv-déla)*, snows.

English Gypsy verbs, in the ordinary dialect, are frequently merely contracted forms of this termination. This is generally the case if the root ends in a vowel, or the liquid *r*, e.g.,

Root.	3rd Pers. Sing., Pres., according to Paspati.	English Gypsy Verb.	Meaning.
Dé-	*Déla*	*Del*	Give
Ja-	*Jála*	*Jal*	Go
Lé-	*Léla*	*Lel*	Get
Ker-	*Keréla*	*Kel*	Play
Kha-	*Khóla*	*Kol, hol*	Eat
Mer-	*Meréla*	*Mel*	Die
Per-	*Peréla*	*Pel*	Fall
Ter-	*Teréla*	*Til*	Hold
etc.	etc.	etc.	etc.

Examples from the Old Dialect.

Yói jinéla man, She knows me.
Yov jivéla pósha mándi, He lives near me.
Yov peeréla místo, He walks well.

3rd pers., plur., *-éna, -en.*

The old dialect retains this termination, *e.g.*,

Chivénna, They put.   *Ríggerénna*, or *ríggerén*, They carry.
Jinénna, They know.   *Wénna*, or *wen*, They come.

Examples.

Kek né jinénna yon, They do not know.
Chivénna yon kek gorgiokonés adré lésti, They put no English in it (their talk).

PAST FORMS ; *vide* Paspati's AORISTS.

There appears to be no distinction between the imperfect and aorists, but only one form for both.

1st pers., sing. and plur., *-dóm, -óm.*

Bísserdóm, I forgot   *Hónjedóm*, I itched
Dióm, } I gave   *Kairdóm*, I made
Deldóm, }   *Lióm*, I took
Chidóm, I put   *Pedóm*, I fell

Ghióm, I went   *Woóserdóm*, I threw
Hodóm, I ate

Examples.

Ghióm mé, I went.
Ghióm méndi, We went.

These are contracted forms of past participles, + *shom*, as *kaírdo* + *shom* = *kairdóm*, I made ; *see* Paspati.

2nd pers., sing. and plur., *-án*.

Lián, Thou hast got.
Ghián, Ye went.
Múterdán, Ye micturated.

Examples.

Sávo cheérus lián to atch akéi, What time hast thou got to stay here (in prison) ?
Múterdán too ti-kókero ? Have you wet yourself ?

These are contracted forms of past participles + *shan*, as *kaírdo* + *shan* = *kairdán*, Thou hast done.

3rd pers., sing. and plur., *-dás*, *-tás*, *-ás*.

Chingadás, He tore.	*Jivdás*, He lived.
Diás, He gave.	*Kairdás*, He made.
Dookadás, He hurt.	*Kindás*, He bought.
Yon ghiás, They went.	*Liás*, He got.
Pendás, He said.	*Mooktás*, He left.
Yon jindás, They knew.	*Pedás*, He fell.
etc.	etc.

These are contracted forms of past participles + *see*, as *kaírdo* + *see* = *kairdás*, He made.

Occasionally this termination is used for the 2nd person singular, somewhat in accordance with that person of the imperfect of Paspati's conjugation, and in these cases sometimes takes a final ' *a*,' e.g.,

Bísserdás too ? Hast thou forgotten ?
Diktássa too ? Did you see ?

3rd pers., plur., *é*, formed from past participle plural.

Yon hodé, = They ate⎫
Yon pedé, = They fell⎭ (Wester Bos.)

The following sentences, spoken by Sylvester Boswell, well illustrate the above forms, *-óm, -án, -ás,*—

Dióm o bítto joókel, so hodás o mas, o wáver dívvus, too kindás.	I gave away the little dog, which ate the meat, the other day, thou boughtedst.
Dióm les káter bítto tárno rei akéi, ta jivéla pósha mándi, and yov liás les párdel o padni káter Boóko-padni-gav.	I gave it to a little young gentleman here, that lives near me, and he took it over the water to Liverpool.
Too kairdán o mas ?	Have you done the meat ?

Future.

In the Turkish dialect this tense is formed, from analogy to modern Greek, by prefixing the verb *kamáma,* to wish, desire, etc. As already mentioned, the present tense in English Rómanes serves also for the future, the meaning being determined by the context, or accompanying circumstances.

Example.

Dikóva tálla o hótchiwítchi.	I will look after the hedgehog.
Mándi latchóva yek.	I will find one.
Mauróva lésti, ta mórrov lésti.	I will slay it, and shave it.
Yoósheróva lésti.	I will clean it.
Chivóva lésti káter yog,	I will put it to the fire,
Ta kérav lésti, ta hóva lés mónghi.	And cook it, and eat it myself.

SYLVESTER BOSWELL.

IMPERATIVE.

2nd pers., sing. The verbal root, as *dik,* see ! *kair,* do !

Although the forms *dé,* give, and *lé,* take, exist, the English Gypsies generally use *del* and *lel.*

1st pers., plural.

According to Wester Boswell's usage, this is formed by the addition of *-as* to the root, with the accent on the added syllable.

Examples.

OLD DIALECT.	NEW.
J'ás ménghi, Let us go	*Mook's jal*
Dik-ás méndi, Let us look	*Mook's dik*
Latch-ás ménghi, Let us find	*Mook's latçh*
Ker-ás ménghi, Let us make	*Mook's kair*

Harriot (see Pott, vol. i., p. 348) has the following examples :—

Ne pala ! jas amego, (sic) *ti chinnás amege* (sic) *bete giv*,
Now mates, let us go, and let us cut a little corn.
Páravása, Let us change.
Jas omingo, (sic) Let us go.

Pott (vol. i., pp. 346, 475) gives several instances taken by him from Puchmayer's "Románi Czib" (Pott, vol. i., p. 20, Source 25), e.g., *dschas, shas*, and *javas*, let us go; *dikkas* and *te dikas*, let us see ; *ma das*, do not let us give ; and conjectures that the form is borrowed from the 1st person plural of the present conjunctive.

SUBJUNCTIVE.

The Turkish Gypsies form the present subjunctive by prefixing *te* to the present indicative. The English Gypsies do the same.

Examples.

The *Beng te lel doóva Rei*. I'll *chiv* a *choóri adré* his *ráttvali see*.	The Devil take that Gentleman. I'll put a knife in his bloody heart. "The most wishfullest thing as you can say against any one." CHARLIE BOSWELL.
The *Beng te lel toóti*.	The Devil take you. NED BOSWELL.
Beng te lel toot.	Devil take you.
Delóva meéro lav káter mi-Doóvel yov te jal káter yov.	I will give my word (I will pray) to God that he may go to him.
Te wel teéro králisom.	May thy kingdom come. SYLVESTER BOSWELL.

PARTICIPLE.

Present.

They invariably use the English termination -*ing*, which they pronounce -*en'* or -*in'*, e.g.,

Kómin', loving. *Koóren'*, fighting.

Past.

It ends in -*do*, -*no*, or -*lo*, e.g.,

Chórdo, stolen,	from *Chor*,	to steal.
Dándo, bitten,	„ *Dan*,	„ bite.
Moóklo, left,	„ *Mook*,	„ leave.
Násherdo, lost,	„ *Násher*,	„ lose.
Pógerdo, broken,	„ *Póger*,	„ break.
Díkno, seen,	„ *Dik*,	„ see.
etc.	etc.	

In deep Rómanes the past participle ends in *é* in the plural, and is used for the 3rd person plural of the perfect. (See above.)

Some verbs are formed from past participles of verbs which are otherwise believed to be extinct in this dialect, *e.g.*,

And, to bring, vide *andó*, p. part. of Turk. Gypsy *andáva*.
Hínder, cacare, „ *khindó*, „ „ *khidva*.
Kíster, to ride, „ *uklistó*, „ „ *uklidva*.

LOST VERBS.

Besides those last mentioned, there are other verbs which seem to be lost in the English Gypsy dialect, though their roots are retained in derivatives, *e.g.*,

ENGLISH GYPSY.	*See* TURKISH GYPSY.
Beíno, born.	*Bendva*, to lie in,
Bóllesko-dívvus, Christmas Day.	*Boláva*, to baptize, christen (Borrow, "Lavo-lil," p. 24, inserts this verb).
Poósoméngro, fork.	*Pusavdva*, to stick, spur.
Stárdo,	
Stáriben, } prison.	*Astardva*, to seize, arrest.
Stáripen, etc.	

Compound Verbs.

These are numerous and in most cases mere literal translations from the English, *e.g.*,

Atch apré,	Arise,	lit.	Stand up.
Del apré,	Read,	„	Give (attention) on.
Lel apré,	Arrest,	„	Take up.
Jal adré,	Enter,	„	Go in.
Woóser apré,	Vomit,	„	Throw up.
Jal pálla,	Follow,	„	Go after.
etc.	etc.		etc.

In every case the inflection is added to the verb, *e.g.*,

> *Woósedóm apré*, I vomited.
> *Ghióm adré*, I entered.
> *Ghióm pálla*, I followed.

NOTE.—The pure inflections given above are not usually
met with in the ordinary dialect, which inflects its verbs after
the English mode in preference. Even among those who
still retain a knowledge of the old dialect, the inflections
are frequently confused, *-éla* being used for *-ésa*, *-ésa* for
-énna, etc.

Westárus (Sylvester) Boswell asserts that it is only some
of the Hernes and Boswells who know how to use the
'double words' (inflected), and that most Gypsies us
simply the 'dead words' (uninflected).

PRONOUN.

Personal Pronouns.

The following are the inflections of the Turkish Gypsy
pronouns according to Dr. Paspati, "Tchinghianés," pp.
66, 67, and those still in use among the English Gypsies,
arranged in parallel columns for more convenient comparison.

FIRST PERSON.

	TURKISH GYPSY.		ENGLISH GYPSY.	
	SINGULAR.	PLURAL.	SINGULAR.	PLURAL.
Nom.	Mé, I	Amén, we	Mé, mándi	Men, méndi
Gen.	Mángoro	Améngoro	Mánghi's, mándi's	[Amándi's, Lld. Eng. G., p. 251.]
Acc.	Mán	Amén	Man, mándi, mánghi	Men, méndi
Dat. 1.	Mánde	Aménde	Mándi, to mándi, to mánghi	Méndi [amande, Bw., "Zincali," 1861 ed., pp. 19, 262.]
" 2.	Mánghe	Aménghe		
Instr.	Mándja, ménsa	Améndja	Mánsa, with mándi	Ménsa
Abl.	Mándar	Améndar	[Mander, Bw., "Lavo-lil," p. 64]	

SECOND PERSON.

	TURKISH GYPSY.		ENGLISH GYPSY.	
Nom.	Tu, thou	Tumén	Too, tooti	Tumén, tuméndi
Gen.	?	Tuméngoro	Tooti's, tooti's	
Acc.	Tut	Tumén	Toot, tooti, túki	Tumén, tuméndi
Dat. 1.	Túte	Tuménde	Tooti, tooki	Tuméndi
" 2.	Túke	Tuménghe		
Instr.	Túsa	Tuméndja	Toosa, with tooti	
Abl.	Tútar	Tuméndar		

THIRD PERSON, SINGULAR.

	TURKISH GYPSY.		ENGLISH GYPSY.	
	MASCULINE.	FEMININE.	MASCULINE.	FEMININE.
Nom.	Ov, of, he	Oi, ai, she	Ov, yov, yuv, yow	Yói, yoi
Gen.	Léskoro	Lákoro	[Olescro, Bw., "Zinc.," 1843 ed., vol. ii. p. 145*—lescro, Bw., "Lavo-lil," p. 61] lésko, lésti's	Lóki, láki, láti's
Acc.	Les	La	Les, lésti	[La, Bw., "Lavo-lil," p. 60] las, láti
Dat. 1.	Léste }	Láte }	To lésti, to léski	To láti, to láki
,, 2.	Léske }	Láke }		
Instr.	Lésa	Lása	With lésti	{[Lása, Harriot; lasa, lasar, Bw., "Lavo-lil," p. 60]
Abl.	Léstar	Látar	[Lestar, Bw., "Lavo-lil," p. 61]	[Later, Bw., "Lavo-lil," p. 60]

PLURAL, SAME FOR BOTH GENDERS.

	TURKISH GYPSY.		ENGLISH GYPSY.
Nom.	Ol		Yon, yaun
Gen.	Léngoro		Léngheri, lénghi, lénti, léndi.
Acc.	Len		Len, lénti
Dat. 1.	Lénde	Dat. 2. Lénghe	To léndi, to lénghi
		Instr. Léndija	[Lensar, Bw., "Lavo-lil," p. 60]
		Abl. Léndar	[Lendar, Bw., "Lavo-lilp.60],"]

Ló, He; pl., *lé*, They.

Besides the forms *yov* and *yoi*, he and she—pl., *yon*, they—we have met with *lo*, he (of which the feminine would be *li*, she), and *lé*, they. These pronouns are only used after the auxiliary verb *to be*, so far as we can find. Dr. Pott (vol. i., p. 242) quotes the same remark as having been made by Graffunder, though he adduces instances from other writers showing that this is not an invariable rule.

The following sentences we noted down as we heard them :—

> *O rashéi, koóshto sas-ló*, The clergyman was a good man ; lit., good was he.
>
> *'Jaw wáfedo see-ló adré lésko zee*, He is so jealous ; lit., so evil is he in his heart.
>
> *Poókeroméngri see-lé*, They are 'informers.'
>
> *Koshté see-lé konáw*, They (hedgehogs) are good (to eat) now.
>
> *Toblo see-lé*, They are fat.

POSSESSIVES.

Mi, mine ; Pasp., *mo, mi*,	*Ti*, thine ; Pasp., *to, ti*
Mínno, ⎫	*Teéro*, thine ; Pasp., *tinró*
Méero, ⎬ mine ; Pasp., *minró*,	*Lésko*, his ; Pasp., *léskoro*,
Méiro, ⎭	*Láki, lóki*, her ; Pasp., *lákoro*,
Móro, our ; Pasp. *amaró*,	*Léngheri, lénghi*, their ; Pasp.,
	lénguro

Péski, his ; Pasp., *po* (of which the Dative would be *péske*).

N.B.—Mr. Borrow, " Lavo-lil," pp. 13, 174, gives *minro, minri*, my.

DEMONSTRATIVES.

Akóvva, kóvva, This ; pl. *kólla*, These ; Pasp. *aká*, pl. *aklé;* *kadavá*, pl. *kadalé.*

Adóvva, doóva, That ; pl. *dólla, dúlla*, Those ; Pasp., *odova*, pl. *odolé.*

INTERROGATIVES, RELATIVES, ETC. ETC.

Kei, Where ; Pasp., *ka*,
adv. locat., *q.v.*
Kókero, Self (*Ipse*)
Kon, *ko*, Who ; Pasp., *kon*,
quis
Nógo, Own

Jáfri, Such ; Pasp., *asavkó*
Sávo, so, Which, what ; Pasp.,
savó, so
Sor, All ; Pasp., *sarró*
Ta, who, which, that ; Pott,
ke ; Pasp., *ka*, rel. pron.

These words are classed together in accordance with Pott's and Paspati's arrangement.

NUMERALS.

1 *Yek ;* Pasp., *yek*, p. 75.
2 *Doöï ;* „ *dúi,* „
3 *Trin;* „ *trin*
4 *Stor;* „ *star*
5 *Pansh;* „ *pantch, pandj.*
6 *Shov;* „ *shov.*
7 *Doöï trinydw ta yek; trin ta stor* [*Afta*, Bryant ; *Heftan*, Marsden ; Pasp., *eftá*].
8 *Doöï storáw* [*oitoo*, Bryant ; Pasp., *ohtó*], and see 18.
9 *Doöï stóraw ta yek* [*enneah*, Bryant ; *Henya*, Marsden ; Pasp., *eniá*].
10 *Desh ;* Pasp., *desh.*
11 *Desh ta yek ;* Pasp., *desh u yek*, etc.
18 *Déshto ;* Pasp., *desh u ohtó.*
20 *Bish*, or *doöï desháw ;* Pasp., *bish.*
30 *Trin desháw ;* Pasp., *trianda.*
40 *Stor desháw ;* „ *saránda.*
50 *Pansh desháw ;* „ *peninda.*
60 *Shov desháw*, etc. ; Pasp., *exinda.*
100 *Desh desháw ;* Bw., *shel ;* Pasp., *shel.*
1000 *Mille*, Bw., " Lavo-lil," p. 154.

Besides the above forms, we may note the following :—
6 *Sho*, Bw., " Lavo-lil," p. 89 ; Pasp., *sho.*

7 *Efta*, Lld., Eng. G., p. 218, and *hefta*, p. 15; Bw. "Lavo-lil," p. 42, *eft*.

9 *Ennyo, nu*, Bw., "Lavo-lil," p. 5. Mr. Borrow, "Lavo-lil," pp. 154—162, gives *trianda*, 30; *shovardesh*, 60; and several other numerals.

For 7, 8, and 9 we have ourselves only heard the corrupt compound forms given above.

From the numerals there are formed

> *Yékino*, adj., single; and *yékorus*, adv., once.
> *Panshéngro*, n., five pound bank-note. Pasp., p. 77, *pantchengeré*, gen. pl.; of five piastres.

Mr. Borrow supplies the following :—

> *Duito*, second, "Lavo-lil," p. 408.
> *Trito*, third, "Lavo-lil," p. 96; and "Zinc.," 1843 ed., vol. ii., p. 145*.

PREPOSITIONS.

Adrál, 'dral, Through.

Adré, 'dré, Into, in.

Aglál, 'glal, Agál, 'gal, } Before, in front of.

Apósh, Against; v., *Pósha*.

Apré, opré, 'pré, Upon, on, up.

Avrée, 'vree, Out of, out, away, off, from.

Fon, from.

Katár, kátar, káter, To, unto, at.*

Ke, To (*ke-divvus*, to-day).

Palál, Pálla, Paúli, } After, behind, back.

Párdel, Pérdal, Paudál, Paúdel, } Over.

Posh, Pósha, } Opposite, near, by, besides.

Sar, With.

Talé, alé, 'lé, Down, under, beneath.

Tálla, Under, beneath, behind, after, except.

Te, To

Tooostál, Trróstal, } About, concerning.

---

* Katár, prep., = Hel., ἀπό; M. G., ἐκ; Paspati.

The following variations and additions are taken from Borrow's " Lavo-lil," etc. :—

Ando, In.

Anglo, Before.

Inna, inner, In, within.

Hir, By, " Lavengro," 1851 ed., vol., iii., pp. 53, 172.

Pa, For,   „   „   vol. i., p. 325.

Mr. Leland, " English Gypsies," p. 232, gives *muscro*, Through, in the centre of.

Of these, *te, ke*, and *sar* are also postpositions, *te* and *ke* forming the dative, and *sar* forming the instrumental case of the pronouns in this dialect, and of those cases of the nouns also in the Turkish and other dialects.

N.B.—Many of these prepositions are also used adverbially.

SYNTAX, IDIOMS, ETC.

The arrangement of words in a Gypsy sentence, with few exceptions, is strictly in accordance with the English language. The following peculiarities may, however, be mentioned :—

(1) The order of a sentence is often reversed, in deep Rómanes in connection with the verb *to be*, e.g.,

> *Tátcho see*, It is right.
> *Bókalo shom*, I am hungry.
> *Hóχano shom*, I am a liar.
> *Beéno shó'mas*, I was born.
> *'Jaw see*, It is so.
> *Tíkno chor see yov*, He is a little child.

(2) The nominative case often follows the verb it governs, *e.g.*,

> *Kobrombngro sas metro dad*, My father was a soldier.
> *Tóogono shom mé to dik toot akéi*, I am sorry to see thee here.

Kek na jinбva mé, I do not know.

Kek na jinéna yon, They do not know.

(3) The verb *to be* is frequently used without pronouns, *e.g.,*

Sar shan, How are you?

Bókalo shan, Are you hungry?

See also (1).

(4) In asking questions, the sense is frequently determined only by the tone, the pronoun when expressed often preceding the verb, *e.g.,*

Too dids o baúro chбori káter moosh? Did you give the big knife to the man?

Too rígherdás o koбshni keré? Did you bring the basket home?

Lon see tóoti? Have you got any salt?

Kek shoonésa too? Don't you hear?

Examples of the following will be found in other parts of the grammar :—

(5) The article, definite and indefinite, is frequently omitted.

(6) The adjective precedes the noun.

(7) Possession is denoted by the auxiliary verb and the pronoun in the dative case (*cf.* Pasp., p. 29).

(8) The use of the present tense for the future.

(9) The formation of the subjunctive by the optative particle *te* preceding the verb.

(10) Intensity is denoted by a repetition of the word, *e.g.,*

Dobvoreé dobvoreé, Very far indeed,—*cf.* Pasp., p. 171,

Nakéla sigó sigó o bersh, The year passes very quick.

(11) The elision of *or* between two numerals, *e.g.,*

Yek doбï, One or two; *Doбï trin*, Two or three, etc.,—*cf.* Pasp., pp. 594, 610.

(12) The use of double negatives for emphasis,—*cf.* Pott, ii., p. 321.

(13) Negation.   There are three classes of negatives:

(*a*) *Kek*, with derivatives *kéker, kékero, kékeno.*

(*b*) *Ma*, variously pronounced *maa, maw, mo,* usually *maw.*

(*c*) *Na, naw, né,* with derivatives *nei, nanéi, nastíssa, nestís.*

Class (*a*) are used chiefly in giving negative answers; (*b*) with the imperative in prohibiting; and (*c*) in making negative assertions.

It is remarkable that *kek*, which is so frequently used in this dialect, should be apparently without a representative in the Turkish, except perhaps *kánek,* Any, some, none,—about which, however, see Pasp., p. 266.

GYPSY-ENGLISH VOCABULARY.

NOTE.—Cross references are given between brackets ( ).

A.

Aáva, | *adv.*, Yes, truly, certainly, verily (óurli). Pasp.,
Aávali, | *va; beli* (As.) ; Lieb., *auwa*

Adói, *adv.*, There ('doi, odói). Pasp., *otid;* abl., *otár*

Adoósta, *adv.* and *adj.*, Plenty, enough ('doósta, 'dósta).
Lieb., *docha*

Adoóva, *pron.*, That ('doóva, adúvel). Pasp., *odová*
Adúlla, *pl.*, Those

Adrál, *prep.*, Through ('dral). Pasp., *andrál*, from within

Adré, *prep.*, In, into, to ('dré). Pasp., *andré*, in.
Kaíred adré, enclosed, fenced in ; lit., made in

Adróm, *adv.*, Away ('drom)

Adúlla, *pron. pl.*, Those
Adúlla *folk*i, so kek nanéi koméla mándi, Those
people who do not love me

Adúvel, *pron.*, That (adoóva)

Agál, | *prep.*, Before, in front of, in the presence of ('gal,
Aglál, | 'glal). Pasp., *anglál, angál*
Póshaglál, Opposite ; lit., close before

Ajáw, *adv.*, Thus, so ('jaw). ? Pasp., *adjái*, yet, still, again;
aveká, thus

Akéi, *adv.*, Here ('kei). Pasp., *aká*
Dídakeis, or Dítakeis, *n.pl.*, Half-bred Gypsies, who,
instead of '*dik-aket*,' say '*did-*, or *dit-, aket*,' for
' look here '

Akónyo, *adv.*, Alone (bikóyno)

Akóva, *pron.*, This ('kova). Pasp., *akavá*

Aládj, *adj.*, Ashamed ('ladj). Pasp., *ladj*, shame

Alé, *prep.*, Down ('lé, talé). Pasp., *telé*

    Besh alé, Sit down

    Chin alé, Cut off, cut down

Amándi, *pron.*, To me (mándi)

Améndi, *pron.*, We (méndi). Pasp., dat. pl., *aménde*

And, *v.a.*, To bring, fetch, etc. (hand). Pasp., *andáva*

    Andóva, I do, or will, bring, etc.

    Andéssa, You bring

    Ánlo, *p. part.*, Brought

    Ánlo apré, Brought up, educated

    Andadóm, I brought

    Andás, } He brought, they brought
    Andadás, }

Ángar, *n.*, Coals (vángar, vóngar). Pasp., *angár*, coal

Ánghitérra, *n., pr.*, England. French, *Angleterre*

Apópli, *adv.*, Again (pópli)

Apósh, *prep.*, Against

Apré, *prep.*, Upon, on, up ('pré, opré). Pasp., *opré*

    Atch apré, To awake, get up

    Dé, or del, apré, To read

    And apré, } To educate, bring up
    Hand apré, }

    Jiv apré, To live uprightly

    Lel apré, To arrest, take up

    Pand apré, To close, shut up

    Til apré, To raise, hold up

    Woóser apré, To vomit, throw up

    Yoóser apré, To sweep, clean up

Asár, ? *adv.*, ? Also. This word, or particle, is in frequent use, sometimes separately, apparently for emphasis, and sometimes as an adjunct to a *gáujo lav*, in order to disguise it. It frequently follows verbs in the imperative ; *cf.* Vaill., Gramm. Romm., 71, *Gati sar londis'*, prépare la salade ; and Mikl., ii., 5, 6. Mr. Borrow, in his " Lavo-lil," gives

(p. 18), "*Asā, asau,* ad., also, likewise, too ; *meero pal asau,* my brother also. *Asarlas,* ad., At all, in no manner ; " (p. 110) " It is my *Dovvel's kerrimus,* and we can't help *asarlus ;* " (p. 144) " But it was *kek koskipen asarlus.*" Our examples are:—

Besh pduli, asdr ? *Do* sit down (lit., back), won't you ?

Dik, odbi, asdr, mi Dobvelénghi ? *Do* look there, won't you, for God's sake ?

Rak, asdr, tl tobvlo. *Do* mind your tobacco

Too rbker asdr, sar see dbva chido talé ? Do you speak as it is put down ?

Mdndi rbker asdr misto kendw sig. I will speak well immediately

Pand asdr lésti opré káter rook. *Do* tie him up to (a) tree

Meéro rom pands asdr mandi opré. My husband shuts me up

And asdr mdndi a *kobsi padni.* *Do* bring me a little water

Help *asdr men, kair o wdrdo jal opré o drom.* *Do* help us (to) make the cart go on the road

Méndi forgive *asdr tobti.* We *do* forgive you

There's the *Béngesto-hév,* and the *Béngesto-mél asdr.* There's the devil's ditch, and the devil's die (dyke) too

Shan tobti jálin' to Stockport *asdr ?* Are you going to Stockport too ?

O bitto chávo wants *asdr* to *jin, kon shan too.* The little boy wants to know who you are

So too want *asdr ?* What do you want ?

Shobnedbm lésti kbrin' asdr mdndi. I heard him calling to me

Dboï méndi had *asdr kbmeni o' léndi.* Both of us had some of them

Mdndi did *asdr kombva* to *jal.* I did want to go

Yov kom'd asdr láti. He pitied her

Sas so yov promised *asdr.* It was what he promised

Kair too sus asár koméssa. Do just as you like

Well, if I wasn't thinking *asár ajáw !* Well, if I
wasn't thinking so !

Atch, *v.,* To stop, stand, halt, etc. (hatch). Pasp., *atchdva*

Atchóva, I stand, I do stand, I am standing, I will
stop, stand, arise, etc.

Atchéssa, You stop, thou stoppest

Atchéla, He stops

Atchénna, They stop

Átch*ing*, Standing, floating

Átchlo *p. part.* and *adj.,* Stopped, still

Átch*ed,* Stood

Atchdás,⎫
Atchtás, ⎭ He stood, arose

Atchdém, We stopped

Yon atchté, They stood

Atch apré, Awake, get up

Átch*ing* apré apópli, Resurrection ; lit., standing up
again

*A*trásh, *adj.,* Afraid (trash). Pasp., *trashdva*, to fear

Aúra, *n.,* Watch, hour (óra, háura, yórra)

Av, *v.,* To come (hav, 'wel, 'vel). Pasp., *avdva*

Avél, *or* awél, *v.,* To come, *eg.,* yon sas avél*in'*,
They were coming

Avéla, He comes

Avéssa, Thou wilt come

Ava tá, Come ye, come along !

Av pálla, Follow ! lit., come after

Av*in'*,   ⎫
Av*ering,*⎭ Coming

Wéla, wénna, vióm, viás, vié. See Vel

Avrée, *or* Avrí, *prep.* and *adv.,* From, out, out of, off, away
('vree). Pasp., *avrí*

Avrí-rig, Outside, crust

*A*wóver, *adj.,* Another (ovávo, wóver, wáver). Pasp., *yavér,*
other

Avávеré, *pl.,* Others

Azer, *v.*, To lift (had) ; *cf.* Pasp., *lásdava, ushtídva ;* Vaill., Gramm. Romm., *asarao*

    Ázerdás, He, or they, lifted

B.

*Badja*árus, *n.*, Badger

Báiro, *n.*, Ship. See Béro. Pasp., *beró*

Bal, *n.*, Hair. Pasp., *bal*

    Bálaw, *pl.*, Hairs

    Bal, *sing.,* ⎫ Grays, a Gypsy tribe ; as if *grey hairs.*
    Bálaw*s, pl.,* ⎭ Compare Borrow's Spanish Gypsy, *bullas,* grey hairs

    Bálaw*s, pl.*, Hernes, a Gypsy tribe

    Bálaw- ⎫
    Báleno- ⎭ mátcho, Herring

    Báleno, ⎫
    Bál*y*, ⎭ *adj.*, Hairy

    Kralisí's baúro báleno joókel, Dandelion (flower) ; lit., Queen's big hairy dog

    Bal-choóri, Knife

Bálans, ⎫
Bálanser, ⎭ *n.*, One pound sterling, a sovereign

Báleno-mas, ⎫
Bálovás, ⎭ *n.*, Bacon (baúlo). Pasp., *balanó-mas*

Bang, *n.*, Devil (Beng). Pasp., *beng*

Bángarée, *n.*, Waistcoat

Bánga, *n. pl.*, Whiskers. ? German *Wange*, cheeks, or is *bánga* due to the assonance of *waistcoat* and *whiskers* ?

Bar, *n.*, Stone. Pasp., *bar*

    Baráw, *pl.*, Stones

    Báryaw, *pl.*, Stones, testicles, pillars

    Baréngri, *n., pr.*, Stanleys, a Gypsy tribe ; as if ' stonely.' Pasp., *baréngoro*, stony

    Baréngro- ⎫
    Baréskro- ⎭ grei, Stallion, horse

Bísh'*ning* báuro bars, Hailing ; lit., raining big stones

Meéästo-
Poóker*ing*-} bar, Milestone

Soónakei *with* tátcho bars adré lis, Jewelry ; lit., gold with real stones in it

Bar, *n.*, One pound sterling, sovereign.　Pasp., *paró*, heavy

Bárvalo, *adj.*, Rich, wealthy.　Pasp., *barvaló*

Bárvalo-tem, Yorkshire

Bárvalopen, *n.*, Wealth, riches.　Pasp., *baravalipé*, wealth

Bárvalo bar, Diamond

Déshbár, *n.*, Ten-pound note

Barséngri,} *n.*, Shepherd.　Lieb., *Bershero ;* ? French, *Ber-*
Baséngro,} *gère*

Bastárdo, *n.*, Bastard (Boshtárdus)

Báulo, *n.*, Pig.　Pasp., *baló*

Baulé, *pl.*, Pigs

Baúlesto-fóros, Pig fair, pig market

Baúlesko-mas, Pork

Bálovás,　·
Báleno-mas,} *n.*, Bacon

Baúlesko-moór, Pigface, a nickname

Baúleski túlopen, Lard ; lit., pig's fat

Baúro, *adj.*, Great, big, large, broad, deep, etc.　Pasp., *baró*

Baúri, *adj., f.*, Pregnant, '*big* with child '

Baúri-chérikl,}
Baúro-chériklo,} Pheasant

Baúri-dei, Grandmother

Baúrodár, *comp.*, Bigger.　Pasp., *baredér*

Baúro-béresto-gav, Liverpool ; lit., big-ship-town

Baúro-bíshno, Hail

Baúro-choóri, Sword

Baúro-díklo, Shawl

Baúro-dood, Lightning

Baúro-gav, London

Baúro-hóloméngro,⎫
Baúro-hóloméskro, ⎬ Glutton
Baúro-hóbenéskro, ⎭

Baúro-paáni, Ocean, sea, deep water

Baúro-rei, Gentleman

Bauryó,⎫ *n.*, Assizes ; due to the assonance of
Baúri, ⎬ ' *Assize*' and ' *a size*' (a big thing)

Baúri, *n.*, Snail (boúri)

Bával, *n.*, Wind. Pasp., *balvál*

Bavéngro,⎫
Pógado-bávaléngro,⎬ *n.*, Broken-winded horse

Bával-pógaméngri, Windmill

*Be*chō'vihóni*ed*, Bewitched (chō'vihóni)

Beébee, *or* Beébi, *n.*, Aunt. Pasp., *bíbi*

Beéno, *p. part.*, Born. Pasp., *bendó*, delivered

Beené, *pl.*, Born

Posh-beénomus, *Placenta*, after-birth

. Beénopen, *n.*, Birth

Bei, *n.*, Sleeve, bough. Pasp., *bái*, sleeve

Gádesto-bei, Shirt-sleeve

Beng, *n.*, Devil (Bang). Pasp., *Beng*

Béngaw, *pl.*, Devils

Beng, *adj.*, Evil, wicked

Béngalo, *adj.*, Wicked, devilish, diabolic. Pasp.,
bengaló

Béngesko,⎫
Béngesko-dík*ing*,⎬ ditto, ditto

Béngesko-gaíro, *n.*, Enemy

Béngesko-tan, Hell ; lit., Devil's place

Béngeski-⎫ hev, ⎧The Devil's Ditch, near Balsham,
Béngesti-⎭ ⎨ Cambridgeshire

Béngesko-mel, The Devil's Dyke, near New-
market

Berk. See Burk

Béro, *n.*, Ship, boat, barque (Baíro). Pasp., *beró*

Beréngro,⎫
Béroméngro,⎬ *n.*, Sailor. Pasp., *beréskoro*

Béresto-sheréngro,⎫
Tátcho-beréngro,　⎬ Captain

Béresto-plóχta, A ship's sail

Béro-gav,　　　　　⎫
Baúro-béresto-gav,⎬ Liverpool

Besh, v., To sit. Pasp., *beshdva*

　　Beshóva, I sit

　　Beshéla, He sits

　　Beshtás, He sat

　　Beshás, Let us sit

　　Béshoméngro, n., Chair

　　Béshto, n., Saddle (bóshto). Pasp., *beshtó*, sat

　　Béshopen, n., Sessions. Pasp., *beshipé*, residence

　　Baúro-poókinyuski-béshopen, Assizes ; lit., great
　　　　judges' session

Besh, n., Year. Pasp., *bersh*

　　Béshaw,⎫
　　Besháw,⎬ *pl.*, Years

　　Beshéngro, n., A one-year-old horse, a yearling. This
　　　　word is also used with other numerals in stating a
　　　　person's age ; so Pasp., *Isí bish-u-pandj bershéngoro*,
　　　　He is twenty-five years old, which in the English
　　　　dialect would be ' *You see* a *bish-ta-pansh beshéngro*'

*Besom*aári, Besom-makers

Beúrus, n., Parlour, the best room of a house ; *cf.* Vaillant,
　　　　Gramm. Romm., *buro*, cavern

Bíkin,⎫
Bik,　⎬ v. a., To sell. Pasp., *biknáva*

　　Biknóva, I do, or will, sell

　　Bíkinéssa,⎫
　　Bíkinássa,⎬ Thou sellest

　　Bíkinéla, He sells

　　Bíkindé, They sold

　　Bíkindás, He sold

　　Bíkinás, Let us sell

　　Bíkinoméngro,⎫
　　Bíkoméngro,　⎬ n., Pedlar, licensed hawker

Bíknomus, *n.*, Auction sale

Bikónyo,⎫ *adv.*, Alone, unbegun, not done (akónyo, pokén-
Bikónya,⎭ yus). Pott, ii., 345, *pokoino, bokōno,* quiet
     Muk lésti bikónyo, Leave it alone

Bíssio,⎫
Bísko,⎭ *n.*, Spur. Pasp., *bust,* a spit

Bish, *adj.*, Twenty. Pasp., *bish*

Bíshno, *n.*, Rain (bríshindo)
     Baúro bíshno, Hail
     Bíshn*ing*, Raining
     Bíshn*ing* baúro bar*s*, Hailing

Bísser, *v.*, To forget. Pasp., *bistráva*
     Bíssadóm, I forgot
     Bíssadás, He forgot

Bísser, *v.*, To avoid (nísser)

Bísser, *v.*, To send. See next

Bítcher, *v.*, To send, to sentence. Pasp., *bitchaváva*
     Bítcherénna, They send
     Bitchadás, He sent
     Bítchadi paúdel, Transported ; lit., sent over. Pasp.,
        bitchavdó
     Bítchama, *n.*, Sentence, judgment
     Bítchaméngro, *n.*, A convict

Bítto, *m.*,⎫ *adj.*, Small, little, thin, narrow, lean. ? French,
Bítti, *f.*,⎭   *petit.* Sundt, *bittan,* a bit
     Bítta ta bítta, Little by little
     Bitadér, *comp.*, Smaller, less

Biván, *adv.*, Raw. Pott, ii., 406, *Bivant mass,* raw meat
     (taken by Pott from Zippel)
     Bívano, *adj.*, Raw
     Bívan-kosht, Green-wood

Blue-ássa, *adj.*, Blue

Blue léggi, *n. pl.*, Toadstools ; lit., *blue legs,* because one
     variety (Agaricus personatus), much esteemed by
     the Gypsies as a delicacy, has blue stalks

Bŏ′bi,⎫
Bóbbi,⎭ *n.*, Pea (bóobi). Pasp., *bóbi*

Baúro-)
Hólin'-} bóbbi, Broad-bean
　　Grei-bóbbi, Horse-bean
Bok, *n.*, Hunger.　Pasp., *bok*
　　Bókalo, *adj.*, Hungry.　Pasp., *bokaló*
　　Baúro bókaloben, Famine
Bok,)
Boꭔt, } *n.*, Luck, fortune.　Pasp., *bakht*
　　Bókalo,)
　　Bóky, } *adj.*, Lucky.　Pasp., *bakhtalo*
　　Koóshko bok, Health, happiness
　　Koóshki bóky, Happy
Bókocho, *n.*, Lamb (vákasho, bókoro).　Pasp., *bakritchó*
　　Bókochésto-pur, Tripe
Bókoro,)
Bókro, } *n.*, A sheep (bókocho).　Pasp., *bakró*
　　Bokré, *pl.*, Sheep
　　Bókoroméngro,)
　　Bókroméngro, |
　　Bókoméngro, } *n.*, Shepherd (barséngri)
　　Bókoréngro,)
　　Bokré's-peeré, Sheep's feet
　　Lávines-bókro, Goat ; lit., Welsh sheep
Bólesko-dívvus, *n.*, *Christ*mas Day.　Pasp., *boldva*, to bap-
　　tize, to *christen*
Bóngali-gáiro, *n.*, Rich man.　Only heard once ; ques-
　　tionable ; *cf.* Vaillant, Gramm. Romm., *banik*,
　　richard
Bóngo, *adj.*, Left, wrong, crooked, lame.　Pasp., *bangó*
　　Bóngo-wast, Left hand
　　Bónges, *adv.*, Wrongly
　　Bóngo-grei, Spavined horse
Bónnek, *To* lel bónnek, to lay hold of.　Pasp., *búrnek*,
　　handful
Boóbi, *n.*, Pea, bean (bōbi).　Pasp., *bóbi*, bean
　　Kaúlo-boóbi, Black bean
　　Boóbi bóshno, Peacock

Boódega,⎱ *n.*, Shop (boórika). French, *boutique;* Italian,
Boódika, ⎰ *bottéga;* Spanish, *bodega*
    Boódegaméngro, *n.*, Shopkeeper
    Símmer*ing* boódega, Pawnshop
Boogénya, *n.*, A pock (boóko). Pasp., *pukní,* abscess ; Pott,
    ii., 396 ; Mikl., i., 5
    Boogénya*s*, *pl.*, Smallpox
Boóko, *n.*, Liver. Pasp., *bukó,* intestine
    Boókesto-paáni-gav,⎫
    Boóko-paáni-gav,   ⎬ *n. pr.*, Liverpool
    Boóko-paáni,   ⎪
    Bookésto-gav   ⎭
Boóko, *n.*, Smallpox (boogénya)
Bool, *n.*, Rump. Pasp., *bul*
    Booléngri*es*,⎱ *n. pl.*, Breeches, knee-breeches
    Boóliéngri*es*,⎰
    Boóloméngro, *n.*, Contra naturam peccator
    Bool-koóva, Chair
    Grō'vneski-bool, Beef-steak
Boóīno, *adj.*, Proud, boasting, swaggering ; Pott, ii.,
    407
    Boóīnélopus pénsa rei, As stuck-up as a lord ; lit.,
    swaggering like gentleman
    Boóīnus-, or boóīno*us*-, moosh, A swaggering fellow
Boot, ⎱ *adj.*, Much. Pasp., *but*
Boóti,⎰
    Boótodair, *comp.*, More. Pasp., *butedér*
    O bootodaír, *superl.*, Most
    Boot adoósta, Very many, very much
Boóti, ⎱ *n.*, work. Pasp., *butí*
Boótsi,⎰
    Boóti, ⎱ *v.*, To work
    Boótsi,⎰
    Boótiéngro, ⎱ *n.*, Servant, worker
    Boótsiéngro,⎰
    Boótiesto-várdo, Knifegrinder's barrow
    Boótsi-*ing* gáiro, Working man

Shov divvusáw too boótiéssa, Six days shalt thou labour

Bor, *n.*, Mate, friend. ? In too general use to be the common Eastern Counties provincial word

Bor, *n.*, Hedge. Pasp., *bári*, garden

    Bóryaw, *pl.*, Hedges

    Boréngri, *n.*, Hedge-stake

Bórlo, Pig. See Baúlo

Bóro, Great. See Baúro

Boryó, Assizes. See Bauryó

Bosh, *v.*, To fiddle. Pasp., *bashaváva*, to play on any instrument

    Bosh, *n.*, Fiddle

    Bóshero, *n.*, Fiddler

    Bósherus, *n.*, Cough

    Bóshervénna, They are fiddling

    Bóshoméngri, *n.*, Piper, fiddler, a fiddle, music

    Bóshoméngro, *n.*, A fiddle, fiddler

    Wásto-bóshoméngro, *n.*, Drum

Bosh, *v.*, To bark. Pasp., *basháva*, to cry, call, sing

    Boshéla, It barks

    Bóshadé, They barked

    Bóshno, *n.*, Cock. Pasp., *o bashnó bashél*, the cock crows

Boshtárdus, *n.*, Bastard (bastárdo)

Bóshto, ⎫
Boshtó, ⎬ *n.*, Saddle (béshto). Pasp., *beshtó*, sat
Bóshta, ⎭

Boúri, *n.*, Snail (baúri). Vaill., Gramm. Romm., *buro*

*Breed*open, *n.*, Breed

Bríshindo, *n.*, Rain. Pasp., *brishindó*

    Brísheno, *adj.*, Rainy

    Bríshinéla, It rains

    Bishn*ing*, Raining

    - Bíshn*ing* baúro bar*s*, Hailing

    Baúro bíshno, Hail

Brŏ'gi*es*, *n.*, Knee-breeches

Búmbaros, *n.*, Monkey. ? Bw.'s Span. Gypsy, *bombardo*, lion, and *bomboi*, foolish

*Bung*aárus, *n.*, Bung, cork
Bur, *n.*, Gate
Burk, *n.*, Breast. Pasp., *brek*
  Burkáari, *pl.*, Breasts

CH.

Chábi, *n.*, *s.* and *pl.*, Child, children (chávi). Pasp., *tchavé*
Cháho, *n.*, Coat (chúkka, choófa, choóko). ? Pasp., *sharga*,
  ridinghood, " probably Turkish *chóha*, cloth, which
  the Greeks call τσόχα."—Extract from a letter
  from Dr. Paspati
Cháirus, *n.*, Time (cheérus). Pasp., *keros;* " καιρος, pro-
  nounced in Crete and Cyprus τσαιρὸς."—Extract
  from a letter from Dr. Paspati
  Mi-dúvelésko-cháirus, ⎫ Heaven, universe, world,
  Doóvelésto-cháirus, ⎭ eternity
  Gívesto-cháirus, Harvest
  Vénesto-cháirus, Winter
Chal, *n.*, Fellow, chap
  Rómani-chál, A Gypsy
  Rómani ⎧ -chaláw, ⎫
         ⎨ -chálaw, ⎬ *pl.*, Gypsies
         ⎩ -chalé, ⎭
Chálav, *v.*, To touch, meddle (chárvo). Pasp., *tchardva*, to
  lick ; *tchalaváva*, to beat
Cham, *n.*, Leather, cheek, tin. Pasp., *tcham*, cheek ; Lieb.,
  leather
Chárdoka, *n.*, Apron (choróva, to cover ; járifa, járika,
  jórjoχa, jorjóffa, shárdoka, yárdooka, yárduχa).
  Pasp., *utchardó*, covered. Baudrimont ("Voca-
  bulaire de la langue des Bohémiens habitant sur
  les pays Basques Français," Bordeaux, 1862,) has
  uruka, mantle, and Francisque Michel (" Pays
  basque," Paris, 1857,) has *uraka*, cape, both con-
  jecturally referred by M. Ascoli (p. 157) to *urav*,
  to dress

Chára, } *v.*, To touch, meddle, tease (chálav).   Pasp., *tcha-*
Chárvo, } *ráva*, to lick

    Charás, Let us tease

    Chárer opré, To vomit

    Cháver, *v.*, To betray, inform, tell, *sed quære*

Chávo, *m.*, } *n.*, Child.   Pasp., *tchavó, m. ; tchaví, f. ;*
Chávi, *f.*, } *tchavé, pl.*

    Chávi, }
    Chavé, } *pl.*, Children
    Chávies, }

    Kóshno-chávi, Doll ; lit., wooden-child

    Moósh-chávi, Boy ; lit., man-child

    Chavorí, *n.*, Chicken.   See Pott, ii., 199, *czarvi*, das
        Huhn ; dimin., *czarvóri*

Cheérus, } *n.*, Time (cháirus).   Pasp., *keros*
Cheer, }

Chei, *n.*, Lass, daughter, girl.   Pasp., *tchéi*

    Chéiaw, }
    Cheiáw, } *pl.*, Girls.   Pasp., *tchaiá*
    Chéias, }

Chein, *n.*, Moon (choom, shool, shoon).   Pasp., *tchon*

. Chellé mauré, *pl.*, Loaves (Chóllo):   Lieb., *zĕlo*

Chériklo, *m.*, } *n.*, Bird (chíriklo).   Pasp., *tchiriclĭ*
Chérikli, *f.*, }

    Baúro-chériklo, *m.*, } Pheasant
    Baúri-chérikli, *f.*, }

    Rómani-rókering-chériklo, A parrot

    Chériklesto-kair, Birdcage

Cheúri, *n.*, Knife (choóri).   Pasp., *tchorí, tchurí*

Chib, *n.*, Tongue (chiv, jib).   Pasp., *tchip*

Chíchi, } *n.*, Nothing.   Pasp., *hitch*
Chi, }

    Chíchikeni-dróm, ' No thoroughfare,' a private road

Chidé, They put. }
Chído, *p. part.*, Put. } See Chiv
Chidóm, I did put. }

Chik, *n.*, Dirt, filth, mud, ashes, sand, earth, soil, etc.   Pasp.,
    tchik

Chíkesko chúmba, Dunghill

Chíklo, *m.*,
Chíkli, *f.*, } *adj.*, Dirty. Pasp., *tchikaló*

Chikéngrie*s*, *n.*, 'Bankers,' who repair canal banks

Chin, *v.*, *a.*, To cut, dig. Pasp., *tchináva*

Chinóva, I do, or will, cut

Chinéla, He cuts

Chínlo,
Chin'*d*, } Cut

Chindóm, I did cut

Chínoméskro,
Chínoméngro, } *n.*, Bill, chopper, cleaver, hatchet,
Chínomóngri, } knife, letter

Poóvo-chínóméngri, Plough

Chínoben, *n.*, Wound, cut

Chin talé, *or* alé, To cut off, or down

Chíngar, *v.*, To quarrel, scold, tear. Pasp., *tchingdr*, misfortune, the origin of a quarrel, brawl

Chíngerénna, They quarrel

Chingadás, He tore, quarrelled, etc.

Chíngariben, *n.*, Quarrel

Chíriklo, *n.*, Bird (chériklo). Pasp., *tchiriklí*

Chiriklé, *pl.*, Birds

Chíti, *n.*, Chain. ? German, *kette*

Chiv, *v.*, To put, place, pour, etc. Pasp., *tchiváva*, to throw

Chivóva, I do, or will, put

Chivés,
Chivéssa, } Thou puttest

Chivéla, He puts, will put

Chivénna, They put

Chidóm,
Chivdóva, } I did put

Chivdás,
Chidás, } He placed, put

Chidém, We put, did put

Chído,
Chidé, *pl.*, } *p. part.*, Put

Yon chidé, They put

Chiv it *adré* your *shéro*, Remember; lit., put it into your head

*Chiv*ed upon, Cheated; lit., put upon, imposed on

*Chiv*ed to *woódrus,* Confined (of a woman); lit., put to bed

Chiv, *n.,* Tongue (chib). Pasp., *tchip*

Chívoméngro,⎫
Chívoméngri, ⎭ *n.,* Letter, lawyer, knife

Chívlo-górjer, Magistrate, justice of the peace (chúvno-górjer). Lieb., *tschiwalo rai,* der Polizei-direktor

Chivéngro, *n.,* Lawyer

Chok,   ⎫
Chókker, ⎭ *n.,* Shoe, boot. Pasp., *tchekmi* (As)

Chókaw, ⎫
Chóχaw, ⎭ *pl.,* Shoes, boots

Chokéngro, ⎫
Chokéngri, ⎭ *n.,* Shoemaker

Gréi-esto chok, Horseshoe

Néi-esto chók, Hobnailed boot

Chókka,⎫ *n.,* Coat (chúkka, cháho). Sundt, *tjokka,* Skjœrt;
Chóχo, ⎭   Pott, ii., 178

Pállani chókka, Petticoat; lit., behind-coat

Chóllo, *adj.,* Whole, entire (chellé). Pasp., *tchaló,* satisfied. Pott, ii., 256; Mikl., i., 7

Chóllo maúro, Loaf; lit., whole bread

Chellé mauré, *pl.,* Loaves

Chong, *n.,* Knee, hill (choong). Pasp., *tchang,* leg

Chóngaw, *pl.,* Knees

Chooáli, ⎫ *n., voc. pl.,* Mates! (choováli, chowáli). Pasp.,
Choobáli,⎭   *tchavále*

Choófa, *n.,* Coat (cháho, choóko, chúkka, chókka)

Chúffas, *pl.,* Petticoats (shoóba)

Choófihóni, *n.,* Witch (chō'vihóni, choóvikon). Pasp., *tcho-vekhanó,* ghost

Choókni,   ⎫
Chooknée, ⎭ *n.,* Whip (choópni). Pasp., *tchukní*

Choóko, *n.*, Coat (cháho, etc.)

    Yogéngri-choóko, Shooting-coat

Choom, *n.*, Moon (chein, shoon, shool). Pasp., *tchon*, *tchomút*

Choóma, *n.*, Kiss. Pasp., *tchumí*

    Choóma, *v.*, To kiss

    Choómeróva, I do, or will, kiss

    Choómadóm, I kissed, I did kiss

    Choomadás, He kissed

    Choómaben, *n.*, Kissing

Choómba,} *n.*, Hill, chin (choónga, chúmba, dúmbo). Pasp.,
Choómbo,}   *túmba*, hillock

Choómoni, *n.*, Something (chúmoni). Lieb., *tschomoní*

Choónga, *n.*, Hill (choómba, dúmbo). Pasp., *túmba*, hillock

Choong, *n.*, Hill, knee (chong). Pasp., *tchang*, leg

Choóngar, *v.*, To spit (chúngar). Pasp., *tchungardva*

    Choóngarben, *n.*, Spittle

Choópni, *n.*, Whip (choókni). Pasp., *tchupní*

Choóralo, *adj.*, Bearded. Pasp., *tchor*, beard

    Choóralo-moóí, Bearded face

Choóri, *n.*, Knife. Pasp., *tchorí*, *tchurí*

    Baúro choóri, Sword

    Choóresto-gav, Sheffield

    Poóvesto-choóri, Plough

Choóro, *m.*,} *adj.*, Poor, humble (chóro). Pasp., *tchoró*
Choóri, *f.*,}

    Choóreno, } *adj.*, Poor
    Choórokno,}

    Choórokné, *pl.*, Mumpers

    Choóroméngro,} *n.*, Tramp
    Choórodo, }

    Choórodé, } *pl.*, Tramps
    Choórodoné,}

    Choórodár, *comp.*, Poorer

    Choórones-gav, Wakefield ; lit., poorly town (poorly
      = weak = wake)

    Choórokono-lav, A mumper's word

Choováli, *n.*, *voc. pl.*, Mates, companions (chawáli, etc.)

Choóveno, *adj.*, Poor (chúveno)

    Choóvenes, *adv.*, Humbly

Choóvikon, *n.*, Witch (chō'vihóni). Pasp., *tchovekhanó*, ghost

    Choóvihóneski mátchka, Bewitched cat

Chor, *n.*, Grass. Pasp., *tchar*

    Choréngri, *adj.*, Grassy, green

    Chór-dik*ing*, *adj.*, Green ; lit., grass-looking

    Chor-óχtaméngro, Grasshopper

    Dándiméngri-chor, *pl.*, Nettles

    Chórkeno-tem, Yorkshire

Chor, *v. a.*, To steal. Pasp., *tchordva*

    Choróva, I do, or will, steal

    Chórdo,
    Chórno,
    Chórdeno,   } *p. part.*, Stolen. Pasp., *tchordó*
    Chordné, *pl.*,

    Chor,
    Chóroméngro, } *n.*, Thief. Pasp., *tchor*

Chor, *n.*, Son, lad. Pasp., *tcho*, child ; *gor* (As), boy

    Givéngro chor, Farmer's lad

Chóro, *adj.*, Poor (choóro). Pasp., *tchoró*

    Chórokonés, *adv.*, Humbly

Chóro,
Chóra, } *n.*, Plate, dish. Pasp., *tcharó*
Chor,

Choróva, I cover, wrap up. Pasp., *utchardva*

    Choróva les pardál *o'* yog, I will cover it up with
    ashes

    Chordás, They covered

Chórda, *v.*, To ' cover' (in coïtu). Pasp., *utchardva*, to cover,
    or *tchordva*, to pour ; *tchoraibé*, seminal fluid

Chóvono, *adj.*, Poor (chúveno, choóveno)

Chōvihóni, *n.*, Witch (choófihóni, choóvikon). Pasp., *tcho-*
    vekhanó, ghost

Chúffas, *n. pl.*, Petticoats (choófa, shoóba)

Chúkka, *n.*, Coat (cháho, choóko, etc.)

Chukkéngro,
Chukkéngri, } *n.*, Policeman

Chúmba, *n.*, Hill, chin (choómba, choónga, dúmbo). Pasp.,
    túmba, hillock

Chúmba kálesko tem, Derbyshire

Chúmoni, *n.*, Something (choómoni). Lieb., *tchomoní*

Chúngar, *v.*, To spit (choóngar). Pasp., *tchungardva*

    Chúngar, *n.*, Skewer, spit

Chúveno,
Chúvni, } *adj.*, Poor (choóveno, chóvono)

    Chúvno-górjer, Magistrate, justice of the peace
    (chívlo górjer)

D.

Dad,
Dádus, } *n.*, Father. Pasp., *dad*

    Daádi, *voc.*, Father !

    Dadéngro,
    Dadoméngro, } *n.*, Bastard ; because 'fathered' on
    Dádlo,   .   the putative parent

    Poóro-dad, Grandfather

    Stíffo-dad, Father-in-law

    Dádesko kair, Father's house

    Mi dádeski boótsiéngri, My father's servants

Dan, *adv.*, Than

Dánder,
Dand, } *v. a.*, To bite. Pasp., *dantáva*
Dan,

    Dándo,
    Dánlo, } *p. part.*, Bitten. Pasp., *dantó*

    Dan, *n.*, Tooth

    Dányaw,
    Danáw, } *pl.*, Teeth

    Choóro-bítto-dándoméngro, Mouse ; lit., poor little
    biter

    Dándiméngri-chor, Nettles ; lit., biting-grass

Dánderméskri, *n.*, Pepper

Dánoméskri, *n.*, Mustard

Dánd*ing*-píshum, Wasp; lit., biting-fly

Dash, *n.*, Cup. Pasp., *tási*

Doódás, } *n.*, Cup and saucer; lit., two cups, or
Doói-dash, } cuplike things

Dásko. See Dei

De, article, The

Dé. See Del

Deáro, } *adj.*, Dear
Dedri, }

Dei, *n.*, Mother. Pasp., *déi, dái*

Déiesko, } *gen.*, Mother's. Pasp., *daiáskoro*
Dásko, }

Déiä, *voc.*, Mother!

Baúri-dei, } Grandmother
Poóri-dei, }

Stíffi-dei, Mother-in-law

Del, *v. a.*, To give, kick, hit, read (dé). Pasp., *dáva,* to
give, kick, hit, speak

Dé, To give, kick

Dóva, } I do, or will, give, etc.
Delóva, }

Delóva meéro lav káter mi-Doóvel, I pray; lit., I give
my word to God

Déla, } He gives, will give, etc.
Deléla, }

Deldóm, } I gave, etc.
Dióm, }

Méndi dióm, We gave

Diás, He gave, forgave, etc.

Diás drován opré o woóda, He knocked hard at the
door

Díno, *n.*, Gift; lit., given. Pasp., *p. part.,* dinó

Dié, They gave

Dé } opré, *v.*, To read
Del }

Délomus-opré, Writing

Del-*to*-mándi, Present ; lit., a give to me

Peéro-délli*ng*-tem, Lancashire ; lit., foot-kicking
country

Déloméngro, *n.*, Parson, lucifer match, kicking horse

Déloméskro, *n.*, Hammer

Den, adv., Then

Desh, *adj.*, Ten. Pasp., *desh*

Deshbar, Ten-pound bank-note

Déshto-haúri,⎱ Eighteen-pence. Pasp., *desh-u-shtó*,
Déshti-kórri, ⎰ eighteen

Desh-ta-yék, Eleven. D. ta doói, -trin, -stor, -pansh,
-doói-trináw, 12, 13, 14, 15, 16. and so on ; doói
desháw, 20

Dídakeís, *n. pl.*, Half-bred Gypsies. See Akéi

Diás, He gave.⎱ See Del
Dióm, I gave. ⎰

Dik, *v. a.*, To see, look. Pasp., *dikáva*

Dikóva, I look, see

Te dikóv avrí, dikóva, If I look out, I see

Dikéssa, ⎱ Thou lookest, ye look, see
Too dikés,⎰

Dikéla, He sees

Dikéla pénsa raúni, She looks like a lady

Diktóm, ⎱ I saw
Diktoóm,⎰

Diktássa, Thou didst see, ye saw

Diktás, He saw, looked

Dikás, Let us look

Too diktás? Have you seen? (Properly *diktán;* see
p. 37)

Diktás kómeni? Did you see anything? (Properly
diktán; see p. 37)

Diktána, They saw, (properly *diktás*)

Díkto, ⎱ *p. part.*, Seen. Pasp., *diklô*
Díkno,⎰

Dik pálla, *v.*, To watch, attend to; lit., look after

Béngesko-díking, Diabolic, ugly ; lit., devil-looking

Koóshko-díking, Handsome, good-looking

Dídakéis, pl., Half-bred Gypsies.   See Akéi

Díkoméngro, n., Looking-glass

Door-díkoméngro, Telescope; lit., far-seeing thing

Díkoméngri, n., Portrait, likeness, photograph, picture

Díkimus, ⎫
Díkomus, ⎬ n., Sight

Wáfedo díkomusti chei sas yóɪ.   She was an ugly girl

Díklo, n., Handkerchief, necktie, etc.   Pasp., diklô

Baúro-díklo, Shawl

Dínilo, ⎫
Dínlo, ⎪
Dinlée, f., ⎬ n., Fool.   Pasp., dinilô
Dínvero, ⎭

Dinlé, pl., Fools

Dínveres, adv., Foolishly

Dínveri, adj., Silly, foolish

Diás. ⎫
Dié, Díno. ⎬ See Del, to give
Dióm. ⎭

Dívio, ⎫
Dívioo, ⎬ adj., Mad, wild.   Lieb., dîwio; Mikl., i., 9

Díviaw, pl., Lunatics

Dívio-kair, Asylum, madhouse

Dívi-gáiri, Midwife ; lit., madwife.   Due to assonance

Dívvus, n., Day.   Pasp., divés

Divvusáw, pl., Days

Ke-dívvus, ⎫
Kóvva-dívvus, ⎬ To-day
Te-dívvus, ⎭

Kóliko-dívvus, yesterday

Kroókingo-dívvus, Sunday

Mi-dúvel's-dívvus, ⎫
Mol-dívvus, ⎬ Christmas Day
Bólesko-dívvus, ⎭

Ovávo-dívvus, To-morrow

Trin-dívvus*es*-pálla-koóroko, Wednesday; lit., three days after Sunday, and so on for the other days of the week

Dívvus*ly*, *adv.*, Daily

Dívvus*y* roózha, Daisy

'Doi, *adv.*, There (adoí, odói). Pasp., *otíd ;* abl., *otár*

Dólla, *pron.*, Those (dúlla). Pasp., *odolé*

Dood, *n.*, Light. Lieb., *tüt*

Doódaw,
Doódyaw,} *pl.*, Lights, stars

Doódoméngro, *n.*, Lantern

Doódoméngro,
Doódeno, } *adj.*, Light (lucidus)
Doódengi,

Doódoméskri, *n.*, Lucifer-match

Doódesko moólo, Will-o'-th'-Wisp

Baúro-dood, Lightning

Midoóvelésko-dood, Moon, lightning

Dood-yógengi-kóshter*s*, Firebrands; lit., light-fire-sticks

Kaúlo-dood, Dark-lantern

Doódás, *n.*, Cup and saucer (dash)

Doódum, *n.*, Belly, womb. Pasp., *dudúm*, gourd

Doóï, *adj.*, Two. Pasp., *dúi*

Doóï-méndi, We two, or both of us

Doóï-léndi, They two, or both of them

Doóï kólli, Florin, a two-shilling piece; lit., two things

Doóï-dash,
Doódás, } Cup and saucer (dash)

Doóï trin, Two or three

Yon ghién avrí doóï ta doóï ketané, They went out by twos (*ghién*, for *ghiás*)

Doóker, *v.*, To hurt, pain, ache. Pasp., *dukáva*, to feel pain

Doóker, *n.*, An ache. Pasp., *duk*

Doókeróva, I punish

Doókadás, He did hurt

Doókadno, *p. part.*, Tormented

Doómo, *n.*, Back. Pasp., *dumó*

Dooméngro,   } *n.*, Broken-backed horse ; *doom-*
Dooméksno-grei, } *éksno* for *doomískano*

Door, *adj.* and *adv.*, Far, long. Pasp., *dur*

Door, *n.*, Distance

Door door dósta,} A very long way, very far off
Doovorí-doovorí, }

Doórdair, } *comp.*, Farther. Pasp., *duredér*
Doóroder, }

Door-díkoméngro, *n.*, Telescope ; lit., far-seer

Doóri, *n.*, String, twine (dóri). Pasp., *dorí*

Doórik, *v.*, To tell fortunes, predict (dúkker). Lieb., *turke-wawa*

Doórikapen, *n.*, Fortune-telling, prediction. Lieb., *turkepenn*

Doosh, *n.* and *adj.*, Evil ; bad, unlucky, etc. Lieb., *dosch*

Doóshalo, *adj.*, Unlucky, etc.

Doósta, *adj.* and *n.*, Enough, many, much, plenty, very (adoósta, dósta). Lieb., *docha ;* Mikl., i., 10

Door doósta, Long enough

'Doóva, *pron.*, That (adoóva). Pasp., *odová*

'Glal doovéski kair, In front *of that* house

Dúlla kólla, *pl.*, *Those* things

Doóvel, n., God (dúvel). Pasp., *devél*

Doóvelkanésto, *adj.*, Divine, holy. Pasp., *devlicanó*

Mi doóveléski cháiros, Eternity, for ever, the World, universe ; lit., my God's time

Dúvelésko chávo, Christ ; lit., God's Son

Mi-doóvelésko, *adj.*, Religious. Pasp., *devléskoro*

Mi-doóvelésko-dood, The moon

Mi-dúveléski gairé, Saints

Mi-dúvelésko maúroméngri, Jews ; lit., my God's slayers

Mi-doóvelésko bítta fólki, Fairies ; lit., my God's little people

Dúveléski Joóvel, The Virgin
Mi-dúvelésto-tem, Sky
Mi-doóvelésko-gódli, Thunder; lit., my God's voice
Mi-dúvelésko-kéri, Heaven
Mi-doóvelénghi, }
Mi-doóvelésti, } For my God's sake
Mi-dúvel, By God !
Mi-dúvel's moosh, Clergyman
Mi-dúvel's dívvus, Christmas Day

Doovorí, A long way off. (Door.) ? A contraction of
 door-avrée; compare, however, Böht., part i. (*adj.*) : "A
 lengthened form, *-oro, m.,* and *ori, f.,* is much affected
 by both adjectives and nouns, *e.g., terno,* young, *ternoró,
 ternorí,* very young "

Dórdi', *interj.,* Lo, behold, see, look ! ? Pasp., *otár dik*
Dóri, *n.,* String, twine, riband, navel (doóri). Pasp., *dorí*
Doriŏ'v, *n.,* Ocean, sea, river (doyáv). Pasp., *daráv*
Dósta, *adj.* and *n.,* Plenty, etc. See Doósta
 Dósta kómeni, A great multitude
 Dósta dósta besháw, Very many years
 Dósta ta dósta, Enough and to spare

Dóva, *pron.,* That, it. See Doóva
Dóva, I give. See Del
Dovál, }
Dovyál,} *n.,* Sea. Pasp., *devryál*
Doyáv, *n.,* Sea (doriŏ'v). Pasp., *daráv*
Drab, *n.,* Poison, drug, medicine. Pasp., *drab,* herb, root,
 physic
 Drabéngro, }
 Drabéngri, } *n.,* Druggist, doctor
 Tátcho-drabéngro, Doctor of medicine
'Dral, *prep.,* Through (adrál). Pasp., *andrál,* from within
'Dré, *prep.,* In (adré). Pasp., *andré*
Dríllaw, *n. pl.,* Berries, gooseberries (dúril)
Drom, *n.,* Road, way, path, lane, street, etc., fashion,
 manner. Pasp., *drom,* road; Mikl., i., 10
 Dromáw, *pl.,* Roads

Bauré drómaw, Highroads
Baúri-gávesti-drómaw, Streets; lit., big town-roads
Bítti-gávesti-drómaw, Lanes ; lit., little town-roads
Droóven, *adv.*, Slowly.   Pott, ii., 318, *dirwanés, drovven*, etc.
Droóveno,⎫
Droóven, ⎭ *adj.*, Tiresome, wearisome
Drován, *adv.*, Hard, forcibly, slowly
Dúkker, *v.*, To tell fortunes, predict (doórik).   Lieb., *turke-
wawa*
Dúkkeróva, I tell fortunes
Dúkker*in*', *n.*, Fortune-telling
Dúkkeriben, *n.*, Fortune
Dúkkadno, *p. part.*, Predicted
Dúlla,⎫
Dúlli, ⎭ *pl.*, Those (doóva).   Pasp., *odová ;* pl., *odolé*
Dúmbo, *n.*, Hill, mountain (choómbo, etc.)   Pasp., *túmba,*
hillock
Dúril, *n.*, Gooseberry (dríllaw).   Lieb., *heril*, a pea ; Pott,
ii., 167
Duriléski-gót, Gooseberry-tart
Dúvel, *n.*, God, sky, star.   See Doóvel.   Pasp., *devél*, God, sky

E.

Ei, an ejaculation of woe, alas !
'Es, *pron.*, It (les)
Eézaw, *n. pl.*, Clothes.   Sundt, Beretning om Landstryger-.
folket, 1852 ; *isar*, (*pl.*), Klœder

F.

Fáirus, *n.*, Fair (fóros)
Greésto-faírus, Horse fair
Férradair, ⎫
Féttadair, ⎬ *adj., comp.*, Better.   Lieb., *fedidir*
Féttadáiro,⎭
Féttedaíro toóti, Better than you

So komóva féterdáir, What I want most

O feterdáir plóχta, The best robe

Fílisin, *n.*, Hall, mansion.   Lieb., *filezzin*

Fíno, adj., Fine

First-adáir, *adj.*, First

    First-adáir *o'* liléi, Spring ; lit., first of summer

Fiz, *n.*, Enchantment, charm

*Folk*i (pron. fŏ'ki), *n.*, Folk, people

Follasé, }

Follasáw, } *n. pl.*, Gloves.   Lieb., *forlozzo ;*   Pott, ii., 394

Fóllasi*es*, }

Fon, *prep.*, From.   German, *von*

Foozhaári, *n.*, Fern

*Ford*é, }

*For*del, } *v.*, To forgive (dé, del)

    Forgive-asár, Forgive

    *For*delo*ness*, *n.*, Forgiveness

Fóros, *n.*, Market town (faírus).   Pasp., *fóros*

    Baúlesto-fóros, Pig fair

Fóshono, *adj.*, False, counterfeit, imitation

    Fóshono wóngushi*s*, False rings ; rings made of imitation gold

    Maw kair toóti kek kómeni fóshono koókelo, Thou shalt not make any graven image ; lit., don't make to thee not any false doll

Full, }

Fool, } *n.*, Dung, excrement.   Pasp., *ful*

    Full-várdo, Dung-cart

G.

This letter must be invariably pronounced hard, as in *go*, and not as in *gin*.

Gad, *n.*, Shirt.   Pasp., *gad*

    Gádaw, *pl.*, Shirts

    Gádesto-bei, Shirt-sleeve

    Gad-kosht-koóva, Clothes-peg

Gáiro, *n.*, Man. Only applied to *gaújos*. Pasp., *kur ; gor* (As), boy ; Sundt, *gaer* (*pl.*), Folk

Gáiri,
Gairí, } *f.*, Woman

Gairé, *pl.*, Men

Peévlo-gáiro, Widower

Peévli-gáiri, Widow

Vardéngro-gáiro, Miller

Yek *o'* mi doóvel's tátcho gairé, An angel

'Gal, *prep.*, Before (agál, 'glal). Pasp., *anglál, agál*

Gárav,
Gárer, } *v. a.*, To hide. Pasp., *gheraváva*

Garóv, I do, or will, hide

Gárido,
Gáridnó, } *p. part.*, Hidden
Gárer*ed,*

Gáridnes,
Gárones, } *adv.*, Secretly, hidden, unknown

Gáradóm,
Garavóm, } I hid

Gáradás,
Garavás, } He hid

Gaújo, } *n.*, Stranger, English person, one who is not a
Gaújer, } Gypsy. (Górjo.) Pasp., *gajó*

Gav, *n.*, Town, village. Pasp., *gav*, village

Gaváw, *pl.*, Towns

Gavéngro,
Gavéngri, } *n.*, Policeman

Baúro-gav, London

Baúro-béresto-gav,
Boóko-paáni-gav, } Liverpool

Stéripen-gav, County town ; lit., prison town

Méndi jal*s* yek gáver káter wáver, We go from one town to the other

Ghián, You went.
Ghiás, He, she, they went. } See Jal
Ghién, They went.

Ghil, *v. a.*, To sing (ghiv). Pasp., *ghilidbava*

Ghíli, *n.*, Song (ghíveli). Pasp., *ghill*

Ghílyaws, *pl.*, Songs, broadsheets, handbills, newspapers

Ghilyéngri, *n. pl.*, Newspapers

Ghílo,
Ghilé, } *p. part.*, Gone. See Jal. Pasp., *gheló, ghell*

Ghínjer,
Ghínya, } *v.*, To count, reckon. Pasp., *Ghendva;* pass.,
ghenghiovdva

Ghióm, I went. See Jal

Ghiv, *v. a.*, To sing (ghil)

Ghivóva, I do, or will, sing

Ghíveli, *n.*, Song (ghíli)

Ghivénna, They sing

Ghiv, *n.*, Corn, wheat. Pasp., *ghiv*

Ghivéngro,
Ghivéskro, } *n.*, Farmer

Ghivésto-cháiros, Harvest ; lit., corn-time

Ghivésto-kair, Farmhouse

Ghivésto-shéro, Ear of corn

Ghiv-pooséngro, Wheat-straw stack

Ghiv-poov, Wheat-field

Lívena-ghiv, Barley ; lit., beer-corn

Ghiv, *n.*, Snow (iv, hiv, shiv, yiv). Pasp., *iv, hiv, biv, vif*

'Glal, *prep.*, Before ('gal, agál, aglál). Pasp., *anglál, angál*

Póshaglál, *adv.*, Opposite ; lit., close before

Tátcho-'glal, *adv.*, Opposite ; lit., right before

Gódli, *n.*, Noise, dispute, quarrel, row, summons (gúdli,
goódli)

Mi-doóvelésko-gódli, Thunder

Góı, *n.*, Pudding, pie, tart. Pasp., *gói*, a thick sausage

Gō'ıa, *pl.*, Puddings

Góıóngo-gúnno, Pudding-bag

Góno,
Gonnó, } *n.*, Sack (gúnno, kányo). Pasp., *gonó*

Goódlo, *m.*,
Goódli, *f.*, } *adj.*, Sweet. Pasp., *gudló*, gentle, sweets

Goódli, *n.*, Sugar, summons

Goódlopen, *n.*, Sweets, sweetmeats. Pasp., *gudlipé*, gentleness

Goóroni, *n.*, Bull. Pasp., *gurí*, ox ; adj., *guruvanó*

Goóshum, *n.*, Throat

Górishi, trin-górishi, Shilling. Pasp., *ghroshia*, piastres, from the Turkish *ghrush ;* compare also German *groschen ;* Sundt, *gurris ;* Skilling ; Pott, i., 52 ; Mikl., i., 13

Gorjo, } *n.*, Englishman, stranger, alien, gentile, any one who
Gorjer, } is not a Gypsy. Pasp., *gadjó ;* Mikl., i., 11

    Górji, *f.*, Stranger. Pasp., *gadjí*

    Gorjé, *pl.*, English persons, Gentiles. Pasp., *gadjé*

    Górjikana-drom, non-Gypsy fashion

    Gaújikana jínomus, Learning fit for an alien

    Boot gaujé-kani *fólk*-i see-lé konáw, They are all like Gentiles now

    Górjikanes, }
    Górjokanes, } *adv.*, English
    Górjones, }

    Chívlo- }
    Chúvno- } górjer, Magistrate

    Paanéngro-górjer, Sailor ; lit., water-gentile

    Poovéngri-górjer, Irishman ; lit., potato-gentile

    Yogéngri-górjer, Gamekeeper ; lit., gun-gentile

Gózvero, *adj.*, Artful, sly. Lieb., *godswěro ;* Pasp., *godialó*

Gráinsi, }
Gránza, } *n.*, Barn. Lieb., *granscha*, stable

Grásni, *n. f.*, Mare. Pasp., *grasní*

    Grásni-méila, She-ass

Greíno, *adj.*, Green

Grei, *n. m.*, Horse. Pasp., *grái*

    Gréiaw, }
    Greiáw, } *pl.*, Horses

    Greiéngro, *n.*, Horsedealer, groom

    Gréiesto-chok, Horseshoe

    Gréiesti-chóχaw, *pl.*, Horseshoes

Gréiesto-chúkni, Horsewhip
Gréiesto-faírus, Horse-fair
Gréiesto-kóppa, Horse-rug
Gréiesko-menéngro, Horse-collar
Gréiesto-prástering, Horse-race
Baréngro-⎫ grei, Stallion
Baréskro-⎭
Deloméngro-grei, Kicking horse
Dooméksno-grei, Brokenbacked horse
Grúnchi-grúnchi-grei, Insatiable horse; by onoma-
    topœa
Grésti, n., The *mayor* of a town. (The form of this word is
    the dative of *grei,* but it is probably a corruption
    of *grásni*)
Groóvni,⎫ n., Cow. Pasp., *guruvnó*
Groóven,⎭
    Groóvenesko-mas, Beef
    Moóshkeni-groóvni, Ox, bull; lit., male cow
    Groóvni roózha, Cowslip (flower)
Grōv, n., Bull. Pasp., *guruv*
    Grōvneski-bool, Beef-steak
Gúdli, n., Noise (gódli)
Gúnno, n., Sack, bag (gónno). Pasp., *gonó*
Gur, n., Throat (kaúri, kur, kárlo). Pasp., *korí;* Mikl., i., 13

H.

This letter is in many instances interchangeable with K, and in such cases is a
    relic of an original aspirated *K,* e.g., *hol* and *kol,* to eat (*khála,* Pasp.)

Had, v. a., To raise, lift (ázer). Lieb., *hadawa*
'Hámyas, n. pl., Knee-breeches (rokámyas)
Hand, v. a., To bring (and). Pasp., *andva*
Hánik,⎫ n., Well. Pasp., *khaník*
Hánikos,⎭
Hárri, n., Penny (hórro, haúro, kórro). Lieb., *cheiro*
Hatch, v., To stand, halt, stay, stop, etc. (atch). Pasp.,
    atcháva, to remain

6

Hatch-paúli-kánni, Guineafowl; lit., stay-back fowl, because provincials call them 'comebacks,' from their cry

Hav, *v.*, To come (av, 'vel).   Pasp., *aváva*

Haw, *particle*, ? eh

Too shánas náfelo wáver dívvus, haw ?   You were ill the other day, eh ?

Haw, *v.*, To eat (hol, kol).   Pasp., *kháva*

Hawméskro, *n.*, Table

Haúrini, *adj.*, Angry, cross, savage (hóino, kórni).   Pasp., *kholinákoro*

Haúro, *n.*, Copper (hárri, hórro, kórro)

Haúrongo, *adj.*, Copper (hólono)

Haúro, *n.*, Sword.   Pasp., *khanró*

Héka, *n.*, Haste (yéka, hókki).   Pott, ii., 173, suggests *sik*, quick as the etymon

Héro, ⎫
Hérer, ⎭ *n.*, Leg, wheel.   Lieb., *hero.*   Pasp., *gher*, thigh

Heré, *pl.*, Wheels

Wárdesko-heré, Cart-wheels

Heréngri*es*, *n. pl.*, Leggings

Hérengro-mátcho, Crab ; lit., legged-fish

Hev, *n.*, Hole, window, grave (kev).   Pasp., *khev*

Hévaw, ⎫
Hévyaw, ⎬ *pl.*, Holes, windows
Hévyaw*s*, ⎭

Hév*ly*, ⎫ Holy.   From the assonance of *Hole* and
Héveski, ⎭   *Holy*

Moósheno-hev, Armpit

Hínder, ⎫
Hind, ⎭ *v.*, Cacare (kinder).   Pasp., *khendáva*

Híndo, ⎫
Híndi, ⎭ *adj.*, Dirty, wretched, squalid, filthy

Híndi-kair, Privy.   Pasp., *khéndi*

Híndi-kákarátchi, Parrot ; lit., dirty magpie

Híndo-tem, ⎫ Ireland.   ? *cf.* Pasp., *hindyemi*, the
Híndi-teméskro⎭   end of the world

Híndo-kóvva, A coarse expression sometimes used for mustard; *cf.* múterimóngeri

Híndi-teméngro, Irishman

Híndi-teméngri-gairé, *pl.*, Irishmen

Híndi-teméngri kóngri, Catholic Church; because so many Irish are Roman Catholics, or, in common parlance, Catholics

Hiv. *n.*, Snow (iv)

Hoax, *v.*, To cheat (hókano). Pasp., *khokhaváva*

Hóben, *n.*, Food, victuals, eatables (hólben, kóben). Pasp., *khabé*

  Hóben-cháiros, Supper-time

  Hóbenéngro, *m.*,
  Hóbenéngri, *f.*, } *n.*, Cook, one who sells food

  Hóbenéskro, *n.*, Table

  Baúro hóbenéskro, A glutton; lit., big eater

Hodás, He ate. See Hol

Hódjerpen, *n.*, Gonorrhœa (hótchopen)

Hódno,
Hodóm, } I ate, eaten. See Hol

Hóïno, *adj.*, Angry (hō'no, etc.) Lieb., *hoino;* Mikl., i, 12

  Hóïnomus,
  Hóïben, } *n.*, Anger, vexation

  Hóïn*ed*,
  Hóï*ed*, } Vexed

  Hoïn*ous*, *adj.*, Angry

Hóχaben,
Hóχani, } *n.*, Lie, falsehood (hoókapen, hoax)

  Hókano,
  Hóχanó, } *n.*, Liar, lie; *adj.*, false. Pasp., *khokhavnó*

  Hokané, *pl.*, Lies

Hóχter,
Hókter, } *v.*, To jump (óχta). Pasp., *ukhkidva*, to arise, get
Hok, } up

  Hókki! Look! Here! (heka, yéka). Pott, ii., 173

Hol, *v.*, To eat (haw, kol). Pasp., *khidva*, to eat; *khaló*, eaten

Hóva, }
Holóva, } I do, or will, eat

Hóla, He eats

Holéssa, Thou eatest, you eat

Hodóm, I ate

Hodás, He ate, he has eaten

Hodé, }
Hodén, } They ate

Hódno, }
Hólled, } *p. part.*, Eaten

Hólben, }
Hóloben, } *n.*, Food (kóben). Pasp., *khabé*
Hóben, }

Hóleno, }
Hólono, } *n.*, Landlord
Holéskro, }

Hólomus, *n.*, Feast, supper. Vaill., p. 70, *Andeas o hamos*, On a servi ; p. 71, *To hamos pe meseli*, Mets le plat sur la table

Baúro-hóloméngro, Glutton

Baúro-hóloméngro-joókel, }
Baúro-hóloméskro-joókel, } Wolf ; lit., big-eating dog

Lólo-hóloméngri, Radish

Gréi-esko lólo-hólomengri, Horse-radish

Hólono, *adj.*, Copper (haúrongo)

Honj, *n.*, The itch

Honj, *v.*, To itch. Pasp., *khándjiovava*

Hónjedóm, I itched

Hónji*fied*, *adj.*, Mangy

Hŏ'no, *adj.*, Angry, cross, etc. (hóino, haúrini, kórni). Lieb., *hoino*

Hoófa, *n.*, Cap, captain (koófa). Dr. Paspati says in a letter, "from the Greek κούφια, a cap"

Hoókapen, *n.*, Lie, falsehood (hóχaben). Pasp., *khokhamnibé, khokhaimbé*

Hoólavers, *n. pl.*, Stockings (*oúlavers*). Lieb., *cholib;* Mikl., i., 4

Hoóra, *n.*, Watch (óra). Pasp., *óra*

Hórro,
Hórri, } *n.*, Penny (hárri, kórro, haúro)

    Posh-hórri, Halfpenny
    Shoo-khórri, Sixpence
    Désto-hórri, Eighteenpence

Hótcher,
Hotch, } *v. a.*, To burn (káchar).   Lieb., *chadschewawa*

    Hótcheróva, I do, or will, burn
    Hótcheréla, It burns
    Hótchedo, *p. part.*, Burnt
    Hótchedé, *pl.*, Burnt, also They burnt
    Hótchedóm, I burnt
    Hótchedás, He burnt
    Hótcheropen,
    Hótcheroben, } *n.*, Gonorrhœa (hódjerpen)
    Hótchopen,

Hótchi-wítchi, Hedgehog. Vaill., Gramm. Romm., *Hoc'a,*
    épic, pique ; *hoc'aviça*, porc, épine, hérisson ; *hoc'lo,*
    herissé, piquant

Hótcher mé, I said.   An irregular verb ; used in narration,
    like 'quotha.' Vaill., *hiotosarao*, jeter les hauts
    cris ; Pasp., *khuyásava*, to call, cry to any one
    Hótchi-yov, He said
    Hótchi-yóï, She said
    Hótch'ov, He said, I said

Hóva, I eat.   See Hol

I.

I, *f.*, *def. art.*, The. Pasp., *i*
I'ngrin*ies*, *n. pl.*, Welsh Gypsies, ? Ingrams
Iv, *n.*, Snow (ghiv, hiv, shiv, yiv).   Pasp., *iv*, etc.
    Iv-bar, Snowball

J.

Jáfra,
Jáfri, } *adj.*, Such.   Pasp., *asavkó*

Maw kel jáfri gódli, Don't make such a noise

Kek na komóva jáfri tanáw si kóli, I do not like such places as these

Jal, v., To go (jaw, jil, jol, ghílo). Pasp., *djáva*

Jóva, ⎫
Jalóva, ⎬ I do, or will, go

Jalássa, ⎫
Jássa, ⎬ Thou goest, you go

Jála, He goes

Jalóm méndi, We will go

Yov te jal, That he may go

Ghióm, I, or we, went

Ghiás, He went

Ghián, Ye went

Ghilé, They went

Ghílo, *p. part.*, Gone. Pasp., *ghelô*

Jas ménghi pardál kóla poovyáw, Let us go over those fields

Jál*ed*, Went

Jal pálla, To follow; lit., go after

Jal shookár, Go softly

Jámba, *n.*, Toad (jómba). Pasp., *zámba*, frog

Járifa, ⎫
Járika, ⎬ *n.*, Apron (jorjóffa, etc.)

Jas, Let us go. ⎫
Jássa, You go. ⎬ See Jal

Jaw, v., To go (jal, etc.) Pasp., *djáva*

Jaw paúli, v., To return, go back

'Jaw, *adv.*, Thus so (ajáw). Pasp., *adjái*, yet, still, again ; *aveká*, thus

'Jaw see ta 'jaw see, Amen ; lit., so it is and so it is

'Jaw mándi, So do I

Jeer, *n.*, Rump. Pasp., *ghür*, groin

Jib, *n.*, Tongue, language (chiv). Pasp., *djib* (As); *tchip*

Jído, *adj.*, Alive, lively. See Jiv

Jil, *v.*, To go. See Jal

Jin, *v.*, To know. Pasp., *djináva*

Jinóva,
Jináw, } I know

Kek na jinóm mé, *I* don't know (? jináw mé)

Jinéssa, Ye know, thou knowest

Jinéla, He knows

Jinénna, They know

Jindóm, I knew

Jindássa, Thou didst know, you knew

Jindás, He knew, they knew

Jínlo, *p. part.*, Known

Jínoméskro, *adj.*, Wise, clever, knowing, sharp, 'fly'

Jínoméskro,
Jínoméngro, } *n.*, A knowing person, wise man

Jínoméskri, *pl.*, Wise men

Jiv, *v.*, To live. Pasp., *djiváva*

Jivóva, I live

Jivéssa, Thou livest, ye live, thou shalt live

Jivéla, He lives

Jivénna, They live

Jivdás, He lived

Jívdo,
Jívo, } *adj.*, Alive, living. Pasp., *p. part.*, *djivdó*
Jído,

Jívoben, *n.*, Livelihood, life. Pasp., *djibé*

Jiv apré, *v.*, To live uprightly

Job, *n.*, Oats (jōv). Pasp., *djov*, barley ; Mikl., i., 47

Jób-pooséngro, Oat straw stack

Jō'l-ta, A signal-cry, the meaning of which is obsolete.
? Bryant, *shulta*, here (sed q., *shulta = shoonta*, hear!), Leland, Engl. G., p. 227, *jōter*

Jol, *v.*, To go. See Jal

Jómba, *n.*, Toad (jámba). Pasp., *zámba*, a frog ; Mikl., i., 47

Jóngher, *v.*, To awake. Pasp., *djangáva*

Joókel,
Jook, } *n. m.*, Dog (yákel). Pasp., *djukél*

Joókli, *f.*, Bitch.   Pasp., *tchukli*

    Kanéngro-joókel, Greyhound ; lit., hare-dog

    Vesh-joókel, Fox ; lit., wood-dog

    Baúro-hóloméngro-joókel, ⎫

    Baúro-hóloméskro-joókel, ⎭ Wolf ; lit., big-eating dog

    Kralisí's baúro báleno joókel, Dandelion (flower) ; lit., Queen's big hairy dog

Joóva, *n.*, Louse.   Pasp., *djuv*

    Joové, *pl.*, Lice

    Joóvli, *adj.*, Lousy.   Pasp., *djuvaló*

Joóvel, *n.*, Woman.   Pasp., *djuvél*

    Joóvyaw, *pl.*, Women

    Joóvni, *adj.*, Feminine, female.   Pasp., *djuvlicanó*

    Joóvni-kóllaw, *pl.*, Women's clothes

    Joóvisko-más, ⎫ Mutton ; lit., female meat ; or,

    Joóviko-mas, ⎭ The flesh of a cow which has died in calving

    Joóvioko-st ádi, Bonnet ; lit., female hat

Jorjóffa, ⎫ *n.*, Apron (járifa, chardókka, etc.) Böhtlingk,

Jorjóχa, ⎭ Part i., p. 35, *jäudäräka*, shawl

Jōv, *n.*, Oats (job).   Pasp., *djov*, barley

Jóva, I go.   See Jal

Justa konáw, Just now

K.

This letter in some words is interchangeable with '*h*,' and, in such cases, is a relic of an original aspirated '*k*,' e.g., *kol*, *hol*, originally *k-hol*, to eat.

Kaáfni, *adj.*, In foal (kávni).   Pasp., *kabní*

Káchar, *v.*, To burn (hótcher). Lieb., *chadschewawa ;* Pasp., *kisdízava*, to take fire

Kair, *n.*, House.   Pasp., *ker*

    Kairáw, *pl.*, Houses

    Kairéngro, *n.*, Housedweller, housekeeper

    Káiriko-tan, Brickfield

    Kéri, ⎫

    Keré, ⎭ *adv.*, At home.   Pasp., *keré*

Chíriklésto-kair, Birdcage
Ghivésto-kair, Farmhouse
Híndi-kair, Privy
Králisko-kair, Palace
Loódopen-kair, Lodging-house
Kair, *v. a.*, To do, make, etc. (kérav, kel). Pasp., *ke-ráva*

Kairóva,
Keróva,
Kelóva, } I make, do make, I will make, or do, etc.
Keráw,

Keréssa,
K'éssa, } Thou makest
Kerés,

Kairéla,
Keréla,
Keléla, } He, she, it, does, or will, make, do, etc.
Kéla,

Kairénna, } They make, dance, etc.
Kerénna,

Kédo,
Kaírdo, } *p. part.*, Done, made. Pasp., *kerdó*
Kaíred,

Te. kérav teéro drom, To make thy way
Kedóm, I did, I made, I did do, I have done
Kedás, } He made
Kerdás,
Kedás wáfedo, He sinned, he suffered; lit., he did bad
Kairdán, Thou hast cooked, done
Yon kerdé, They cooked
Kedé *a* baúro gódli, They made a great noise
Kerás ménghi, Let us cook, make, dance, play
Kair posh, To help; lit., do half
Kair tátcho, To cure; lit., make right
Káired adré, Enclosed, fenced in
Káiropen, *n.*, Doings, dealings, actions

Kériben, }
Kérimus, } *n.*, Behaviour, doing

Káiroméngro, }
Kéroméngro, } *n.*, Creator, maker

Kal-kélimus-tem, Cheshire ; lit., cheese-making
    country

Kaij, }
Kaish, } *n.*, Silk. Pasp., *kesh*

Káijino, }
Káisheno, } *adj.*, Silken. Pasp., *keshanó*

Kákarátchi, *n.*, Magpie. Pasp., *karakáshka, kakaráshka*
    Híndo-kákarátchi, *n.*, Parrot ; lit., dirty magpie

Kal, *n.*, Cheese. Pasp., *kerál*
    Kaléngri, *n.*, Buttermilk, whey
    Kál-márekli, Cheesecake
    Kálesko- }
    Kal-kélimus- } tem, Cheshire, as if *Cheese*shire
    Kal-kélin'- }
    Chúmba-kálesko-tem, Derbyshire ; lit., hill-cheese-
      county

Káliko, *n.*, Yesterday, to-morrow (kóliko)
    Lóva léndi *to* mándi's hóben adré káliko saúla, I will
      have them for breakfast (lit., to my food) (in) to-
      morrow morning
    Káliko koóroko, Last Sunday

Kam, *n.*, Sun. Pasp., *kam*
    O kam see opré (or, átch*ed* opré), The sun has
      risen
    O kam see bésh*ed* (or, bésh*ed* talé), The sun has set

Kámora, }
Kamóra, } *n.*, Chamber, room. Lieb., *kamóra;* see Mikl.,
    i., 17 ; Pasp., in a letter, says "Greek κάμερα,
    from κάμαρα, a vault"

Kánder, }
Kan, } *v.*, To stink. Pasp., *kandáva*

    Kand, }
    Kan, } *n.*, A stink, unpleasant smell
    Kanéla, It stinks

Kánlo,
Kánelo,
Kánloo, } *adj.*, Stinking
Kanlé, *pl.*,

Kánlo-poóruma, Garlic ; lit., stinking onion
Kan, *n.*, Ear. Pasp., *kann*
    Kánaw, *pl.*, Ears
    Kanéngro,} *n.*, Hare
    Kanéngri,
    Baúri-kanéngri-moosháw, *pl.*, Hernes ; lit., big-hare-
      men
    Kanengré, *pl.*, Hares
    Kanéngro-joókel, Greyhound
    Kanéngro-moosh, Gamekeeper
    Kanéngro,
    Kanéngri, } *n.*, Earring
    Kánoméngro,
    'Shoóko kanéngri, Deaf person
Kánna, *adv.*, When, now (kónna). Pasp., *kánna*
    Kánna yuv sas lell*ed* opré, When he was arrested
    Kánna sig, Immediately (kenáw sig)
Kánni,} *n.*, Hen, fowl. Pasp., *kagní;* Liebich, *kachnin.* See
Káχni, Mikl., i., 16
    Kánniaw,} *pl.*, Hens, fowls
    Kánnia,
    Hatch-paúli-kánni, Guineafowl, called 'comebacks'
      by provincials, from the cry
Kányo, *n.*, Sack (góno). Pasp., *gonó*
Kárlo, *n.*, Throat (kur, gur). Pasp., *kurló*
Kas, *n.*, Hay. Pasp., *kas*
    Kaséngro, *n.*, Hayrick
    Kásoni, *n.*, Billhook
Káter,} *prep.*, To, unto, at. Pasp., *kátar*, from where,
Kátar,} whence; *katár*, from; *akatár*, from here ; *okatár*,
Katár,} from there. Lieb., *gatter*, hither
Kátsers,} *n.*, Scissors. Pasp., *kat*
Kátsi*es*,

Káteni, }
Kátenes, } *adv.*, Together (kétané, *to*-ketané). Pasp., *ketané*
Kátené, }

Kaúlo, *m.;* Kauli, *f.;* Kaulé, *pl.*, Black. Pasp., *kaló*

>Kaúlo, *n.*, Common, heath, a term which is said to have originated with the large black waste lands about Birmingham and the Staffordshire Potteries

>Kaúloben, *n.*, Blackness

>Kaúloméskro, *n.*, Blacksmith

>Kaúloméskro-koóva, Anvil ; lit., blacksmith-thing

>Kaúlo-boóbi, Black bean

>Kaúlo-dood, Dark-lantern

>Kaúlo-gav, Birmingham, London ; lit., black town

>Kaúlo-tem, 'The Black Country,' either Manchester, Birmingham, the Staffordshire Potteries, or Lancashire

>Kaúli-raúni, Turkey ; lit., black lady

Kaur, *v.*, To shout, call (kor). ? Pasp., *tchárdava*

Kaúri, *n.*, Penis (kórri)

Kaúri, *n.*, Neck (kur). Pasp., *kort*

Kávakéi, This here

Kávodói, That there

Kávni, *adj.*, In foal (kaáfni). Pasp., *kabní*

'Kávi, *n.*, Kettle (kekávi)

Kedás, He made. See Kair

Ke-dívvus, *n.*, To-day

Kédo, *p. part.*, Made. } See Kair
Kedóm, I made. }

Kei, *adv.*, Where. Pasp., *ka*

'Kei, *adv.*, Here (akeſ)

Kekávi, *n.*, Kettle ('kávi). Pasp., *kakkávi*

Kek, *adv.*, No, not. ? Pasp., *kaných*, none

>Kéker, *adv.*, No ; *adj.*, None

>Kékero, *adj.*, None

>Kékera mándi, }
>Kéker mándi, } No, not I ; an emphatic negation

Kéker adré lin, Empty ; lit., none in them

Kek-kómi, *adv.*, Never, no more

Kék-kom, *v.*, To hate ; lit., not-love

Kek-kómeni, None, nobody, no one (kómeni)

Kel, *v.*, To do, act, play, dance, make, cook, etc. (kair).
　　Pasp., *keráva*, to make ; *keláva*, to dance

　　Kelóva, I will make

　　Kéla, It will do

　　Keléla péias, It is playing ; lit., it makes fun

　　Kell*ed*, Made

　　Kell*ing*, Dancing

　　Kélopen, *n.*, Spree, dance, dancing, ball.　Pasp.,
　　　　kelibé

　　Kéloméngro, *n.*, Doer, performer

　　Spingaáro-kéloméngro, Skewer-maker

　　Kélimus, *n.*, Play.　Vaill., *kelimas'*

　　Kal-kélimus-tem, Cheshire ; lit., cheese-making
　　　　country

Kenáw,⎫
Knaw,　⎭ *adv.*, Now (kánna).　Pasp., *akaná*

　　Kenáw-sig, Just now, immediately (kánna-sig) ; lit.,
　　　　now soon, or quick

Képsi, *n.*, Basket (kípsi)

Kérav, To cook.⎫
Keráw, I do.　　⎭　See Kair

Keré,⎫
Kéri,⎭ *adv.*, At home.　Pasp., *keré*

Kériben,　⎫ Behaviour.
Kérimus,　⎭

Kerénna, They make.　⎫ See Kair

Keréssa, Thou makest, etc.⎭

Kérmo, *n.*, Worm (kírmo),　Pasp., *kermó*

Keróva, I do.　See Kair

Késser, *n.*, Care ; *v.*, To care

　　Késseréla, He cares

Késter, *v.*, To ride (kíster).　Pasp., *uklistó*, mounted

　　Kesterdás, He rode

Késterméngro, *n.*, Jockey

Kétané, } *adv.*, Together (káteni).　Pasp., *ketane*
Kétanes,

Kév, *n.*, Hole, window (hev).　Pasp., *khev*

Kil, *n.*, Butter.　Pasp., *kil*

　　Kil-maúro, Bread and butter
　　Kil-kóro, Buttercup (flower)
　　Kil-píshum, Butterfly

Kílli, *n.*, Earring.　Pasp., *tcheni*

Kin, *v.*, To buy.　Pasp., *kindva*

　　Kindóm, I have bought
　　Kindás, He bought

Kínder, *v.*, To relieve the bowels (hínder).　Pasp., *khen-dáva*

Kíndo, *adj.*, Wet, sweaty.　Pasp., *tünde* (As).　Pott, ii., 103

Kínger, *v.*, To tease, bother, weary, vex.　Pasp., *khíniovava*, to be tired

　　Kínno,
　　Kinó,　} *p. part.*, Tired, weary.　Pasp., *khinó*
　　Kíni,
　　Kiní,

Kípsi, *n.*, Basket (képsi)

Kírmo, *n.*, Worm (kérmo).　Pasp., *kermó*

Kísi, *n.*, Purse.　Pasp., *kisí*

Kísi, *adj.*, Much ; sar kísi, how much.　Lieb., *gizzi*
　　Sávo kísi, What a lot of

Kíster, *v.*, To ride (késter).　Pasp., *uklistó*, mounted

Kítchema, *n.*, Inn.　Lieb., *kertschimma.*　See Mikl., i., 19

　　Kítchemáw, *pl.*, Inns
　　Kítcheméngro, *n.*, Innkeeper

Klérin, *n.*, Key.　Pasp., *klidí*

　　Klérin,
　　Klísin,　} *n. and v.*, Lock

　　Klísináw, *pl.*, Locks, a Gypsy tribe
　　Klísoméngro, *n.*, Bridewell, lock-up, police-station, rabbit-trap

Klísi, *n.*, Box

K'naw, *adv.*, Now (kenáw)

Ko, *pron.*, Who (kon). Pasp., *kon, ka*

Kóko, *n.*, Uncle. Pasp., *kak*

Kokálos,⎱ *n.*, Bone, rib, thigh (kokoólus). Pasp., *kókkalo*
Kókalo, ⎰

Kókero,⎱
Kokeró,⎬ *adj.*, Self, lonely, alone. Pasp., *kórkoro,* alone
Kókeri, ⎰

    Kokeré, *pl.*, Selves

Kókerus, *n.*, Week (koóroki, kroóko, etc.) Pasp., *kurko*

Kokoólus, *n.*, Bone (kokálos). Pasp., *kókkalo*

    'Kólyaw, *pl.*, Bones

    Koókelo, *n.*, Doll. Lieb., *gukkli*

Kol, *v.*, To eat (hol, haw). Pasp., *khava*

    Kóben, *n.*, Food, victuals, eatables (hóben, hólben).
        Pasp., *khabe*

Kóliko, ⎱ *n.*, Yesterday (káliko). Pasp., *korkoro,*
Kóliko-dívvus,⎰   *kólkoro,* alone ; Lieb., *kokeres,* retired,
        alone

    Kóliko-'saúla, To-morrow morning

Kólla,⎱ *n., s.* and *pl.*, Thing, things, shillings (kóvva, koóva).
Kólli,⎰   Pasp., *ková.* This is really a plural form ; compare
       '*kova,* this, and '*doóva,* that

    Kóllaw,⎱ *pl.*, Things, shillings
    Kolé, ⎰

    Doói-kólli, Florin, two-shilling piece

    Joóvni-kóllaw, Woman's clothes

    Múttering-kólla, Urinal

    Pansh-kólla, Crown, five-shilling piece

    Pansh-kólenghi-yek, A five-shilling one

    Práastering-kólli, Railway train

    Wáfedi-kólli, Misfortunes ; lit., evil things

'Kólyaw, *n. pl.*, Bones (kokoólus)

Kom, *v.*, To love, owe, wish, desire, want, like, etc. Pasp.,
    kamáma

    Kómer, *v.*, To love

Komóva, I do want, I want, like, wish, etc.

Koméssa,}
Komés,   } You like, thou lovest, thou wantest

Komés too ? Do you like ?

Koméla, He wants, or will want, he likes

Koménna, They wish

Kom asár, *imperat.*, Love thou

Kómoben, *n.*, Love, friendship, mercy, pity

Kómomus, *n.*, Love

Kómoméskro,}
Kómelo,   } *n.*, Lovell, a Gypsy tribe

Kómomúso,}
Kómomusti,} *adj.*, Loving, kind, dear
Kómelo,   }

Kómelo-gáiro, Friend

Komyáw, *pl.*, Friends

Kómyaws, *pl.*, Lovells. See above

Kek-kom, *v. a.*, To hate ; lit., not love

Kómeni, *adj.*, Some, somebody (choómeni, kúmeni)

  Kek-kómeni, None, nobody, not any

  Dósta-kómeni, A great multitude

Kómi, *adj.*, More. Pott, ii., 90

  Kómodair, *comp.*, More

  Kek-kómi, *adv.*, Never, no more, not again

Kon, *pron.*, Who (ko). Pasp., *kon, ka*

Kon, *adv.*, Then, therefore

  Besh toóki 'lé kon, Sit down then

Kon, Sor-kon, All, every. Mikl., ii., 35, *sekon;* Vaill., *se kono;*
    Mikl., i., 46

  Sór-kon kólli, All things, everything

Konáfni,   }
Konaáfi,   } *n.*, Turnip (kráafni)
Konáfia, *pl.*,}

  Gréiesko-   }
  Baúlesko-   } konaáfi, Beetroot
  ·Bókro-   }

Kóngali, *n.*, Comb. Pasp., *kanglí*

Kónga,
Kóngl, } *v.*, To comb

Kóngeri,
Kóngri, } *n.*, Church. Pasp., *kangheri*

    Kóngri lil, Bible

Koófa, *n.*, Cap (hoófa)

Koókelo, *n.*, Doll, goblin (kokoólus). Lieb., *gukkli*

Koóko, *n.*, Week (koóroko)

Koónjonés, *adv.*, Secretly, unknown ; ? connected with
    Koónsus, a corner. See also Bikónyo, Akónyo

Koónsus,
Koónshi, } *n.*, Corner. Lieb., *guntsch*

Koor, *v.*, To fight, beat, strike, knock, etc. Pasp., *kuráva*

    Kooróva, I do, or will, fight

    Koórdno, *p. part.*, Beaten

    Koorás, Let us beat

    Koordás, He beat

    Koordém ménghi, We fought

    Koóroben,
    Koórimus, } *n.*, Battle

    Koóroméngri, *n.*, Drum, tambourine

    Koóroméngro, *n.*, Soldier, pugilist, etc.

    Koórimóngeri, *n.*, Army

Koóroko,
Koóroki, } *n.*, Sunday, week (kókerus, kroóko, koóko, etc.)
    Pasp., *kurkó*, Sunday, week

    Yórakána-koóroko, Easter Sunday ; lit., egg Sunday

    Koóroko, *n.*, Thunder ; by a lisping assonance of
    thunder and *Sunday*

    Yek dívvus pálla koorokéss, Monday ; lit., one day
    after Sunday

Koórona, *n.*, Crown, five-shilling piece. French, *couronne*

Koóri, *n.*, Cup, pot (kóro, kúra). Pasp., *koró*

Koósi, *n.*, A little. Pott, ii., 96, *kutti*

Kooshné, *pl.*, Baskets (kúshni). See Mikl., i., 18

Koóshto,
Koóshko, } *adj.*, Good (kóshto, kúshto). Lieb., *gutsch*,
    happy ; Böhtl., *känsto*, good ; Sundt, *kiska*,
    good ; Pott, ii., 93, *kucz*, theuer

Koóshtiben, ⎫
Koóshtoben, ⎬ *n.*, Goodness, good
Koóshkopen, ⎭
Koóshko-bok, Happiness, good health
Koóshko-bóky, Happy
Koóshko-díking, Handsome, good-looking
Koóva, *n.*, Thing (kólla, kóvva). Pasp., *ková*
   Koóvaw, *pl.*, Things
   Bool-koóva, Chair
   Gad-kosht-koóva, Clothes-peg
   Kaúloméskro-koóva, Anvil
   Mútterimóngeri-koóva, Teapot
   Tátto-koóva, Pepper
   Lálo-koóvaw, Cherries, currants
Kóppa, *n.*, Blanket. Lieb., *gappa ;* Pasp., *kírpa*, a dish-clout
   Greſesto-kóppa, Horserug
   Peéresto-kóppa, Carpet
Kor, *v.*, To call (kaur). ? Pasp., *tchárdava*
   Koróva, I do call
   Kórdo, *p. part.*, Called
   Kordóm, I called
   Kordás, He called
   Kordé, They called
   Kóroméngro, *n.*, One who calls at shops, and steals
     money by sleight of hand
   Mookás méndi kor asár dúla *folki*, Let us call those
     people
Kor, *n.*, Brow, eyebrow
Kóro, ⎫
Kóredo, ⎬ *adj.*, Blind. Pasp., *koró*
Kórodo, ⎪
Kórdi, ⎭
   Kordé, ⎫ *pl.*, Blind people
   Kóredé, ⎭
   Kórodomus, *n.*, Blindness
Kórni, *adj.*, Cross, ill-tempered (haúrini, hóno, hórno).
   Pasp., *kholinákoro*

Kórro,⎫ *n.*, Penny (hórro, hórri, hárri).   Lieb., *cheiro,* cheir-
Kórri, ⎭ *engero*

Déshti-kaúri, Eighteenpence

Shookhaúri, Sixpence

Kóro, ⎫ *n.*, Cup, pot (koori, kúra).   Pasp., *koró*
Kórro, ⎭

Koréngro, *n.*, Potter

Koréngri, *pl.*, Potters

Koréngri-tem, ⎫ Staffordshire
Kóresko-tem, ⎭

Kórri,⎫ *n.*, Thorn, tent-peg, pudendum virile (kaúri). Pasp.,
Kóro, ⎭ *kar,* penis ; *kanró,* thorn

Baúro-kauréngro-moosh, A descriptive appellation

Kor'ri, *or* Kaúri, *n.*, Throat (kur).   Pasp., *korí*

Kósher,⎫ *v.*, To lick, to clean (yoóso).   Pasp., *koshdva*
Kósser, ⎭

Kósserin' plóxta, Towel ; lit., cleaning-cloth

Kósseróva les yoózho, I will cleanse it

Kossadé, They licked

Kóshno-chávi, Doll (kóshteno)

Kóshto, *adj.*, Good (koóshto)

Koshté, *pl.*, Good

Kóshtoben, ⎫ *n.*, Goodness, peace
Kóshtomus, ⎭

Keróva mi kóshtodaír les, I will do my best

Kosht, *n.*, Stick.   Pasp., *kasht, kash*

Koshtáw, *pl.*, Sticks

Koshténgro, *n.*, Woodcutter.   Pasp., *kasht'skoro*

Kóshteno-tíkno, Doll (kóshno-chávi).   Pasp., *kashtu-
nanó*

Dood-yógengi-kóshters, Firebrands

Gad-kosht-koóva, Clothes-peg

Moóshkero-kosht, Constable's staff

Poókering-kosht, Signpost

Yoósering-kosht, Broom

Kósser.   See Kósher

Kótor, *n.*, Piece, part, guinea-piece. Pasp., *kotór*, a piece indeclinable

    Kotoré,   } *pl.*, Pieces
    Kótoráw, }

    Kótoréndri, *n.*, Fragment

    Kótoréndi, Pieces, to pieces

Kóvva, *n.*, Thing (koóva, etc.) Pasp., *ková*

    Lílesko-kóvva, Paper ; lit., book thing

    Moóesto-kóvva, Looking-glass

'Kóvva, *adj.*, This (akóvva). Pasp., *akavá*

    Kóvva-dívvus, To-day

Kraáfni, } *n.*, Nail, button, turnip (konáfia, konáfni). Pasp.

Kráfni, } (p. 451), *kárfia ;* Mikl., ii., 37, 132 (Kolomyjer Kreise Galiziens Vocab.), *karfín,* nail

Krális, *n.*, King. Pasp., *krális.* See Mikl., i., 18

    Kralisí, }
    Králisi, } *n.*, Queen. Pasp., *kralítcha*
    Krallíssi, }

    Králisko-kair, }
    Králiskésko-kair, } Palace

    Králisko-poóro-kair, Castle

    Králisko-rook, Oak ; called frequently 'royal oak'

    Krális*om*, *n.*, Kingdom

    Kralisí's } baúro báleno joókel, Dandelion (flower);
    Kraliskésko } lit., Queen's }
                   King's } big hairy dog

Krámbrookos, *n.*, Drum. Lieb., *tambuk*

Kreéa, *n.*, Ant. Pasp., *kirí*

    Kreéaw, *pl.*, Ants

Kroóko, *n.*, Week (koóroko, etc.) Pasp., *kurkó*

    Kroókingo-dívvus, }
    Kúlfo,   } *n.*, Sunday

Kúmbo, *n.*, Hill (dúmbo)

Kúmeni, *adj.*, Some, somebody (kómeni)

    Vániso-kúmeni, Anybody

Kur, *n.*, Throat (kárlo, kor'ri, gur). Pasp., *kurló, korí*

Kúra, *n.*, Cup (kóro)

Kúrri, *n.*, Tin, solder. Pasp., *kaldi*, tin
Kúshni, *n.*, Basket (tushni, trooshni, etc.) Pasp., *kóshnika*
    Kooshné, *pl.*, Baskets
Kúshto, *adj.*, Good (koóshto)
    Kúshto-moóshi, Right arm

L.

Ladj, *n.*, Shame (aládj). Pasp., *ladj*
    Ládj-*fully*, *adv.*, Shamefully
Ládjipen, *n.*, Goodness (látcho). Pasp., *latchipe*
Láki, } *pron.*, Her (láti, lóki). Pasp., 2nd dat., *lake;* gen.
Lákro, }   *lákoro*
Lálo, *adj.*, Red (lólo). Pasp., *loló*
    Lálo-gav, Reading ; lit., red-town
    Lálo-píro, Redford ; lit., red-foot
    Lálo-koóvaw, Cherries, currants ; lit., red things
Las, He, or she, got (lel). Pasp., *lids, las*
Las, *pron.*, Him, it (les, lis, 'es). Pasp., *les*
Lása, With her. Pasp., *lása*
Latch, *v.*, To find. Pasp., *lasdáva*, to pick up
    Latchóva, I do, or will, find
    Latchénna, They find
    Látchno, *p. part.*, Found
    Latchdóm, I found
    Latchás ménghi, Let us find
Látcho, *adj.*, Good, fine (ládipen). Pasp., *latchó*
Láti, *pron.*, To her, with her, her (láki). Pasp., 1st dat., *láte*,
    to her
Lav, *n.*, Word, name. Pasp., *lav*
    Lávaw, }
    Laváw, } *pl.*, Words
    Lávyaw, }
    Lávines, *adv.* used as a *noun*, Gibberish
    Lávines-tem, Wales ; lit., wordy country
    Lávines-rókerben, Welsh language ; lit., wordy talk
    Lávines-gaújo, Welshman

Lávines-gairé,   } *pl.*, Welshmen
Lávinéngri-gaujé, }

Del lav, *v.*, To answer, pray

Del koóshto lávaw, To pray ; lit., give good words

Delóva meéro lav káter mi-doóvel, I pray God

Law, I take. See Lel

Lé, *pr. pl.*, They.   Pott, i., 242

 Boot gaujákani *fólk*i see-lé konáw, Very Englishified
  folk are they nowadays

 Poókeroméngri see-lé, They are informers

 Koshté see-lé konáw—toólo see-lé, They (hedge-
  hogs) are good now (to eat)—they are fat

 Kanlé see-lé, They are putrid

Lé, Take !   See Lel

'Lé, *prep.*, Down (alé, talé)

Leéno, *p. part.*, Taken.   See next

Lel, *v.*, To take, get, obtain, catch, etc.   Pasp., *láva*

 Lóva,   )
 Lelóva,   } I do, or will, get, take, etc.
 Law,   )

 Léla, He takes, catches, he will take, etc.

 Lióm, I got, obtained, etc.

 Liás,)
 Las, } He, or they, got.   Pasp., *liás, las*

 Lián, You took, got, etc.

 Lié, They took

 Leéno,)
 Linó,   } *p. part.*, Got, taken, begotten.   Pasp., *linó*
 Lélo,   )

 Beng te lel toóti, Devil take you

 Lel kóshtoben, Please ; lit., take the goodness

 Lel mótti, To get drunk

 Lel opré, To apprehend ; lit., take up   *Lel bonnek*

 Lel trad, Take care ! mind !

 Lel veéna, Take notice

Len, *pron.*, Them (lin).   Pasp., acc., *len*

Léndi, *pron.*, To them, them, their (lénti).   Pasp., 1st dat., *lénde*

Shoon léndi, Remember! lit., hear them

Léngheri,
Lénghi, } *pron.*, Their (léndi)
Lénti,

Lénsa, With them. Pasp., *lénsa*

Les, *pron.*, Him, it (las, 'es, lis). Pasp., acc., *les*

Lésko, *pron.*, His. Pasp., gen., *léskoro*

Lésti, *pron.*, His, her, it. Pasp., 1st dat., *léste*

Lián, Ye got.
Liás, He, or they, got. } See Lel

Líbena, *n.*, Beer (lívena, 'víni). Lieb., *lowina*

Lié. See Lel

Lik, *n.*, Nit. Pasp., *lik*

   Líkyaw, *pl.*, Nits, flies

Lil, *n.*, Book, paper. Pasp., *lil*

   Liláw,
   Lílyaw, } *pl.*, Books

   Lílesko-kóva, Paper; lit., book-thing

   Liléngro, *n.*, Star, because ' read' by astrologers

   Mi doóvelésko lil, } Bible; lit., my God's book, or
   Kóngri lil,   } church book

   Pansh bálanser lil, Five-pound note

Lilef,
Lílei, } *n.*, Summer. Pasp., *nilái*

   Bíg*n*omus } *o'* lilef, { Spring; lit., beginning, or first,
   Fírstadair }   { of summer

   Pálla-lilef-see-párdel, Autumn; lit., after summer is
      over

Linó, *p. part.*, Taken. See Lel

Lióm, I took. See Lel

Lívena, *n.*, Beer (líbena, lovína, 'víni). Lieb., *lowina;* Mikl.,
      i., 28

   Livenéngro, *n.*, Brewer, beerseller

   Livenéngries, *n. pl.*, Hops

   Póbesko lívena, Cyder; lit., apple-beer

   Lívena ghiv, Barley

Lo, *pron.*, He. Pott, i., 242

Yov ghiás káter tan kei sas-ló, He went to the place where he was

O rashéi, koóshto sas-ló, The priest was a good man ; lit., the priest, good was he

'Jaw wáfedo see-ló adré lésko zee, He is so jealous

Lod, *v.*, To lodge. Pasp., *lodáva*

    Loódopen, *n.*, Lodging

Lóki, *pron.*, Her (láki)

Lóko,⎫ *adj.*, Heavy. Pasp., *lokó*, light (*levis*) ; Mikl., i., 22.
Lokó,⎭   This is an example of the confusion of opposite meanings remarked by Mr. Leland, Eng. Gypsies, p. 126

    Kek naneí lóko, It is light

    Chómoni sas adré, lokó, Something was inside, heavy

Lólo, *adj.*, Red (lálo, lúller). Pasp., *loló*

    Lóli-mátcho, Red-herring

    Lólo hóloméngri, Radish ; lit., red-eating thing

    Greíesko lólo hóloméngri, Horseradish

    O lólo wéshkeno-joókel, The fox

    Lólo-matché, *pl.*, Salmon ; lit., red-fish

Lóli, *n.*, Farthing (lúli)

Lónderi, *n. pr.*, London (Lúndra). French, *Londres*

Lon, *n.*, Salt. Pasp., *lon*

    Lóndo, *adj.*, Saline, salt. Pasp., *londó*

    Lóndo-paáni,⎫ The sea ; lit., salt water
    Lóndudno-paáni,⎭

    Lóndo mátcho, Salt fish

    O hõ'mo lóndo paáni, The angry waves

Long, *adj.* and *v.*, Lame, to lame. Vaill., *lang ;* Sundt, *longaló ;* Pott, ii., 337

    Longé, *pl.*, Lame people

Loóbni,⎫ *n.*, Harlot (lúbni, lúvni). Pasp., *lúbni ;* Mikl., i.,
Loódni,⎭ 21

    Loóbniaw, *pl.*, Harlots

    Loóberiben, *n.*, Prostitution

Loódopen, *n.*, Lodging, barn (lod)

Loódopen-kair, Lodging-house

Loor, *v.*, To rob, plunder, steal

Loórdo,
Loór*ed*, } *p. part.*, Robbed

Loóroméngro, *n.*, Thief

Loóripen, *n.*, Booty, plunder

Loóvo,
Lóvo, } *n.*, Money (lúva). Pasp., *lové*

Lóva, I take. See Lel

Lovína, *n.*, Beer (lívena)

Lúbni, *n.*, Harlot (loóbni). Pasp., *lubní*

Lúli, *n.*, Farthing (lóli)

Lúller, *v.*, To blush (lóló). Pasp., *lóliavava*

Lúlleróva, I do, or will, blush

Lúndra,
Lúndro, } *n. pr.*, London (Lónderi). French, *Londres*

· Lúva, *n.*, Money (loóva). Pasp., *lové*

Lúvni, *n.*, Harlot (loóbni)

M.

Maa, *prohibitive particle*, Do not (maw). Pasp., *ma*

Maloóna, *n.*, Thunder. Mikl., i., 24

Mályaw, *n. pl.*, Companions, mates. Pasp., *mal*

Man,
Mándi, } *pron.*, I, me (ménghi, mónghi). Pasp., acc., *man;*
Mánghi, } 1st dat., *mánde;* 2n l dat., *mánghe*

Mándi see lésti, It is mine ; lit., to me is it

A del-*to*-mandi, A gift, present

Manoósh, *n.*, Man, male (moosh). Pasp., *manúsh*

Manoóshni, *n.*, Woman (mónoshi). Pasp., *manushní*

Mánsa, *pron.*, With me. Pasp., instr., *mánsa*

Mántchi too,
Mántcha too, } Cheer up ! Vaill., *manjao*, I console

Márikli, *n.*, Cake. Pasp., *manrikló*

Kal-márikli, Cheesecake

Mas, *n.*, Meat, sheep. Pasp., *mas*

Masáw, *pl.*, Meats, victuals
Maséngro, *n.*, Butcher. Pasp., *maséskoro*
Maséngro's maúr*in'* kair, Slaughter-house
Masáli, *n.*, Frying-pan
Joóvioko-mas, Mutton
Moóshkeno-mas, Beef
Balovás, Bacon
Moólo-mas, Carrion

Mátchka, *n.*, Cat. Pasp., *mátchka;* Mikl., i., 23
 Tíkno mátchka, Kitten ; lit., little cat

Mátcho,
Mátchi, } *n.*, Fish. Pasp., *makchó*

 Mátchaw,
 Matcháw, } *pl.*, Fish
 Matché,

 Mátcho, *n. pr.*, Heron, Herne, a Gypsy tribe; as if
  herring
 Mátchoméngro, } *n.*, Fisherman. Pasp., *matchíngoro*,
 Matchéngro, } fish-seller
 Sápesko mátcho, Eel ; lit., snaky-fish
 Hérengo-mátcho, Crab ; lit., leggy-fish
 Báleno-mátcho, Herring
 Lólo-mátcho, Red-herring
 Lóli-matché, *pl.*, Salmon
 Moóshkeno-
 Pelé- } mátcho, Cod-fish
 Rínkeni bar mátcho,
 Rínkeni mátchaw ta jals talé o baryáw, } Trout
 Reíeski matché, *pl.*,

Maur, *v.*, To kill. See Mor. Pasp., *maráva*
Maúro, *n.*, Bread. Pasp., *manró, maró*
 Mauréngro, *n.*, Baker
 Chóllo maúro, Loaf
 Chellé mauré, *pl.*, Loaves
 Kil-maúro, Bread and butter
Mávi, *n.*, Rabbit
Maw, *prohibitive particle*, Do not (maa). Pasp., *ma*

Mé, *pron.*, I. Pasp., *me*

Meéa, *n.*, Mile. Vaill., *miga ;* Sundt, *mijan;* Pott, ii., 454 ;
 i., 88

    Meéasto-bár, Milestone

Meéro, *m.*,⎫ *pron.,* My (meíro, míno). Pasp., *minró*
Meéri, *f.*, ⎭

Meíla, *n.*, Donkey, ass (móila). Pott, ii., 454, suggests
 for etymon Lat. *mulus*, Gael. *muil, muileid,*
 etc.

    Meílesto-gav, Doncaster; as if, donkey's town

    Meílesko-tem, Yorkshire

    Grásni-meíla, She-ass

    Posh grei ta posh meíla, Mule

Meíro,⎫ *pron.*, My (meéro). The first syllable appears to
Meíri, ⎭ have been influenced by the English word

Mel, *v.*, To die (mer)

    Béngesko-mel, The Devil's Dyke, near Newmarket,
    Cambridgeshire

Men, *n.*, Neck. Pasp., *men*

    Gréiesko-menéngro, Horse-collar

    Men-wériga, Necklace

    Dúla baúro-menéngri-cheriklé, Herons; lit., those
    great-necked birds

Men, *pron.*, We, us. Pasp., *amén*

Méndi, *pron.*, To us, we, us. Pasp., 1st dat., *aménde*

Ménghi, *pron.*, Me, we (mánghi). Pasp., 2nd dat. s., *mánghe;*
 pl., *aménghe*

    Koordém ménghí, We fought

Ménsa, With us. Pasp., instr., *améndja*

    Kek yon te wel pósha ménsa ? May they not come
    along with us ?

Mer, *v.*, To die (mel). Pasp., *meráva*

    Meróva, I do, or will, die

    Merénna, They do, or will, die

    Merdás, He died

    Merdé yon besh ghiás konáw, They died a year ago
    now

Mériben,⎫ *n.*, Death, life. Pasp., *meribé*. Life is, to
Méripen,⎭ a Gypsy, an abstract idea or state, and
  death is a fact. It terminates life. The Gypsies
  have therefore taken the preceding state as part
  of the terminating fact, making death part of a
  man's life, and thus call life and death by the same
  name. See also remarks on Lóko

Méripen tánaw si dikéla, Murdering places as they
  look (lit., looks)

Shō'mas te meróva, I must have died

Mérikli, *n.*, Bead. Pasp., *minriklб*

Mérikl*ies*,⎫ *pl.*, Beads, bracelets
Mérikios,⎭

Meróva, I die. See Mer

Mi-, *adj.*, My. The words *Doóvel, Dúvel,* God, generally
  take this word as a prefix. Pasp., *mio, mi*

Mindj,⎫ *n.*, Pudendum muliebre, woman. Pasp., *mindj, mintch*
Minsh,⎭

Míno, *adj.*, My (meéro, meíro). Pasp., *minrб*

Mísali,⎫ *n.*, Table. Pasp., *mesáli*, towel; Lieb., *messelin,*
Misáli,⎭ tablecloth; Mikl., i., 24

Míshto,⎫
Místo, ⎬ *adv.*, Well. Pasp., *mishtб, mistб*
Mistó, ⎭

Míshto,⎫ *adj.*, Good, glad
Místo, ⎭

Moíla, *n.*, Donkey, ass (meíla)

Moílesto-gav, Doncaster; lit., donkey's town

Móker, *v.*, To foul, dirty. Pasp., *makáva*, to spot, stain

Móχodo, ⎫ *adj.*, Dirty, filthy, etc. Pasp., *maklб,*
Moókedo,⎭ stained; *makavdб*, painted

Móχadi *fólk*-i, Dirty people

Pardál sor moχodé posh-kedó Rómani-chal*s*, Over
  all dirty half-breed Gypsies

Mókto,⎫ *n.*, Box (moókto). Lieb., *mochton*
Móχto,⎭

  O múllo móχto, The coffin

Mol, *n.*, Wine (mul). Pasp., *mol*

    Kóla so kel*s* o mol, Grapes ; lit., things which make the wine

Moll, *adj.*, Worth (mool). Lieb., *moll*

    Yek shósho adré o kóro see moll doói adré o wesh, One rabbit in the pot is worth two in the wood

Mólos, } *n.*, Lead. Lieb., *molewo*
Mólov, }

Mong, *v.*, To beg, pray, request. Pasp., *mangáva*

    Mongóva, I do beg, pray, etc.

    Mong asár ! Beg !

    Móngaméngro, *n.*, Beggar

Mónghi, *pron.*, I, me (mánghi)

    Jaw mónghi káter woódrus, I will go to bed, or, Let me go to bed

Mónoshi, *n.*, Woman (manoóshni). Pasp., *manushní*

    The commonest words for 'woman' are *mónoshi*, *joóvel*, and *gaíri*, and they are generally used indiscriminately, though *gaíri* is seldom, if ever, applied to a Gypsy

Moói, *n.*, Mouth, face. Pasp., *múi*

    Mooíáw, *pl.*, Faces, mouths

    Moói-éngro, } *n.*, Lawyer
    Moo-éngro, }

    Moóesto-kóva, Looking-glass, mirror

    Moói-kokálos, Jawbone

    Choóralo-moói, Bearded face

Mook, *v.*, To let, allow, leave, lend (muk). Pasp., *mukáva*

    Mookóva, I will leave

    Moóklo, *p. part.*, Left, lent. Pasp., *muklö*

    Mooktás, He left, let

    Mookté, They left

    Mookás, Let us leave

Moókedo, *adj.*, Dirty, filthy (móχodo). Pasp., *makavdó*, painted ; *maklö*, stained

Moókto, *n.*, Box (mókto). Lieb., *mochton*

Mool, *adj.*, Worth (moll). Lieb., *moll*

Moólo, *adj.*, Dead. Pasp., *muló*

    Moólo, *n.*, Ghost, devil (múlo)

    Tátcho-moólesko tan, A regular haunted spot; lit., true ghost's place

    Doódesko-moólo, Will-o'-th'-Wisp

    Moolé, *pl.*, Ghosts

    Moóloméngro, *n.*, Halter

    Moólo-más, Carrion. Pasp., *mulanó-mas*

    Moóleno-rook, Yew; lit., dead-tree, because common in churchyards

Moónjer, *n.* and *v.*, Nudge, pinch, squeeze; *cf.* Borrow, "Lavo-lil," *munjee*, a blow on the mouth or face

    Moónjeróva toot, I will give you a nudge

    Moónjadóm lati's wast, jindás yói so mándi ker'd, I squeezed her hand, (and) she knew what I meant

Moosh, *n.*, Man. Pasp., *mursh, mrush*, boy, male

    Mooshaw, } *pl.*, Men
    Moóshaw, }

    Moosh, *adj.*, Male

    Moósh-chávi, Boy; lit., male child

    Moóshkeno, *adj.*, Masculine, male. Pasp., *murshnó*, manly

    Moóshkeni-gav, Manchester

    Moóshkeni-groóvni, Ox, bull

    Moóshkeni-groovné, Oxen

    Moóshkeno-grei, Stallion

    Moóshkeno-más, Beef

    Moóshkeno-mátcho, Cod-fish

    Kanéngro-moosh, Gamekeeper

    Peiáskro-moosh, Actor

    Mi-dúvel's-moosh, Parson

Moóshi, } *n.*, Arm. Pasp., *musi*
Moósho, }

    Moóshaw, *pl.*, Arms

    Moósheno-hev, Armpit

    Kék-mooshéngri, Maimed people; lit., armless people

    Kúshto-moóshi, Right arm

Moóshaw *of the* rook, Branches

Wásteni-moóshaw, Arms

Moóshkero, \
Moóshero, } *n.*, Policeman, constable. Dr. Paspati, in a letter, says, " = one who looks, observes = *móskero*"

Moóshkero-kosht, Constable's staff

Mooténgri, *n.*, Tea (múterimángeri)

Moótsi, \
Moótska, } *n.*, Skin. Pasp., *mortí; meshín, mezin* (As.), leather; Lieb., *mortin, mortgin,* leather; Mikl., i., 25

Mor, *v.*, To kill, slay, murder (maur). Pasp., *mardva*

    Moróva, I do, or will, kill

    Moréla, He does, or will, kill

    Mordás, He killed

    Mórdeno, \
    Mordené, *pl.,* \
    Mórdno, } *p. part,* and *adj.,* Killed. Pasp., *mardó* \
    Márdo, \
    Móred,

    Mi-Dúvelésko-maúroméngri, Jews

Móro, *pron.*, Our. Pasp., *amaró*

Mórov, *v.*, To shave. Pasp., *muravdva,* to shave; from *murdva, mordva,* to rub

    Mórovóva, I do, or will, shave

    Móroméngro, \
    Mórovméngro, } *n.*, Razor

    Morméngro, *n.*, Barber, razor (múravmángro)

Mótto, *m.,* \
Mótti, *f.,* } *adj.*, Drunk, intoxicated. Pasp., *mattó*

    Móttoméngro, *n.*, Drunkard

    Móttoben, \
    Móttopen, } *n.*, Drunkenness. Pasp., *mattipé*

    Lel mátty, To get drunk

Moúseus, n., Mouse

Muk, *v.*, To let, leave, allow (mook). Pasp., *mukdva*

    Mukóva, I do, or will, leave, etc.

    Mukéla, He leaves

    Muktás, He left

Mul, *n.*, Wine (mol). Pasp., *mol*

Mul, *adj.*, Worth (moll). Lieb., *moll*

Múlo, *n.*, Ghost, devil (moólo)

    Múloméngro, *n.*, Halter

    Wéshni-múlo, Owl

    Múlo-chériklo, Goatsucker; lit., death-bird. " It cries kek-kek, and some one will die"

    Adré o múlo raáti, In the middle, or dead, of night

Múmbli,
Múmli, } *n.*, Candle. Pasp., *momell, mumell*, wax taper

Munkáros, *n.*, Monkey

Múravmángro, *n.*, Barber (mórov). Pasp., *muravdva*, to shave

Múter, *n.*, Urine. Pasp., *mutér*

    Múter, *v.*, To micturate. Pasp., *mutráva*

    Múterdán too ti-kókero ? Hast thou wet thyself ?

    Mútering-kóla, Urinal

    Múterimóngeri, *n.*, Tea (mooténgri)

    Múterimóngeri-koóva, Teapot

N.

Na, *negative*, No, not. Frequently used for emphasis (naw). Pasp., *na*

    Kek na jinóva mé, I do *not* know

    Kek na jóva, I am *not* going

    Kek na jinénna yon, They do *not* know

    O dínilo kek na jinéla, The fool doesn't know

Na, *conj.*, Nor

    Diktóm chíchi, na shoondóm chíchi, I saw nothing, nor heard anything

Náfalo, *m.,*
Náfali, *f.,* } *adj.*, Ill, sick, poorly (násfalo). Pasp., *nasvaló, nasfalo*

    Náfloben,
    Náflopen, } *n.*, Illness, sickness. Pasp., *nasvalibé*

    Shílalo-náflopen, Ague ; lit., cold-illness

Yógenghi-náflopen, Fever; lit., fiery-illness

Nágo, *adj.*, Own (nógo)

Naish, *v.*, To run (nash). Pasp., *nasháva*, to depart

Naneí, *negative*, Not, nor (na, nei). Pasp., *nándi*

    Kek naneí, No, it is not; not at all

    Kek naneí yek, nanéi wáver, Neither one, nor the other

    Kek naneí komóva, I do not wish, like, want, etc.

    Kek naneí yek kosht, Not a single stick

    Kóvva póbo see naneí goódlo, This apple it not sweet

    Kek lúva naneí lésti, He has no money. Pasp., *lové nándi*

Násfalo, *adj.*, Ill, sick (náfalo). Pasp., *nasfaló, nasvaló*

Násher,
Nash, } *v.*, To run (naish). Pasp., *nasháva*, to depart

    Nashénna, They run

    Nashdás, He ran

    Násherméngro, *n.*, Runner, policeman, constable

    Náshing-joókel, Greyhound; lit., running dog

    Náshin' paáni, A stream, running water

Násher, *v.*, To lose, waste, hang. Pasp., *nashaváva*, to lose

    Násheréla, He hangs, he will lose

    Nashedás, He lost, wasted, hanged

    Náshedo,
    Náshado,
    Náshdo,
    Náshered, } *p. part.*, Lost, hung, hanged. Pasp., *nashtó*

    Nashedé, *pl.*, Tátcheni Rómani-chals *are* sor nashedé, True Gypsies are all lost

    Náshedo gáiro, Hangman

Nastíssa,
Nastís, } Cannot; I, you, he, they cannot; unable, etc. (nestís). Pasp., *násti, nástik;* see Pott, vol. i., pp. 367—380; Böhtl., *nashti;* Lieb., *nasti*

    Nastís mándi jinóva-les, I cannot understand it

    Nastís yov latchéla láti, He cannot find her

8

Nav, *n.*, Name. Pasp., *nav*

Návo, *adj.*, New (névo)

Naw,⎱
Né, ⎰ *negative*, No, not (na). Pasp., *na*

    Né shom mé bókolo, I am not hungry

Né, *adv.* or *interj.*, Now

    Né moóshaw! Now, men!

    Né chawóli! Now, mates!

Nei, *negative*, No, not (na, nanef)

    Kek nei jinénna yon, They do not know

    Nei ler kek lóvo, He has no money

Nei, *n.*, Finger nail, any kind of nail. Pasp., *nái*, finger nail

    Nefaw, *pl.*, Finger nails

    Nefesto-chókker, Hobnailed boot

Nestís, *negative*, Cannot (nastíssa). Pasp., *násti*

Névo, *m.*,⎱
Névi, *f.*, ⎰ *adj.*, New (návo). Pasp., *nevó*

Névus, *adj.*, Own (nógo)

Nísser, *v.*, To miss, avoid ; *cf.* Pasp., *nikáva*, to pass ; *niglistó*,
    p. part., gone out ; *nispeláva*, to hide

Nok, *n.*, Nose. Pasp., *nak*

    Nokéngro, *n.*, Snuff, glandered horse

Nóngo, *adj.*, Naked, bald, bare. Pasp., *nangó*

    Nóngo-peéro, *adj.*, Barefoot

*North*eréngri-gairé, Scotchmen ; lit., Northern-men

    *Nöth*eréngri-tem, Scotland ; lit., Northern-country

    *Nöth*erénghi chiriklé, *pl.*, Grouse ; lit., Scotch birds

*Nú*fi, *pl.*, Nuts

O.

O, *m. def. art.*, The. Sometimes indeclinable, like English
    the. Pasp., *o*

Odof,⎱
Odór,⎰ *adv.*, There (adof, 'doi). Pasp., *otiá*

Ókki. Mándi poókeróva too *ókki* yek rínkeno tárno rei, I
    tell you *there is* a handsome young man

Óχta,
Óχter, } v., To jump (hókter). Pasp., *ukhkidva*, to arise

    Oχténna, They jump

    Jánna ti oχtén, They will jump ; lit., they are going
      to jump

    Óχter*er*, *n.*, Jumper

    Chor-óχtaméngro, *n.*, Grasshopper

Ólivas,
Oúlavers, } *n. pl.*, Stockings, socks (hoólaver*s*). Lieb., *cholib*

Opré, *prep.*, Upon, on, up (apré, 'pré). Pasp., *opré*

    Diás opré adré o raáti, It appeared in the night

Óra, *n.*, Watch, hour (aúra, hóra, yóra). Pasp., *óra*

Our, } *affirmative particle*, Yes, truly, etc. (aáva). Pasp.,
Oúr*ly*, }   *va ;*· Lieb., *auwą*

Ov, *pron.*, He (yov). Pasp., *ov*

Ovávo-dívvus, To-morrow (awáver). Pasp., *yavér*

P.

Paáni, páni, *or* paúni, *n.*, Water. Pasp., *paní*

    Paanéngro, *n.*, Boat

    Paanéngro-gaújo, Sailor

    Panéngro, *n.*, Turnip

    Paánesto-
    Panéngri- } shok, Watercress
    Paáni-

    Paánisko-kóva, Bucket, pail, anything to hold water

    Paánisko-tan, Swamp, moss, watery place

    Paániski-hev, Well

    Paúdel-i-paáni, } Transported
    Paúni-*ed*, }

    Baúro-paáni,
    Lóndo-paáni, } The sea
    Londúdno-paáni,

    Tátto-páni, Any kind of spirituous liquor, *e.g.*, brandy

Pal, *n.*, Brother, mate. Pasp., *pral*

    Stíffo-pal, Brother-in-law

Palál,) *prep.*, After, behind, ago, bygone (paúli). Pasp.,
Pálla,∫ *palál, palé*

    Av pálla, To follow; lit., come after

    Dik pálla, To watch; lit., look after

    Jal pálla, To follow; lit., go after

    Pállani-chókka, Petticoat

    Beng pálla man, An enemy; lit., devil after me

Pályaw, *n. pl.*, Rails, palings. Pott, ii., 361, *pall*, board,
    plank; ? Pasp., *belí*, post

Pánder,)
Pand, } *v.*, To shut, fasten, close, tie, bind, etc. Pasp.,
Pan,   ) *pandáva*

    Pánd-asóva, I fasten, etc.

    Meéro rom pand*s* asár mándi opré adré o kair, My
        husband shuts me up in the house

    Pandadóm, I shut, did shut

    Pandadás,)
    Pandás, } He, she, they bound, fastened, etc.
    Pándadas,)

    Pánlo,
    Pándado,) *p. part.*, Shut, etc. Vaill., p. 54, *is pandado*
    Pánd*ed*,) *udar*, the door is shut

    Pándoméngro,) *n.*, Pound for stray cattle, sheepfold,
    Pánoméngro,)   pen, fold, pinfold; *n. pr.*, Pinfold,
        a Gypsy tribe

    Pand opré, Shut up! be silent

Pándjer, *v.*, To wheedle? ? cf. *pánder*, to fasten, enclose, *take
    in;* also Pott, ii., 374, "*panscheraf*, biegen; p. durch,
    durchkriechen"

    They lel'*d* jaw kíssi lúvva *by* pándjer*in' the* gaújo*s,*
        They got so much money by wheedling the Gen-
        tiles

Páni, Water. See Paáni

Pandj,)
Pansh,} *adj.*, Five. Pasp., *pandj, pantch*

    Panshéngro, *n.*, A five-pound bank-note

    Pansh-kóla, Crown, five-shilling piece

Stor-pansh, Twenty

Pápin, *n.*, Goose. Pasp., *papín*

 Papínyaw, *pl.*, Geese

 Pápini,   } *n.*, Goose ; sometimes applied to ducks
 Pápinéngri, }   or turkeys

 Moóshkeno pápin, Gander

 Pápini-driláw, Gooseberries (drílaw)

Pára, *v.*, To change, exchange (púra). Pasp., *paruváva*

 Párapén, *n.*, Change, small money (púraben). Pasp.,
 paruibé, change of clothes

Párav, *v.*, To thank, bless (párik)

Párdal,} *prep.*, Over, across (paúdel). Pasp., *perdál*, beyond
Párdel,}

Párdel, *v.*, Forgive. Párdel mándi *for* yéka, Forgive me for
 once

*Párdon*os, *n.*, Pardon, forgiveness

Párik, *v.*, To thank, bless (párav). Lieb., *parkerwawa*

 Párikaróva,}
 Párik'ró,   } I thank
 Páriko,   }
 Párik'raw, }

 Párikabén,} *n.*, Thanks
 Párik*ing*, }

 Páriktóm, I thanked

Párno, *adj.*, Cloth. Pasp., *paríd, beránd*, tent-cloth ; Lieb.,
 párne, die Windeln

Pártan, *n.*, Cloth (póktan). Pasp., *pokhtán*

Pásheréla, He believes. See Pátser

Pátrin,} *n.*, Leaf, trail-sign. Pasp., *patrín*
Pátin, }

 Patrínaw,} *pl.*, Trails
 Patréni, }

Pátser, *v.*, To believe (pázer). Pasp., *pakidva ;* Lieb., *pat-
 schäwa*

 Patsóva, I believe

 Patsdóm, I believed

 Pásheréla, He believes

Yon kek naneí patserénna, They will not believe

Pátsadé, They believed

Pátsaben, n., Belief. Lieb., patschápenn

O raúni pátsied so yóï pen'd, The lady believed what
she said

Paudál,⎫
Paúdel,⎭ prep., Over (párdal).   Pasp., perdál, beyond

Bítchadi-paúdel,⎫
Paúdel-i-paáni, ⎭ Transported

Paúli, ⎫
Paulé,⎭ prep., Behind, back (pálla).   Pasp., palé

Hatch-paúli-káni, Guineafowl

Jal-paúli, To return

Paúni, Water.   See Paáni

Paúno, adj., White (pórno).   Pasp., parnó

Paúpus, n., Grandfather.   Pasp., pápus

Pázer, v. a., To trust (pásseróva).   Pasp., pakiáva

Pázorus, adj., Indebted

Pázeróva, I obtain credit, get on trust

Pázeroben, n., Credit, trust

Pedás, He fell. ⎫
Pedé, They fell.⎭ See Per

Pédliaw, n. pl., Nuts (pétliaw, pévliaw). Lieb., pendach,
walnut

Pee, v., To drink.   Pasp., piáva

Pióva, I drink, I will drink

Piéla, He drinks, or will drink

Pidóm, I drank

Pidás, He, or they, drank

Pidé, They drank

Peédlo, p. part., Drunk, drunken.   Pasp., piló

Píaben, ⎫
Píamus,⎭ n., Drink

Peeméngro, n., Teapot, drunkard

Píaméngro, m.,⎫
Píaméngri, f., ⎭ n., Drunkard

Píaméskri, n., Tea

Píaméskri-skoodálin, Teapot

Póbesko-píaméskri-tem, Devonshire

Méndi see dósta te hol ta pi, We have plenty to eat and drink

Peer, *v.*, To walk, stroll (pírav). Pasp., *piráva*

Peeréla, He walks

Peerás, He walked

Peérdo, *n.*, Tramp, vagrant

Posh-peérdo, Half-breed

Peéroméngro, *n.*, Stile

Peéromus,*n.*, Roaming. Vaill., p. 78, *Is nasul pirmasko*, Il est difficile de marcher

Peéri, *n.*, Cauldron, stewpan, copper. Pasp., *pirí*

Peéro,
Peéri, } *n.*, Foot (píro). Pasp., *pinró, piró*

Peeré, *pl.*, Feet

Bokré's peeré, Sheep's feet

Peéresto-kóppa, Carpet

Peéro-déli*ng*-tem, Lancashire; lit., foot-kicking county

Peévlo, *adj.*, Widowed. Pasp., *pivliló*

Peévlo-gaíro, Widower. Pasp., *pivló*

Peévli-gaíri, Widow. Pasp., *pivlí*

Péias, *n.*, Play, fun, sport, game. Lieb., *perjas*

Peiáskro-moosh, Actor

Pek, *v.*, To roast. Pasp., *pekáva*

Pekóva, I do, or will, roast

Pekó, *p. part.*, Roasted. Pasp., *pekó*

Pel, *v.*, To fall. See Per. Pasp., *peráva*

Pél'*d*, Fell

Pelóva, I do, or will, fall

Peléla, He falls, or will fall

Pelé,
Péloné, } *n. pl.*, Testicles. Pasp., *peló;* pl., *pelí*
Pélonos,

Péleno-grei, Stallion

Pélengo-chávo, Boy

Peléngro, *n.*, Stallion

Pelé-mátcho, Cod-fish

Pen, *v.*, To say, tell. Pasp., *pendva*

    Penóva, I say, I will say

    Mándi penóva yór'*ll* mer, I say (think) she will die;
        cf. Pott, ii., 346, "akeàke pennàwamè. So meine
        ich's [eig. doch ich sage s. pchenav]"

    So penéssa? What do you say?

    Penéla, He says

    Pendás, He said

    Pendé, ⎫
    Pendén, ⎬ They said

    So pendán? What did you say?

Pen, *n.*, Sister. Pasp., *pen*

    Pényaw, *pl.*, Sisters. Pasp., *peniá*

    Stíffi-pen, Sister-in-law

Pénna, They will fall. See Per

Pénsa, ⎫
Pénsi, ⎬ *adj.* and *adv.*, Like (péssa). ? Pasp., *pentchya* (As.),
Pénza, ⎭   after

    Dikéla pénsa raúni, She looks like (a) lady

Per, *v.*, To fall (pel). Pasp., *peráva*

    Peróva, I fall

    Peréla, He, or it, falls

    Pelóva, I will fall

    Yon pénna, They will fall (pénna = perénna)

    Pedóm, I fell

    Pedás, He fell

    Yon pedé, They fell

Per, *n.*, Belly, stomach, paunch. Pasp., *per*

    Peráw, *pl.*, Stomachs

    Yoósho adré lénghi peráw, Clean in their eating

    Pér-doóka, Stomach-ache

Péski, *pron. reflective*, Himself. Pasp., *pes;* dat., *péske*

    Ghiás péski, He took himself off

    Diás péski kókeri wáfedo-kérimus, He gave himself
        trouble

    Viás péski akeí, He came here himself

Praásterdás péski pénsa grei, He ran off like a
horse
Péssa, *adj.*, Like (pénsa)
Pésser, *v.*, To pay. Lieb., *pleisserwawa, pozinawa*
Pésseróva, I do, or will, pay
Péssado, *p. part.*,⎫ Paid
Pessadé, *pl.*, ⎭
Péssadóm, I paid
Pétal, *n.*, Horseshoe. Pasp., *pétalo*
Petaléngro, *n.*, Blacksmith ; *n. pr.*, Smith, a Gypsy
tribe
Kekávvi-pétalengré, Tinkers ; lit., kettle-smiths
Soónakei-petaléngro, Goldsmith
Petalésto-kóva, Anvil
Pétliaw,⎫ *n. pl.*, Nuts (pédliaw)
Pévliaw,⎭
Píaben. ⎫
Píamus, etc.⎬ See Pee, to drink
Pidóm, etc. ⎭
Pikó, ⎫
Píkio, ⎬ *n.*, Shoulder. Pasp., *pikó*
Piké, *pl.*,⎭
Pióva, I do, or will, drink. See Pee
Pírav, *v.*, To walk (peer). Pasp., *piráva*
Píriv, *v. a.*, To open, woo, court, make love to. Pasp., *pin-
raváva*
Pírino, *m.*,⎫ *n.*, Sweetheart, lover. Pasp., *pírianó*
Pírini, *f.*, ⎭
Pírivdo, *p. part.*, Opened
Pírivdás, He opened
Píro, *adj.*, Open, loose
Píro, *n.*, Foot (peéro). Pasp., *piró*
Písham, *n.*, Flea, fly, honey (poóshuma). Pasp., *pushúm,*
flea
Goódlo-písham, ⎫ Bee ; lit., sweet flea
Goódlo-píshamus,⎭
Dándin' písham, Wasp

Kil písham, Butterfly

Pláshta,
Plóchta, } n., Cloak, cloth.   Lieb., *blaschda;* Mikl., i., 30
Plóχta,

Béresto-plóχta, Sail

Póbo,
Póbi, } n., Apple.   Pasp., *pabái*

Pobé, *pl.*, Apples

Póbomus, *n.*, Orange

Pobomúski-gav, } *n. pr.*, Norwich ; lit., orange town,
Pobomústi-gav, } from the assonance of *an orange*
and *Norwich*

Pobéngro, } *n.*, Cyder
Póbesko-lívena, }

Póbesko-rook, Apple-tree

Póbesko-gav-tem, Norfolk

Póbesko-pfaméskri-tem, Devonshire

Wáver-témeski-lólo-póbo, Orange ; lit., other-country
red apple

Bítto-lólo-póbi, Cherries ; lit., small red apples

Pŏ'chi, *n.*, Pocket (poótsi).   Pasp., *boshka;* Lieb., *pottizza*

Póger, } *v.*, To break.   Pasp., *pangáva, bangáva*
Pog, }

Bóngo, *adj.*, Crooked.   Pasp., *pangó, bangó,* lame

Bónges, *adv.*, Wrongly

Pogadóm, I broke

Pogadás, He broke

Pógado, } *p. part.*, Broken.   Pasp., *panglό*
Pógered, }

Pógado-shéro, Cocked hat, broken head

Pógado-bávaléngro, } Broken-winded horse
Póga-bával-grei, }

Póga-chóngaw-grei, Broken-kneed horse

Pógaméngri, } *n.*, Windmill
Bával-pógaméngri, }

Pógaroméngro, *n.*, Miller

Pógaroméngri, *n.*, Treadwheel

Pógaromésti, } n., Hammer
Pógaroméskro,

Póga-kairéngro, n., Burglar

Pōkényus, n., Judge, justice of the peace (poókinyus). Lieb.,
   pŏkōnŏ, peaceful; Pott, ii., 345, pokoino, bokŏno,
   quiet; ii., 461, pokoinepen, peace; Mikl., i., 31

Póktan, } n., Cloth (pártan). Pasp., pokhtán
Póχtan,

   Póχtan-gav, Manchester
   Póχtan-keloméngro, Weaver; lit., cloth-maker

Póngdíshler, n., Pocket-handkerchief

Poodj, n., Bridge, sky. Pasp., purt, búrdji, bridge; Pott,
   ii., 382

Poóder, } v., To blow, singe, shoot. Pasp., purdáva, puddáva
Pood,

   Pood toóvlo, To smoke tobacco
   Poódado, p. part., Blown
   Poodéla, He blows
   Poóderénna, They shoot, blow
   Poodélers,)
   Poódaméngro, } n., Bellows
   Poódaméngri,)

Poó-h-tan, n., Tinder; ? cloth; cf. póktan

Poókinyus, n., Judge (pōk-ényus)

Poóker, v., To tell
   Poókeróva, I do, or will, tell
   Poókeróva kek-kómeni ta mándi diktás (diktóm)
      toot akeí adré stéripen, I will tell no one that I
      saw you here in prison
   Pookrás, You told
   Poókadás, He told
   Poókeroméngro, n., Watch, clock
   Poókeroméngri, pl., Betrayers
   Poókering-bar, Milestone
   Poókering-kosht, Signpost

Poórav, } v., To bury
Poóros,

Pórasto, }
Poórose*d*,} Buried (pósado)

Poórostóm mi poóro dad, I buried my old father

Poóro, *m.*, }
Poóri, *f.*, } *adj.*, Old.   Pasp., *phuró, phurí*

Poórokono, *adj.*, Ancient, old-fashioned

Poórodár, *comp.*, Older.   Pasp., *phuredér*

Poóroder-rook, Oak ; lit., older (oldest) tree

Poóro-dád, *n.*, Grandfather

Poóri-déi, *n.*, Grandmother

Poóro-dad'*s* chávo, Grandchild

Poórda*s*, *n. pl.*, Stairs.   Harriot, *padras ;* cf. Pott, ii., 382

Poórumi, *n.*, Onion, leek, garlic (póruma).   Pasp., *purúm ;*
        Mikl., i., 31

Poórum, *n. pr.*, Lee, a Gypsy tribe ; as if *Lee*-k

Kánlo poóruma, Garlic ; lit., stinking onion

Poos, *n.*, Straw.   Pasp., *pus*

Poóskeno, }
Poóskeni, } *adj.*, Straw

Pooséngro, *n.*, Straw rick, stack

Ghiv-pooséngro, Wheat stack

Job-pooséngro, Oat stack

Poóshom, *n.*, Wool.   Pasp., *posóm, poshóm*

Poóshuma, *n.*, Flea, bee (písham).   Pasp., *pushúm*, flea

Poóshuméngro, *n.*, Fork.   Pasp., *pusaváva*, to prick, spur

Poósoméngri, *n.*, }
O greí-esko póssoméngri, } Spur (poshaári)

Pootch, *v.*, To ask.   Pasp., *putcháva*

Pootchóva, I ask

Pootchéssa, Thou askest

Pootchdóm, I asked

Pootchdás, }
Pootchtás, } He asked

Pootchtém, We asked

Pootchté, They asked

Poótchlo, *p. part.*, }
Pootchlé, *pl.*, } Asked, invited

Pootchás, Let us ask

Maw too pootch troóstal vániso kóva ta naneí see teéro, Do not covet (lit., ask for) any thing that is not' thine

Poótsi, *n.*, Pocket (pō'chi). Pasp., *bóshka;* Lieb., *pottissa*

Poov, *n.*, Earth, field. Pasp., *phuv, puv*

Poóvyaw, *pl.*, Fields

Poovéla, *n.*, Field-path

Poovéngri, }
Poovyéngri, } *n.*, Potato

Poovéngri-gav, Manchester. A name used by Cheshire Gypsies on account of the loads of potatoes sent there

Poovéngri-gaújo, Irishman; because potatoes enter largely into the diet of the Irish

Poóvesto-choóri, }
Poóvo-chínoméngri, } Plough
Poóv-várdo, }

So o ghivéngro chinéla o poov opré, Plough; lit., what the farmer cuts the field up (with)

Pópli, *adv.*, Again (apópli). Pasp., *pálpale*, Derrière; Vaill., p. 51, *de dûma mandi parpali*, Réponds-moi, *sostar ni dès dûma parpali?* Pourquoi ne réponds-tu pas? Mikl., ii., 52, 1032, "*papále*, adv. von neuem, wieder; *papále* megint Born: 118"

Por, *n.*, Feather (pur). Lieb., *por;* Mikl., i., 29

Pórongo-wúdrus, Feather-bed

Chérikléski-por, Wing

Pórasto, *adj.*, Buried (poórav)

Pórdo, *adj.*, }
Pordé, *pl.*, } Full, heavy. Pasp., *perdó*

Pórdo, *v.*, To fill. Pasp., *peráva*

Póri, *n.*, Tail, end. Pasp., *porí*

Pórno, *adj.*, White (paúno). Pasp., *parnó*

Pórno, *n.*, Flour

Pórnomésti, *n.*, Miller

Pornéngri, *n.*, Mill

Pórni-raúni, Swan

Pórno-sáster, Tin ; lit., white iron

Póruma, *adj.*, Gaelic ; from assonance of *garlic* and *gaelic* (poórumi)

Pósado, *p. part.*, Buried (poórav)

Posh, *adj.*, Half. Pasp., *yék-pásh*

    Posh-hórri, Halfpenny

    Posh-koórona, Halfcrown

    Posh *and* posh,⎫
    Posh-peérdo, ⎬ Half-bred

    Pósh *free*, Turnpike ; lit., half-free, because passengers are not tolled, but carts are

    Kair-posh, Help ; lit., do half

Posh, *prep.*, After. ? from assonance of *half* and *hafter*

    Posh-aglál, Opposite ; ? lit., half before

    Posh-beénomus, Placenta, after-birth

Pósha, *adv.* and *prep.*, Near, by, besides. Pasp., *pashé*

    Pósh-rig, Besides

    Dósta *fólk*-i sas pósha yóı, Much people was with her

Poshaári, *n. pl.*, Spurs (poóshuméngro)

Póshli, *adj.*, Confined. Pasp., *páshlo*, bedfast, bedridden

    Poshlé, *pl.*, Women who have been confined

    Yoı sas poshlé (-f) adré woódrus, She was confined in bed

Práster, ⎫ *v.*, To run. Sundt, *praschta*, springe, hoppe ; Pott,
Praáster,⎭   ii., 244

    Prásteréla, He runs

    Prásterdás, He ran

    Prásterméngro, *n.*, Runner, policeman, deserter

    Prásteroméngro, *n.*, Deserter

    Prásterméngri,⎫
    Prastérimus, ⎬ *n.*, Horse-race
    Greíesto-prástering,⎭

    Prástering-kóli, Railway train

    Prásterin' kíster, Railway journey

    Prástering-wárdesko-átching-tan, Railway station

Wárdesko-prásterméngri, Wheel, cart-wheel

Práster túki! Be off! Run!

Prárchadi, *n.*, Flame. ? Pasp., *práhos*, cinders

'Pré, *prép.*, Upon, on, up (apré, opré). Pasp., *opré*

Pré-éngro, *adj.*, Upper

Pur, *n.*, Feather (por). Lieb., *por*

Pur, *n.*, Stomach, belly, paunch (per)

Bókochésto-pur, Tripe

Púra, *v.*, To change, exchange (pára). Pasp., *paruváva*

Púrer*ed*, Changed

Púraben, *n.*, Exchange (párapen)

R.

Raáti, *n.*, Night. Pasp., *ratt; arattí*, during the night

Raátia, *pl.*, Nights

Raátsenghi-⎱ chíriklo, Owl
Raátenghi-⎰

Raátenghi-chei chíriklo, Nightingale; lit., night-*girl*
(vulg-*gal*) bird

Ke-raáti, To-night

Rak, ⎱ *v.*, To guard, protect, take care of, mind. Pasp.,
Rákker,⎰ *arakáva*

Rak toóti! Take care!

Rak ti toóvlo, Mind your 'baccy

Ráklo, *m. n.*, Boy. Pasp., *rakló*

Rákli, *f. n.*, Girl. Pasp., *rakli*

Ráklia, *pl.*, Girls

Raklé, *pl.*, Boys

Ran, *n.*, Rod, osier, etc. Pasp., *ran*

Rányaw, *pl.*, Rods

Rányaw *to* kair kúshni*es*, Osiers; lit., rods to make
baskets

Ránjer, *v.*, To remove, take off. Lieb., *ranschkirwawa wri*,
I undress

Ráshei, ⎱ *n.*, Parson. Pasp., *rasháí*
Ráshrei,⎰

Ratt, *n.*, Blood. Pasp., *ratt*

Ráttvalo,
Ráttfullo, } *adj.*, Bloody. Pasp., *rattvaló*
Ráttvali,

Dúlla bítta kóla (so) pees o ratt, so see chiv'*d* opré náflo *fólk*i te kair léndi kóshto, Leeches; lit., those little things (which) drink the blood, which are put on sick people to cure them

Raúni, } *n.*, Lady. Pasp., *ránni*
Rauní,

Raúnia, *pl.*, Ladies
Kaúli-raúni, Turkey
Pórni-raúni, Swan

Rei, *n.*, Gentleman. Pasp., *rái*

Réi-aw, *pl.*, Gentlemen
Reíä, *voc.*, Sir!
Doóva reíesko kair, That gentleman's house
Reíesko-kérimus, Gentlemanly behaviour
Reíal*y*, *adj.*, Gentlemanly
Baúro-rei, Gentleman
Reíesko-várdo, Carriage; lit., gentleman's cart
Reíesko roózho-poov moosh, Gardener; lit., gentleman's flower-ground man
Reíeski matché, *pl.*, Trout
Reíakana ta gaújikana jínomus, Learning fit for a gentleman and Englishman

Répper toot, Remember
Réssi toot! Make haste!

Rés-les apré, Rouse him up

Rétsi, } *n.*, Duck (rútsa). Lieb., *retza;* Mikl., i., 35
Rétza,

Retzé, *pl.*, Ducks
Bítto- } rétsa, Duckling
Tíkno-

Ríd*j*il, *n.*, Part*ridge*. Used by Isaac Herne's family
Rído, *p. part.*, Dressed. } See Riv
Rídadé, They dressed.

Rig, *n.*, Side. Pasp., *rik*

Rígher,
Rig, } *v.*, To carry, keep, bring. Lieb., *rikkerwawa*, to
Ríker, } stop

Rígheróva, I do, or will, keep

Rígher toot míshto, Take care of yourself

Rígherénna, } They keep
Rígherén, }

Ríghadóm, I carried

Yon righadás-les, They (that) carried him

Ríkeno, *adj.*, Pretty (rínkeno)

Ríknies, *pl.*, Trousers (rokéngries, etc.)

Ril, *v.*, Pedere; also used as a noun. Pasp., *rül;* Lieb.,
rill

Rínkeno, *m.*, } *adj.*, Pretty (ríkeno). Pott, ii., 264, gives
Rínkeni, *f.*, } *rajkano*, from Puchmayer's Hungarian
Rínkené, *pl.*, } "Rómani Czib," and suggests that the
word *rinkeno* is an adjective formed from the
dative plural of *rai*, i.e., *rénge*. See also Sundt's
"Landstrygerfolket," 1852, *rankanó*, gentle, noble.
Predari has, p. 270, *rincano*, and p. 259, *arincino*,
both apparently taken from Roberts

Rínkenés, *adv.*, Prettily

Rínkenodér, *comp.*, Prettier

Rínkeni mátchaw ta jals talé o baryáw, Trout; lit.,
pretty fishes that go under the stones

Rísser, *v.*, To shake, tremble. Pasp., *lisdráva*

Rísseréla, He trembles

Rísser toot, Be quick (réssi)

Rísser toot apré, Be quick, and get up ; lit., shake
yourself up

Riv, *v.*, To wear (rood). Pasp., *uryáva*

Rído, *p. part.*, Dressed

Rídadé, They dressed

Rívoben, *n.*, Apparel, clothes (ródi, roódopen)

Yov rivdás lésko kókero adré kooshto eezáw sórkon
cheérus, He always dressed in fine clothes

9

Yon sas ridé sor adré kaij, They were dressed all in silk

Rōd,
Rŏ'der, } v., To search, seek.   Pasp., rodáva

Rŏ'dadom, I searched, sought

Rōdé, They searched

Roódopen, n., Search.   Pasp., rodipé

Ródi,
Ródi-ing, } n., Clothing, apparel (roódo, riv)

Roi,
Rói, } n., Spoon.   Pasp., rói

Roíyaws, pl., Spoons

Róiengré, Spoon-makers

Róker, v., To talk, speak.   Pasp., vrakeráva; Mikl., i., 34

Rókeréla, He talks

Kómeni rókeréla troostál mándi, Some one is talking about me—"That's what we say when we sneeze"

Rókerdás,
Rókadás, } He talked
Rókerás,

Rokrás, You talk

Rókerdé, They talked

Rókeropén,
Rókerpén,
Rókeriben, } n., Conversation, language, speech.   Pasp., vrakeribé
Rókerimus,
Rókamus,

Rókeroméngro,
Rókerméngro, } n., Lawyer

Rókeroméskro, n., Talker

Baúro rókeroméngri, pl., Prophets

Rókerin' chíriklo, Parrot

Rokéngries,
Rokónyus,
Rokrényus, } n. pl., Trousers (ríknies)
Roxínyes,
Roxínya,

Rom, *n.*, Husband, bridegroom, a male Gypsy.   Pasp., *rom*

Rómeni,
Rómni, } *n.*, Wife, bride.   Pasp., *romnī*
Rómadi,

Rómano, } *adj.*, Gypsy.   Pasp., *romanó*
Rómani,

Rómano-drab, probably Spurge-laurel (*Daphne lau-reola*), the berries of which, according to Lindley, "are poisonous to all animals except birds"

Rómani-chal, A male Gypsy

Rómani-chálaw, *pl.*, Gypsies

Rómanes, *adv.*, Gypsy, the Gypsy language.   Pasp., *romanés*

Rómano chíriklo, Magpie; lit., Gypsy bird

Rómer, *v.*, To marry

Rómado, } *p. part.*, Married (rómadi)
Rómer*ed*,

Rómadóm, I married

Rómerobén, *n.*, Marriage

Rómeromus, *n.*, Wedding

Rood, *v.*, To dress (riv)

Roódo, *p. part.*, Dressed (rído, ródi)

Roódopen, *n.*, Dress, clothing.   Pasp., *urydibé*

Roódopen, *n.*, Search (road).   Pasp., *rodipé*

Rook, *n.*, Tree.   Pasp., *ruk*

Roókaw, } *pl.*, Trees
Rookáw,

Roókaméngro, *n.*, Squirrel

Roókenghi-chóχas, Leaves; lit., tree-coats

Roop, *n.*, Silver.   Pasp., *rup*

Roópono } *m.*,
Roópno, }   } *adj.*, Silver.   Pasp., *rupovanó*
Roópni, *f.*, }

Roópnoméngro, *n.*, Silversmith

Roózlo, } *adj.*, Strong (rúzlo).   Pasp., *zoraló*
Roózlus,

Sor-roózlo, Almighty

Roózlopen, *n.*, Strength

Rŏv, *v.*, To cry. Pasp., *rováva*

    Rŏvóva, I do, or will, cry

    Rŏvéna, They cry

    Rŏvdé, They cried

Rŏ'zali,
Rŏ'sheo, } *n.*, Flower. Mikl., i., 35

    Roózho-poov, Flower garden

    Roózhaw-poóvaw, *pl.,* Flower gardens

    Groóveni roózha, Cowslip

    Dívusy roózha, Daisy

Rushári, *n. pl.,* Rushes, reeds

Rútsa, *n.*, Duck, goose (rétsi). Lieb., *retza*

Rúzlo,
Rúzino, } *adj.,* Strong, coarse (roózlo). Pasp., *zoralб*

    Rúzlo mas, Coarse meat

S.

'Saála, *n.*, Morning (saúla). Pasp., *disiola*, it dawns ; *disára,*
    early

Sadás, He laughed. See Sav

Sáke-os, *n.*, Sake

Sal, *v.*, To laugh (sárler, sav). Pasp., *asáva*

    Sáling,
    Sálimus, } *n.*, Laughing, laughter, laugh

    Saléla, He laughs

    Saldóva (*for* Sadóm), I laughed

Sálamánca, *n.*, Table. Pasp., *salán*

Sálivárdo,
Sálivárus, } *n.*, Bridle (sólivéngro, solivárdo). Pasp., *sulivári*

Sap, *n.*, Snake, serpent, eel. Pasp., *sapp*, snake

    Sápaw, *pl.*, Snakes. Pasp., *sappá*

    Sápesko-mátcho, Eel

    Sápesko-mátcho-moótsi, Eel-skin

Sápin,
Sápinis, } *n.*, Soap. Pasp., *sapuní ;* Mikl., i., 36

Sar, *prep.*, With

Sar, *adv.*, How, as. Pasp., *sar*, how

    Sar 'shan, How are you?

    Sar koméssa, If you please

Sárler, *v.*, To laugh (sal, sav). Pasp., *asáva*

Sárshta,⎫

Sársta, ⎬ *n.*, Iron. Pasp., *shastír, sastír*

Sáster, ⎭

    Sárstera,⎫ *adj.*, Iron

    Sástera, ⎭

    Sástraméskro, *n.*, Blacksmith. Pasp., *sastiréskoro*

    Sástera-bíkinoméngro, Ironmonger

    Sástermángro, *n.*, An iron-grey horse

Sas, *3rd sing.* and *pl. imperf.* Was, were. Pasp., *isás*

    Yov sas náshedo opré o rook, He was hanged on the

        tree

    Yon sas wáfedo náfalo, They were very

Sáster, Iron. See Sarshta

Sastís, Able, can (sítis, stastís). Lieb., *sasti;* Pasp., *sastó*,

    sound, healthy; Pott, ii., 370—380; *cf.* Lat., valeo

    Sar sastís te yek moosh del, How can one man give?

'Saúla,⎫ *n.*, Morning ('saála). Pasp., *dísiolo, disára*

'Saúlo,⎭

    Kóliko-saúla, To-morrow morning

    Kesaúla, This morning

Sav, *v.*, To laugh (sal, sárler). Pasp., *asáva*

    Sávaben,⎫ *n.*, Laugh, laughter. Pasp., *asaibé*

    Sávapen,⎭

    Sadás, He laughed

Sávo, *pron.*, Who, what (so). Pasp., *savó, so*

    Sávo shan too, Who art thou?

    Sávo cheérus, What time? when?

'See, *3rd sing.* and *pl. pres. ind.*, Is, are, has, have. Pasp.,

    ist

See-éngro, *adj.*, Spirited, lively (zee)

Shab, *v.*, To run away, "A mumper's word." Pott, ii., 14,

    schuf dich! be off! Sundt, p. 394, *skubba!* go!

Sham, We are (shem).   Pasp., *isám*

    Ta sórkon kóvaw sham mé (méndi), And all that we
      have ; lit., and all things are to us

'Shámas, We were (shúmas).   Pasp, *isámas*

    'Sor kíno shámas, We were all tired

'Shan, *2nd sing.* and *pl. pres.*, Art, are, hast, have.   Pasp., *isán*

    Too 'shan kérdo míshto, Thou hast done well
    Too 'shan lésti, You have it
    Sar shan, How art thou ? how are ye ?

'Shánas, *2nd sing.* and *pl. imperf.*, Thou wast, ye were.
    Pasp., *isánas*

    Too 'shánas náfalo wáver dívvus, haw ? You were ill
      the other day, eh ?

    'Shánas kinó ? Were you tired ?

Sháni, *n.*, Mule

Shanéngro, *n.*, Lawyer, liar (shoon).   The two meanings are
    due to their assonance

Shárdoka, *n.*, Apron (chárdoka, etc.)   ? Pasp., *utchardó*,
    mantle, covered.   Pott, ii., 231, 252, " *shaducca*,
    apron, Kog.," is from Roberts; Böht., *jändäráka*

Shaúhaúri, *n.*, Sixpence (shookhaúri)

Shélo, *n.*, Rope, cord (shólo).   Pasp., *sheló, sholó*

    Kóva, so too kairs shélo, Flax ; lit., thing which you
      make rope (of)

Sheléngro, *n.*, Whistler (shol)

'Shem, *1st pl. pres.*, We are ('sham).   Pasp., *isám*

    Méndi 'shem akeí, We are here

Shéro, *n.*, Head (shóri).   Pasp., *sheró*

    Sheréngro, *n.*, Bridle, captain, chief, headman, leader
    Béresto-sheréngro, Captain of a ship
    Shéroméngro, *n.*, Lawyer
    Sheréksno, *n.*, Lawyer ; for sheréskano
    Ghívesto-shéro, Ear of corn
    Pógado-shéro, Cocked hat
    Chiv *it* adré *your* shéro, Remember ; lit., put it into
      your head.   Compare Pasp., *sheráva man ;* Lieb.,
      rikkerwāwa an o schĕro

Shil, *n.*, Cold, catarrh. Pasp., *shil*

    Shílino, *adj.*, Cold (shírilo). Pasp., *shilalб*

    Shílo-tem, The north

Shing, *n.*, Horn. Pasp., *shing*

    Shíngaw, *pl.*, Horns

Shírilo, *adj.*, Cold (shílilo). Pasp., *shilalб*

Shiv, *n.*, Snow (iv, ghiv, hiv, yiv). Pasp., *iv*, etc.

Shok, *n.*, Cabbage. Pasp., *shakh*

    Shókyaw, *pl.*, Cabbages

    Paáni-shok, }
    Panéngri-shok, } Watercress

Shol, *v.*, To whistle (shool). Pasp., *shóndava*

    Sheléngro, *n.*, Whistler

    Sholóva, I whistle. Lieb., *schollewāwa*

Shólo, *n.*, Rope, cord (shélo). Pasp., *sholб, shelб*

'Shom, *1st sing.* and *pl. pres.*, I am, we are (shem). Pasp.,
    1st sing., *isбm;* 1st pl., *isбm*

'Shō'mas, *1st sing.* and *pl. imperf.*, I was, we were (shúmas).
    Pasp., 1st sing., *isбmas;* 1st pl., *isбmas*

    Mandi shō'mas 'jaw kinó, I was so tired

    Beéno shō'mas adré Dovárus, I was born at Dover

    Méndi shō'mas yékera *a* baúro haúro kekávvi, We
    once had a large copper kettle

Shoóba, *n.*, Gown, frock (shoóva)

    Chúffas, *pl.*, Petticoats

Shoóbli, *adj.*, Pregnant (shoóvlo, *q.v.*)

Shookár, *adv.*, Nicely, quietly, slowly. Pasp., *shukár*

    Jal shookár, Go slowly, easily, nicely

    Shookáridáir, *comp.*, Slower, easier

    Shoókar, *adj.*, Quiet, still

    Shoóker! Silence! Keep quiet!

    Shoóko, *adj.*, Dumb

    Róker shookés, *adv.*, Speak low

Shookhaúri, *n.*, Sixpence (shaúhaúri, shov, haúri)

'Shoóko-kanéngri, Deaf person, Pasp., *kashukб*, deaf

Shoóko, *adj.*, Dry. Pasp., *shukб*

Shoóko-maúroméngri-tem, Suffolk; lit, dry bread fellows' county

Shool, *v.*, To whistle (shol). Pasp., *shondáva*

     Shoolóva, I whistle

     Shooldé, They whistled

Shool, } *n.*, Moon. Pasp., *tchon*
Shoon, }

     Shoónaw, *pl.*, Months

Shoon, *v.*, To hear, listen, hearken, etc. Pasp., *shunáva*

     Shoonóva, I hear

     Shoonéssa, Thou hearest

     Shoonéla, He hears

     Shoónta! Listen! Hark!

     Shoonóm, We will hear

     Shoónedóm, } I heard
     Shoóndom, }

     Sar kek shoonénna, If they will not hear

     Shoondás, He heard

     Shoondé, They heard

     Shoon léndi! Remember! lit., listen to them

     Shoon-*to*-kóngri, A bell; lit., hark to church

     Shoónaben, } *n.*, Newspaper
     Shoónaméngri, }

     Shanéngro, *n.*, Lawyer, liar; from assonance

Shoot, } *n.*, Vinegar. Pasp., *shut, shutkó*
Shoóto, }

     Shoótelo, } *adj.*, Sour. Pasp., *shutló*
     Shoótlo, }

     Shoótlo chor, Sorrel; lit., sour grass

     Shoot shokáw, Lettuce, any plant used in making salad

Shoóva, *n.* Gown (shoóba)

Shoóvlo, *adj.*, Swollen. Pasp., *shuvló*

     Shoóvli, *f.*, Pregnant (shoóbli)

Shor, *v.*, To praise. Pasp., *ashardva*

     Shoróva, I do praise

     Shóri*ng his* kókero, Bragging, boasting

Shóroben, *n.*, Boast

Shoró,⎫
Shóro,⎬ *n.*, Head (shéro, shúro). Pasp., *sheró*
Shóri, ⎭

Shoréngro, *n.*, Chief, captain, foreman, headman, lawyer

Baúro-shoréngro, Lord

Shóro jínomus gaíro, A learned man ; lit., head-knowledge-man

Shórokno, *n.*, Chief, master

Shórokno gáiro, A headman, clever fellow, collegian

Shórokné gairé, *pl.*, Clever men

Shórokono moosháw, Disciples ; lit., chief men

Shoshó,⎫
Shóshi,⎬ *n.*, Rabbit (shúshi). Pasp., *shoshói*

Shoshé, *pl.*, Rabbits

Shov, *adj.*, Six. Pasp., *shov, sho*

Shookhaúri,⎫
Shaúhaúri,⎬ *n.*, Sixpence (haúri)

Shúmas, 1*st pl. imperf.*, We were (shõ'mas, shámas). Pasp., *isámas*

Shúro, *n.*, Head (shéro, shóro). Pasp., *sheró*

Shúshi, *n.*, Rabbit (shóshi). Pasp., *shoshói*

Shusheí, *pl.*, Rabbits

Shúshenghi hévyaw, Rabbit-holes

'Si, Is (see). Pasp., *isí*

Si, *conj.*, As. ? From assonance of *is* and *as* when spoken quickly

Jaw door si too, As far as you

Kek na komóva jáfri tanáw si kóli, I do not like such places as these

Méripen tánaw si dikéla, Murdering places as they look (lit., looks)

Sig, *adj.* and *adv.*, Quick, soon, early, just. Pasp., *sigó*

Sígodair, *comp.*, Sooner, earlier, before

Ken sigáw, Immediately ; lit., just now

Sígo toóti, Bestir yourself, be quick

Síker, *v.*, To show. Pasp., *sikáva*

    Síker, *n.*, Gold

    Síkeróva, I show, I will show

    Sikadás, He showed

    Síklo, *adj.* and *p. part.*, Accustomed, used. Pasp.,
        sikló

    Mándi *couldn't* jiv adré *a* gav, mándi*'s so* síklo *to the*
        bával, I couldn't live in a town, I am so accus-
        tomed to the open air

    Síkerméngro, *n.*, Show, showman, circus, pleasure-
        grounds, moon

    Síkeroméngro, *n.*, Signpost

Siménsa, *n.*, Cousin, relation, kin. Miklosich, über die
    mundarten, etc., part ii., p. 71, No. 456, *semence*

    Sor see ménsi, We are all relations

Símmer, *v.*, To pawn, pledge. Lieb., *simmeto*, a pledge;
    Pasp., *simadl*, sign

    Símmer*ing* boódega, Pawnshop

    Símmeroméskro, Pawnbroker

Sítis, If I can (stástis)

Siv, *v.*, To sew. Pasp., *siváva*

    Sivdúm, I sewed

    *Un*sívdo, Unsewn

    Sívoméngro, *n.*, Tailor; the name too of the Taylor
        tribe of Gypsies (soovéngro). Pasp., *súbnáskero*

    Soov, *n.*, Needle. Pasp., *suv*

Skámin, *n.*, Chair. Pasp., *scamni*, stool; Lieb., *stammin*

    Skaminé, } *pl.*, Chairs
    Skáminyaw, }

    Skáminéngro, *n.*, Chair-mender, chair-bottomer

    Ráshei skámin adré o kóngri, kei o ráshei beshéla,
        Pulpit; lit., priest-chair in the church, where the
        priest sits

Sken, *n.*, Sun (kam, tam). Pasp., *kam*

Skŏ'ni, *n.*, Boot. Lieb., *skorni*

    Skŏ'nyaws, *pl.*, Boots (skrúnya)

Skoodálin, *n.*, Plate. ? Italian, *scodella*, porringer

Skoodílin, *n.*, Teapot

Píaméskri skoodálin, Teapot

Kóshtudno skoodílaw, Wooden dishes

Skrúnya, *n. pl.*, Boots (skō′nyaws). Lieb., *skornia;* Mikl.,
 i., 37

*Slug*us, *n.*, Slug

Sménting,} *n.*, Cream. Lieb., *schmindāna;* Mikl., i., 40
Sméntini,

So, *pron.*, What (sávo). Pasp., *so*

Sólivárdo,} *n.*, Bridle (sálivárdo). Pasp., *sulivári*
Sólivéngro,

Sólivaré, *pl.*, Bridles

Sólohólomus, *n.*, Oath (sóverhol, súlverkon). Pasp., *sovél;*
 sovél khalióm, I have sworn

Soom,}
Soon,} *v.*, To smell. Pasp., *sungdva*
Soong,}

Soongóva, I smell

Soongéla, He smells

Soóngimus, *n.*, Smell

Soom *a* kan, Smell a stink

Soónakei, *n.* and *adj.*, Gold. Pasp., *soonakái*

Soónakei-pétaléngro, Goldsmith

Soónaka wériga, Gold chain

Soóti, *v.*, To sleep, coîre (sōv). Pasp., *sovdva,* p. part., *suttó,*
 sottó

Soóto,} *n.*, Sleep (sútto)
Soóti,

Soóto, *adj.*, Asleep, sleepy

Sootéla, He sleeps

Soótadóm, I slept

Sootadás, He slept

Jaw káter sútto, Go to sleep

Yon soótedé, They slept

Dúla kóla (so) kairs toóti te jal *to* soóto, Poppies;
 lit., those things (which) make you go to sleep

Soov, *n.*, Needle (siv). Pasp., *suv*

Soovéngro, *n.*, Tailor (sívoméngro). Pasp., *sübnd-skoro*

Sor, *n* and *adj.*, Everything, all ; *adv.*, quite. Pasp., *sarró, sáore*

    Sor-kon kólli, Everything ; *cf.* Mikl., ii., 35, 133 (Bukowina Vocab.), *sekon shíba*, alle sprachen ; ii., 55, 1271 (Hungarian Vocab.), *sako*, every

    Sór-kon-cheérus,⎫
    Sór-kon-cháirus,⎬ Always, often ; lit., every time

Sórsin, *n.*, Plate ; ? from *saucer*

Sóski, *adv.*, Why ; lit., for what (so). Pasp., dative, *sóske*, for what, why

    Sóski kedás-les tálla ? Why did you do it ?

    Sóski too naneí róker *to* mándi ? Why don't you speak to me ?

Sŏv, *v.*, To sleep, coïre (soóti). Pasp., *sovdva*

    Sovdóm, I slept

    Sovdé, They slept

Sóverhol,⎫ *v.*, To swear, curse (súlverkon, sólohólomus).
Sóvlohol,⎭ Pasp., *sovél-khalióm*, I have sworn ; lit., I have eaten oath

    Sóvlohóloben,⎫
    Sóverhóloben,⎬ *n.*, Curse, oath

Spingl,⎫
Spíngher,⎬ *n.*, Pin. ? French, *épingle*. Pott, ii., 248. *spinaf*,
Spink,⎭   I stick

    Spíngo, *n.*, Brooch

    Spíngo, *v.*, To pin, fasten with wooden skewers

    Spingaárus, *n.*, Skewer, spit

    Spingaáro-kéloméngro, Skewer-maker

Staádi,⎫
Stádi, ⎬ *n.*, Hat. Pasp., *stadík*
Státi, ⎭

    Staádia,⎫ *pl.*, Hats
    Staadé, ⎭

    Joóvioko-staádi, Bonnet ; lit., female hat

Staáni, *n.*, Deer, stag. ? Pott, ii., 247, *stirna*, cat

Stánya, *n.*, Stable. Lieb., *steinia;* Mikl., i., 38

'Stárdo,
'Stárdi, } *n.*, Prison ('stéripen, 'staúri). Pasp., *astardí*, that
'Stáriben, which one holds ; *astaribé*, arrest

Stári, *n.*, Star. Pasp., *stiari* (As.)

Stástis, If it is possible, if he can (sastís, tastís)

'Staúri, *n.*, Prison ('stárdi)

Stékas, *n.*, Gate, turnpike (stígher). ? Provincial English,
 steek, to shut, or from *stakervava*, to tread, walk,
 Pott, vol. i., p. 437 (from Puchmayer's " Románi
 Czib")

'Stérimus, } *n.*, Prison ('stáriben). Pasp., *astaribé*, arrest
'Stéripen,

 'Stéroméngro, } *n.*, Prisoner
 'Stéromésti,

 'Stéripen-gav, *n.*, County town

Stífo-dad, *n.*, Father-in-law. German, *stief-;* English, *step-*
 Stífi-dei, Mother-in-law, } Miklosich, " über die mun-
 Stífo-pal, Brother-in-law, } darten," etc., part ii., p. 69,
 No. 279, and p. 70, No. 376, *shtyfdaj, shtyfdad*
 Stífi-pen, Sister-in-law

Stígher, *n.*, Gate, turnpike (stékas). Pott, ii., 246, gives *i
 stika*, path, and compares fuss-*steig*, footpath ;
 Mikl., i., 39
 Pésser-stígher, Turnpike

Stor, *adj.*, Four. Pasp., *star*
 Trin-stor, Seven ; lit., three-four
 Doói-trinyáw ta yek, Seven ; lit., two threes and one
 Doói storáw, Eight ; lit., two fours
 Stor-pansh, Twenty ; lit., four fives
 Stor-peeréngro, Frog

Strángli, *n.*, Onion. "A mumper's lav, it means poórumi"

*Stúgh*i, *n. pl.*, Stacks. *cf.* Harr., *stagus*, a rick ; Pott, ii.,
 246 ; Mikl., i., 39

Súlverkon, *v.*, To swear, curse (sóverhól, sólohólomus). Pasp.,
 sovél-khalióm, I have sworn

*Sundáy*us, Sunday

Sus. **Kair too sus asár koméssa,** Do just as you like.
　　　　? *Sus* = so as, with the particle *asár* attached, to
　　　　disguise the English words

Sútto, *n.,* Sleep (soóto).　Pasp., *suttó*

Swágler, ⎫
　　　　　 ⎬ *n.,* Tobacco-pipe
Swégler, ⎭

T.

Ta, *conj.,* And.　Pasp., *ta*
　　　　Dad ta dei, Father and mother

Ta, *conj.,* Than (te)
　　　　Yov si bitadér ta mándi, He is less than I.　? Ta
　　　　= Engl. *to,* which is sometimes used provincially
　　　　in this sense.　Some Gypsies similarly use *nor,*
　　　　others *dan, den* (than)

-ta, emphatic suffix to verbs in the imperative.　Pott, vol. i.,
　　　　p. 310
　　　　Shoónta, chawóli! Listen, mates!
　　　　Avatá! Come here!

Ta, *conj.* and *pron.,* That.　Pasp., *ka*
　　　　Yov pendás ta mándi jals pálla wáver mooshᾱw, He
　　　　　was jealous; lit., he said that I go after other men
　　　　Wáfedo bával ta ands kek kóshto bok, A bad wind
　　　　　that brings no good luck
　　　　Yov ta sas moólo, He that was dead

Taf, *n.,* Thread (tav, tel).　Pasp., *tav*

Talé, *prep.,* Down, under, beneath (telé, alé, 'lé).　Pasp., *telé*
　　　　Tálla, *adv.,* After, afterwards, except, without
　　　　Tálla, *prep.,* Under, beneath, behind
　　　　Tall' *of a* baúro wesh, Alongside of a big wood
　　　　Tállani-chóχa, Under-petticoat
　　　　Lel talé, To peel
　　　　Chin talé, To cut off, cut down
　　　　Lel o moótsi talé o póbo, Peel the orange; lit., take
　　　　　the skin off the orange

Tam, *n.,* Sun (kam, sken).　Pasp., *kam*

Támlo, *adj.*, Sunny, light. A corruption of *kámlo*

Támlo, *adj.*, Dark. Pasp., *tam*, blind; Mikl., i., 43

    Támlo raáti, Dark night

Tan, ⎫ *n.*, Camp, place, tent. Pasp., *tan*, place; *katúna*,
Táno, ⎭ tent

    Tánaw, *pl.*, Places

    Tan, *v.*, To encamp

    Kair ti tan tálla o rook avrí o kam, Pitch your tent
        under the tree out of the sun

Tárder, *v.*, To pull, stretch. Pasp., *tradáva*, to draw

    Tardadóm, I pulled

    Tárdadás, He pulled

    Tárdadé, They pulled

    Tárder*ing* shélo kótoréndi, Picking oakum; lit.,
        pulling rope to pieces

    So too tarder*s* matché avrí o paáni troóstal, Fish-
        hook; lit., what you pull fish out of the water with

Tárno, *adj.*, Young (taúno). Pasp., *ternó*

    Tárno, *n.*, Child

    Tárno, *n. pr.*, Young, a Gypsy tribe

    Tárnodar, ⎫ *comp.*, Younger
    Tarnodaír, ⎭

    Tárnomus, *n.*, Youth

Tásser, *v.*, To choke, drown. Pasp., *tasáva*

    Tássado, *p. part.*, Choked

    Tássadás, He choked

Tastís, If he can, if I can, if it be possible, etc. (stastís,
       tússis). A combination of *te sasto isí; vide* Pott,
       i., 370; ii., 242

    Keróva-les, tastís, I will try to do it; lit., I will do
        it, if I can

    Róker too, tastís, Speak, if you can

    Sor o kóli peléla adrál lésti, tastíss, All the things
        (everything) will fall through it, if they can (or
        that can)

Tátcho, ⎫ *adj.*, Good, true, right, real, holy, ready, healthy,
Tátcheno, ⎭ well, safe. Pasp., *tchatchunó*, true

Tátchipen, *n.*, Truth. Pasp., *tchatchipe*

Tátcho wast, Right hand

Tátchené gairé, or *fólki*, Holy men, angels

Tátchnes, *adv.*, Right

Kair tátcho, To cure, comfort; lit., make right

Yov sas o tátcho yek *o'* lésko dei, He was the only son of his mother

Tátcho-'glál, Right opposite, face to face

Tátcho beréngro, Ship captain

Tátcho-bars, Jewels

Tátcho dósta, Sure enough

Táttav,⎫
Tátter, ⎬ *v*, To warm. Pasp., *tattiaráva*

Tátterméngri, *n.*, Frying-pan

Tátto, *adj.*, Warm, hot. Pasp., *tattó*

Táttoben, *n.*, Heat, summer. Pasp., *tattibé*, heat

Tátto-koóva, Pepper

Tátto-páni, Alcohol, ardent spirits; *cf.* American ' *fire-water* '

Tav, *n.*, Thread (taf, tel). Pasp., *tav*

Távesto-gav, Manchester; lit., cotton-town

Taúno, *m.*,⎫
Taúni, *f.*, ⎬ *adj.*, Young (tárno). Pasp., *ternó*

Te, *prep.* and *conj.*, To, for, at, how, with, what, than, but, etc. Pasp., *te*

Tedívvus, To-day

Biknóva-les tei te vániso lúva, I will sell it too for any sum

Te dóva cheérus *o'* raáti, At that time of night

Te goódlo see, How sweet it is

Yon pandás yov opré te lésti, They tied he (him) up with it

Keléla peiás te lésti nógo póri, It is playing with its own tail

Te wáfedo moosh see yov, What a bad man he is

Dórdi, te goódlo pobé see odof, chavóli! Look, what ripe apples are there, mates!

Yói see wáfedodáir te yov, She is worse than he

Kek kómeni sas ker'*d* man koóshto te yov, No one but he cured me

Te, *particle*, used to form the *subjunctive; vide* Grammar, p. 39. Pasp., *te*

Beng te lel toot, Devil take you .

Te wel mándi te bítcheróva-len avrí, If I send them away

Te jinéssa too? Do you know?

Shŏ'mas te meróva, I must have died

Te dikóv avrí, dikóva, If I look out, I see

Teéro, *pron.*, Thine, thy, your. Pasp., *tinro*

Tei, *conj.*, Also, too, indeed. Pott, i., 308, *tai;* Mikl., ii., 58 (1454), *taj*

Dósta bríshno wéla talé ta hiv tei, Much rain comes down and snow too

Biknóva les tei te vániso lúva, I will sell it too for any sum

Tel, *n.*, Thread (tav). Pasp., *tav*

Telé, *prep.*, Down, etc. (talé). Pasp., *tele*

Tem, *n.*, Country, county, district, neighbourhood, etc. Pasp., *tem*, people, world

Temáw, *pl.*, Countries

Teméngro, *n.*, Countryman, rustic

Wáver-teméngro, Foreigner

Híndo-tem, Ireland

Híndi-teméngro, Irishman

Teméskri, *adj.*, Country

Kaúlo-tem, The 'black-country'

Wátchkeni-tem, Wales

Mi-Dúvelésto-tem, Heaven, the sky

Dóla teméski Rómani-chal*s*, The Gypsies of that county

Wáver témeski lólo póbo, Orange; lit., other-country red (yellow) apple

Chórkeno-tem, Yorkshire

Thinkóva,
Thinkasóva, } *v.,* I think

Ti, *pron.,* Thine, thy. Pasp., *ti*

Tíkno, } *adj.,* Small, little. }
Tíkeno, } *n.,* Child. } Pasp., *tiknó,* young, small

    Kóshteno tíkno, Doll

Til, *v.,* To hold. Pasp., *teráva,* to have; 3rd pers. sing.,
    teréla; Vaill., p. 73, *Ti pac'as men, tilas tk kûrdûn,*
    Si tu m'en crois, nous prendrons une voiture

    Til'*d, p. part.,* Held

    Til apré, To raise; lit., hold up

    Tíloméngri, *n.,* Reins, pincers, snaptrap

    Mi Doóvel kek tiléssa (*tiléla*) lésti sor tátcho, God
      will not hold him guiltless

    Yov tildás lésko shóro opré, He held his head up

Tōbár, *n.,* Axe, hammer. Pasp., *tovér,* axe

    Tŏ'ver, }
    Tŏ'fer, } *n.,* Hammer, axe, anvil
    Tŏ'ber, }

Tŏ'ber kōvs (coves), Highwaymen. "That's mumpers' talk"

*T*oketané, *adv.,* Together

Too, *pron.,* Thou, you. Pasp., *tu*

    Toóki, }
    Toóti, } Thy. Pasp., 1st dat., *túte;* 2nd dat., *túke*

    Toot, }
    Toóti, } *pron. acc.,* Thee, you. Pasp., acc., *tut*

    Tússa, *pron. instr.,* With thee. Pasp., *túsa*

    Mántchi too! Cheer up!

Tood, *n.,* Milk. Pasp., *tut*

    Tood, *v.,* To milk

Toof, *n.,* Smoke (toov, túvlo). Pasp., *tuv,* tobacco for
    smoking

Toógeno, }
Toógno, } *adj.,* Sorry, grieved (túgno). Pott, ii., 307; Mikl.,
Toognó, } i., 10, 41
Toógnus, }

    Toógeno, *adj.,* Lonesome, lonely

Toog, {
 v., To grieve
 n., Sorrow
}

Mi toog *is quite* mistó, I am quite well

Toóki, *pron.*, Thee (túki, too). Pasp., 2nd dat., *túke*

Toóshni, *n.*, Basket, faggot (kúshni, trúshni, túshni). Pasp.,
 kóshnika

Toótchi, *n.*, Breast (Lat., *mamma*). Pasp., *tchutchí*

 Tootcháw, *pl.*, Breasts

Toóti, *pron.*, Thee, thy, for thee (too). Pasp., 1st dat., *túte*

Toov, *n.*, Smoke (toof). Pasp., *tuv*, tobacco

 Toov, *v.*, To smoke

 Toóvlo, *n.*, Tobacco (túvlo)

 Toóvlo-gónno, Tobacco-pouch

To-ráati, To-night

Tórro, *adj.*, High. Pasp., *khor*, deep

 Tórropen, *n.*, Height

Tōv, *v.*, To wash. Pasp., *továva*

 Tōvóva, I will wash

Tōver, *n.*, Axe (tōbár). Pasp., *tovér;* Mikl., i., 42

Trad, *To* lel trad, to take care. ? A translation of *prenez
 garde*, corrupted into *grade*, and then *trad*

 Trad, *n.*, Order, notice, etc., e.g., *mándí dels toóti
 koóshto trad* to *kair doóva*, I order you to do so;
 lit., I give thee good order to do that; *del man
 trad*, show me ; ? lit., give me advice

Trash,   } *v.*, To fear, frighten, astonish. Pasp., *trasháva*,
Trásher, }   to fear

 Trashóva, I fear, I am afraid

 Trashéla, He fears, frightens

 Trashénna, They fear

 Tráshedo, } *p. part.*, Frightened, afraid, astonished
 Trásher*ed*, }

 Trásh*ful*, *adj.*, Fearful

 *A*trash, Afraid

 Trash, *n.*, Fear, fright, astonishment

 Trash see mándi, I am afraid ; lit., fear is to me

Tráslo, *adj.*, Thirsty (troóshlo). Pasp., *trushaló*, thirsty

'Tré, *prep.*, In ('dré)

Trin, } *adj.*, Three. Pasp., *trín*
Tring,

    Trin-górishi, Shilling
    Trin-ta-stor, }
    Trín-stor, } Seven
    Doói trinyáw ta yek, }

Troópo, } *n.*, Body, corpse. Lieb., *trupo;* Mikl., i., 42
Troópus,

    Troópus, }
    Troópia, } *n. pl.*, Stays
    Troopé, }

Troosh, *n.*, Thirst. Pasp., *trush*

    Troóshlo, *adj.*, Thirsty (tráslo). Pasp., *trushaló*

Troóshel, } *n.*, A trail formed by three heaps of grass at
Troóshilo, }   cross-roads. Pasp., *trushúl*, cross

Troóshni, *n.*, Can, quart, any large vessel, bundle (kúshni, túshni). Lieb., *tuschni*, flask, bottle

Troostál, } *prep.*, About, of, concerning. Lieb., *trujal*
Troóstal,

    Mándi koméssa (*kombva*) te shoon troostál lésti, I would like to hear about him

    So keréssa o patréni troostál? What do you make trails of?

    So too tárder*s* matché avrí o paáni troóstal, Fishhook; lit., what you pull fish out of the water with

    Troostál meéro kóshto kómomusti Doóvel ker'*d* mándi kóshto, However my good kind God made me well

Túkki, *pron.*, Thee (toóki)

Túllo, *m.*, } *adj.*, Fat, stout, plump. Pasp., *tuló*
Túlli, *f.*,

    Túllopen, } *n.*, Fat, grease, ointment
    Túllipen, }

    Túllo-mas-tem, Lincolnshire; lit., fat-meat county

Túgno, *adj.*, Tiring, fatiguing (toógno)

Tuméndi, *pron.*, To ye, ye. Pasp., 1st dat. pl., *tuménde*

Túshni, *n.*, Faggot, basket (toóshni, etc.) Pasp., *kóshnika* basket

Tússa, *pron.*, With thee, thee. Pasp., *túsa*

Tússis,⎫ If it be possible (tastís)
Tustís,⎭

Túvlo,⎫ *n.*, Tobacco (toov, etc.) Pasp., *tuv*, tobacco
Túvli,⎭

    Túvlopen, *n.*, Tobacco

V AND W.

These letters are almost always interchangeable.

Wáfedo, *adj.*, Bad (vásavo, wásedo)
    Wáfedo *folk*i, Enemies
    Wáfedo gáiro, Enemy
    Wáfedo róker*ing* gaíro, Chatterer
    Wáfedopèn, *n.*, Wickedness
    Wáfedes, *adv.*, Ill
    Wáfedodáir, *comp.*, Worse
    Wáfedo-dík*ing*-tan, Wilderness ; lit., bad-looking place
    Wáfedo bával ta and*s* kek koóshto bok, (An) ill wind that brings no good luck
Wagyaúro, *n.*, Fair, market (walgaúrus)
Vákasho, *n.*, Lamb (bókocho, bókoro). Pasp., *bakritchó*
Válin, ⎫ *n.*, Bottle, glass. Lieb., *walin*
Wálin,⎭
    Válinésko-men, *n.*, Bottle-neck, neck of a bottle
Walgaúrus, *n.*, Fair (wagyaúro, wélingaúro). This word occurs in the following forms in English collections :— Bright, *varingera ;* Harriot, *vail goro ;* Roberts, *waggaulus* (Pott, ii., 77, and Predari, p. 274, give the same word from Kogalnitschan, who took it from Roberts) ; "Illustrated Lond. News," 1851, p. 715, *vellgouris*, pl. ; Leland, *welgooro*, pp. 50, 56, 66, 114, 212 ; *wellgooros*, pl., 137 ; *wellgoóras*, pl., 211 ; Borrow, "Lavo-lil," *weggaulus*,

welgorus, welgaulus. Bryant, Irvine, Simson, and
Borrow's earlier works do not include the word.
Pasp., p. 255, in voce, *inklidv*, "panayiréste (G. M.
πανήγυρις)," to the fair ; Vaillant, Gramm. Romm.,
vagail, foire

Vángar, *n.*, Coals, money (ángar, vóngar). Pasp., *angár,* coal

Wangúshter*s, n., pl.,* Rings (vóngusti, etc.)   Pasp., *angustrí*

Vániso, *adj.* and *n.*, Any, anything (váriso, wóriso). Miklosich, über die Mundarten, part ii., p. 60, No. 1612,
valaso; No. 1622, *vareko;* No. 1626, *vareso*

   Vániso kúmeni, Anybody

*Wán*tasóva, I do want

   Too *wán*tasár, Thou wantest

Várdo, }
Wárdo, } *n.,* Cart. Pasp., *vordón*

   Wardéngro, *n. pr.,* Cooper, a Gypsy gang

   Wárdesko-heré, *pl.,* Wheels ; lit., cart legs

   Wárdesko-kóla, Harness ; lit., cart things

   Wárdesko-prasterméngri, Wheel ; lit., cart runner

   Prástering-wárdesko-atching-tan, Railway station ;
      lit., running-cart's stopping-place

   Boótīesto-várdo, Knifegrinder's barrow ; lit., working
      cart

   Reíesko-várdo, Carriage ; lit., gentleman's cart

   Poov-várdo,   } Plough ; lit., earth-cart (?bavéngro,
   Várdo-bavéngro,}   for poovéngro)

   Wárdi, *n. pl.,* Cards.   From the assonance of *carts*
      and *cards*

   Wárdi, *pl.,* Carts

   Wárdi-gairé, Carters

Váriso. See Vániso

Váro, *n.,* Flour (vóro). Pasp., *varó*

   Varéngro, }
   Vardéngro, } *n.,* Miller, flour

Várter, *v.,* To watch. Lieb., *garda,* precaution

   Raklé vart asár láti, Boys watch her

   Vartínimi, They are watching us

Vast,
Vásti,
Vas, } *n.*, Hand, fist. Pasp., *vast*
Wast,
Wásto,

Vástaw,
Wástaw, } *pl.*, Hands. Pasp., *vastá*

Wasténgri*es*, *n. pl.*, Handcuffs

Wásteni-moóshaw, *pl.*, Arms

Wásto-bóshoméngro, Drum

Yógesto-wástaw, *pl.*, Tongs

Wast hánik, Anvil ; lit., hand-well. Due to assonance

Vásavo, } *adj.*, Bad (wáfedo). ? Formed from, Pasp., *bezeh*,
Wásedo, } sin ; or from *peis*, bad ; Ousely's "Travels in Persia," iii., 400 (see Pott, ii., 368)

Vas, bálo-vas, *n.*, Bacon (mas)

Wáver, *adj.*, Other, others (wóver, etc.) Pasp., *yavér*

Wáveré, *pl.*, Others

Wáver-teméngro, Foreigner; lit., other-country (man)

Veéna, *n.*, Excuse

Veénlo, *adj.*, Excused

Lel veéna, Take notice

'Vel,
'Wel, } *v.*, To come, become (avél, awél). Pasp., *éla*, come !

Wéla, He comes

Welássa,
Weléssa, } Thou comest

'Víssa *wi'* mándi talé koo (k'o) kítchema ? Will you go with me down to the inn ? Welsh Romanes

Wénna,
Ven, } They come

Vióm, I came

Vián, You came

Viás, He came

Sor méndi viám, We all came

Viém akéi o wáver koóroko, We came here last (lit., the other) Sunday

Kánna vián toméndi akeí ? When did ye come here ?

Vién, They came, began, became

Wél'd, *p. part.,* Came

Wel pálla, To follow ; lit., come after

Te 'wel, May it come, or become

Te wel kóva koósi poov meéro nógo, Would that this little field were my own

Yon te vel sor tatchó. Kek yon te wel pánlo. They will be all right. They will not be put in the ' pound '

Te vel yov akeí, If he were to come here

Kek mándi te wel líno opré, I shall not be arrested

Te wel toot rínkeni, If you be pretty

Te wel mándi te mer, If I happened to die

Wélingaúro, *n.,* Fair (walgaúrus)

Ven, They come.   See Vel

Ven, } *n.,* Winter. Pasp., *vent, vend*
Wen,

Vénlo, } *adj.,* Wintry
Wénlo,

Vénesto-chaírus, } Winter, winter-time
Ven-cheérus,

Véndri, *n.,* Gut, intestine.   Lieb., *wenterja*

Wéndraw, *pl.,* Entrails

Wénna, They come. See Vel

Vériga,
Wérigo, | *n.,* Chain. Bw., Span. G., *beriga ;* Pott, ii., 80 ;
Vériglo, | Mikl., i., 44
Wériglo,

Men-wériga, Necklace

Vesh, } *n.,* Forest, wood. Pasp., *vesh*
Wesh,

Wéshaw, } *pl.,* Woods
Wesháw,

Veshéngro, } *n.,* Gamekeeper, one who takes care of
Weshéngro,   a wood, forester

Wéshni-múllo, Owl

Vesh-joókel,
O lólo-wéshkeno-joókel,} Fox
Wéshkeni-tíloméngri, Trap, snare
'Víni, *n.*, Beer (lōvína). Lieb., *lowina*
Vióm, I came. See 'Vel
Wisht,
Wíshto,} *n.*, Lip. Pasp., *vusht*
 'Pré-éngro-wisht, Upper lip
 Tálani-wisht, Under lip
Wólsho, *n. pr.*, Wales (Wótchkeni). Lieb., *walschdo ;* Pott,
 i., 53, *Walldscho*, French
 Wálshenéngro, *n.*, Welshman
 Kek mándi *can* róker Wólshitíkka, I cannot speak
 Welsh. Lieb., '*walschdikko temm*, welschland,
 Frankreich'
Vóngar,
Wóngar,} *n.*, Coals, money (vángar, ángar). Pasp., *angár*,
 coal
 Wóngali-gaíri,
 Wóngaréngries,} *n. pl.*, Colliers
Vónka,
Wónka,} *adv.*, When. ? Mikl., ii., 36 (59), *anké*, noch (in
 Kolomyjer Kreise Galiziens Vocab.)
 Vónka see raáti, When it is night
 Wónka jáfra iv pedás talé, When there was such a
 snowstorm
 Wónka mándi vióm akeí, When I came here
Vóngusti,
Vóngushi,
Wóngushi,} *n.*, Ring, finger. Pasp., *angustré*, ring ; *angusht*
Vóngus,
 finger
 Vongshéngri, *n.*, Glove
 Fóshono-wóngushies, False rings, rings of imitation
 gold
 Vongushté,
 Vongéshters,} *pl.*, Rings
 Wast-vóngushté,
 Vóngustché,} *pl.*, Fingers
Woóder, *n.*, Door. Pasp., *vuddár*

Voódrus, }
Woódrus, } *n.*, Bed (wúdress).   Pott, ii., 78 ; Mikl., i., 27

   Chíved *to* woódrus, Confined

   Woódrus-gav-tem, Bedfordshire

   Opré woódrus, Upstairs ; lit., upon bed, but used for
      upstairs.   O baúro kamóra see opré woódrus, The
      big room is upstairs

Woóser, }
Woósher, } *v.*, To throw

   Woóseróva, I do, or will, throw

   Woóser apré, To vomit

   Woósadóm apré, I vomited

   Woósadás, He threw

   Woóser*ed, p. part.*, Thrown

Vóro, *n.*, Flour (váro).   Pasp., *varó*

Wóriso. See Váriso

Wótchkeni-tem, Wales (Wólsho).   Pott, i., 53, *Walldscho*,
   French

   Wótchkenéngro, *n.*, Welshman

Wóver, *adj.*, Other (awóver, ovávo, wáver).   Pasp., *yavér*

Wúdrus, *n.*, Bed (woódrus)

   Wúdrus-shóroméngro, Pillow

   Wúdrus-dándiméngri, Bug ; lit., bed-biter

Y.

Yákel, *n.*, Dog (joókel).   Pasp., *djukél*

Yárdooka, }
Yárduχa, } *n.*, Apron (jorjóχa, etc.)

Yaun, *pron.*, They (yon).   Pasp., *ol*

Yek, *adj.*, One.   Pasp., *yek*

   Yékino, *adj.*, Single, only

   Yékorus,
   Yékos,
   Yékoro, } *adv.*, Once
   Yékera,
   Yéka,

Yov kom'd asár léndi doói sar yékera, He loved them
both equally; lit., them both as one

Yéka, *n.*, Haste (héka)

Yiv, *n.*, Snow (iv, etc.)   Pasp., *viv, iv,* etc.

Yivyéla, It snows (yiv [d]éla, it gives snow)

Yog, *n.*, Fire.   Pasp., *yag*

Yog-chik, Ashes; lit., fire-dirt

Yogéngro,
Yogéngri,
Yógoméngri, } *n.*, Gun
Yógoméskro,

Yogéngri-choóko, Shooting-coat

Yógoméngro,
Yogéngri gaújo, } Gamekeeper
Yog-moosh,

Yogéngri*es*, *n. pl.*, Lucifer matches

Yógesto-wástaw, *pl.*, Tongs

Dood-yogénghi-kóshter, Firebrand

Yógenghi náflopen, Fever; lit., fiery illness, *pyrexia*

Yógongo-tan, Fireplace

Yói,
Yoi, } *pron.*, She.   Pasp., *ói*

Yok, *n.*, Eye.   Pasp., *yak*

Yókaw,
Yókyaw, } *pl.*, Eyes.   Pasp , *yakd*

Yokéngri*es*, *n. pl.*, Spectacles

Yóky, *adj.*, Knowing, wideawake, sharp

Yóky rívoben, Fine linen

Yóky fólki, Fine people

Cocky yóki, Squinting, cockeyed.   A nickname for
the Boswell tribe about Manchester

Yon, *pron.*, They (yaun).   Pasp., *ol*

Yoóso,
Yoózo, } *adj.*, Clean, clear.   Pasp., *koshdva, ghoshdva,* to
clean; *ushandva*, to sift

Yoóser, *v.*, To clean (kósher)

Yoózheróva, I clean

Yoózhadóm o kair tátcho, I swept the house clean

Yoózhadé, They swept

Yoózhadás, He swept

Yoóser apré, To sweep, clean up

Yoósering kosht, Broom, brush

Yoózhoben, Cleanliness

Yóra, *n.*, Watch, hour, clock (óra, etc.)   Pasp., *óra*, watch

Yóro,⎫
Yóri, ⎭ *n.*, Egg.   Pasp., *vanró, arnó*

     Yórakana-koóroko, Easter; lit., Egg-Sunday

     Yóresko-chóχa, Egg-shell

Yov, ⎫
Yow, ⎬ *pron.*, He (ov).   Pasp., *ov*
Yuv, ⎭

Z.

Zee, *n.*, Heart, soul.   Pasp., *oghí; ghi* (As.)

     Zeeáw, *pl.*, Hearts

     See-éngro, *adj.*, Spirited

Zímen, *n.*, Soup, broth.   Pasp., *zumí;* Lieb., *summin.*

APPENDIX

TO THE

GYPSY-ENGLISH VOCABULARY.

THE words in this Appendix are taken from a variety of Anglo-Romany sources, from which those words only are extracted which we have not ourselves heard, and which have their representatives in foreign Gypsy vocabularies, or seem to us otherwise noteworthy.

The following contractions are used :

Bw. 1 Z., 2 Z.—Borrow, " Zincali," 3rd edition, 1843, in 2 vols.

„ Z.—Borrow, "Zincali," 1861 edition, in 1 vol.

„ 1 L., 2 L., 3 L.—Borrow, "Lavengro," 1851 edition, in 3 vols.

„ 1 R., 2 R.—Borrow, " Romany Rye," 1857 edition, in 2 vols.¹

„ W.—Borrow, "Wild Wales," 1868 ed., 1 vol., post 8vo, ch. xcviii.

„ Ll.—Borrow, " Lavo-lil," 1874.

Bnt.—Bryant's Vocabulary, contained in the "Annual Register," 1784.

Bgt.—Bright's "Travels through Lower Hungary," 1818.

Böht.—Böhtlingk's " Über die Sprache der Zigeuner in Russland, Mélanges Asiatiques," vol. 2, part 2.

Boorde.—Andrew Boorde, " Introduction of Knowledge" (A.D. 1547), reprinted 1870, for Early English Text Society, by Trübner and Co., London, p. 218. See "The Academy," 25 July, 1874, p. 100.

Hotten.—" Slang Dictionary," 1864.

Harr.—Col. Harriot's Vocabulary, published in " Royal Asiatic Soc. Transactions," 1830.

I.L.N.—"Illustrated London News."

Irv.—Irvine's Vocabulary, published in " Bombay Literary Society's Transactions," 1819.

Lld.—Leland, " English Gypsies," 1873.

Lieb.—Dr. Liebich, " Die Zigeuner," etc., 1863.

Mikl.—Miklosich, " Über die Mundarten und die Wanderungen der Zigeuner Europas," Vienna, 1872.

Pasp.—Dr. Paspati, " Tchinghianés ou Bohémiens de l'Empire Ottoman," 1870.

Pott.—Dr. Pott, " Die Zigeuner," etc., 1844

Sim.—Simson's " History of the Gypsies," 1865.

Smith.—Smith's " Tent-life with English Gypsies in Norway," 1873.

Vaill.—Vaillant, " Grammaire Rommane," Paris, 1868.

A.

Afta, Seven.   Bnt. (eft, heft-wardesh); Pasp., *eftá*

Ambrol, } Pear. { Bw., 3 L., 209; 1 R., 245; } Pasp., *ambról*
Ambrell, }   { Boorde; }

Andé, Into. Bw., 1 L., 325; } Pasp., *andé*
Ando, In. Bw., Ll., 17; }

Anglo, Before. Bw., Ll., 17 ; Pasp., *anglé*

Astis, Possible, it is possible. Bw., Ll., 18 (estist)

Artav, To forgive, pardon.} Bw., Ll., 18, 130; *artavávam*,
Artapen, forgiveness. } 210; Vaill., *ertiça*, pardon

B.

Bedra, Pail. Bw., Ll., 264 (pitaree); Pasp., *beláni, beldi*, trough; Mikl., i., 44

Bolla, To baptise. Bw., Ll., 24; Pasp., *boláva*

Bo, Stove. Bw., Ll., 265. Pasp., *bov*

Beshaley, Stanley, a Gypsy tribe. Bw., Ll., 22

C.

Calshes, Breeches. Sim., 300, 315 ; Pott, ii., 170

Chaori, Lasses. Bgt. ; Pasp., *tchaiorí*, lass

Choomomengro, Boswell tribe. Bw., Ll., 82

Chungalo, Void, without form. Bw., Ll., 119; Pasp., *tchungaló*

Colee, Anger. Bnt. ; Pasp., *kholín*

Corbatcha, ? Whip. Bw., W. ; ? Böht., *karbatscho*, whip

Covantza, Anvil. Bw., 3 L., 192 ; Pasp., 42, *govanítcha*

D.

Dearginni, It thunders. Bw., 1 L., 338 ; Bgt., Hungn. G.,
    derguner; Mikl., ii., 42, No. 309, *derginjel*
Devlehi, With God. Bw., 3 L., 186 ; 1 Pott, 191, *devleha*
Deue lasse, For God's sake. Boorde ; Pasp., *devlésa*
Dook, Ghost, spirit. Bw., 2 L., 241 ; 3 L., 66 ; 1 R., 114,
    115, 193, 210, 233. Pasp., *dúkhos;* Lieb., *tucho;*
    Mikl., i., 10
Dugilla, Lightning (? dearginni). Bgt.
Duito, Second. Bw., Ll., 40 ; Lieb., *duito*

E.

Efage, Irish Gypsy. Harr.
Eft, Seven. Bw., Ll. (aft, heft-wardesh). Pasp., *eftá*
Enneah, Nine. Bnt. ; Pasp., *eniá*
Enyovardesh, Ninety. Bw., Ll., 156. Pasp., *iniá far desh*
Estist, May be. Bw., Ll., 138 (astis)

G.

Grommena,⎫
Grovena, ⎬ *s.* and *v.*, Thunder ; to thunder. Bw., Ll., 47 ;
Grubbena, ⎭   Pasp., *kúrmi;* Mikl., i., 13
Grondinni, It hails. Bw., 1 L., 338 ; 1 Pott, 104, *grados ;*
    Polish, *grad;* Russ., *gradi;* Mikl., i., 12

H.

Harko, Copper. Bw., W., 344 ; 1 Pott, 107, *hart'as ;* 119,
    Pchm., *charkom*
Harkomescro, Coppersmith. Bw., 3 L., 53
Horkipen, Copper. Bw., Ll., 51
Heftwardesh, Seventy. Bw., Ll., 158 ; Pasp., *eftá far desh*
Hetavava, To slay, etc. ; Bw., Ll., 49
Hir, By. Bw., 3 L., 53, 172 ; 1 R., 230 ; Bw., Hungn. G.,
    Ll., 126, *heri*

Hushti, Wide awake there. Lld., 102 ; Pasp., *ushtiáva*, I
     get up ; *ushtí!* get up !
Husker, To help. Lld., 209

I.

Inna, In, within. Bw., Ll., 51

K.

Kater (myla barforas ?), How farre (is it to the next
     towne ?) Boorde ; ? Pasp., *kébor*, combien
Kona, A meal. Irv. ; Hind., *khana*, dinner ; Mikl., i., 20
Koppas, Times. Lld., 221 ; Lieb., *koppa*, time

L.

Lach ittur ydyues, Good morow. Boorde ; Pasp., *latchó to*
     divés, bon ton jour = bon j. ; Pott, ii., 331, *latschidir*
     diwes, einen bessern Tag
Later, From her. Bw., Ll., 60 ; Pasp., *látar*
Lendar, From them. Bw., Ll., 60 ; Pasp., *léndar*
Lestar, From him. Bw., Ll., 160 ; Pasp., *léstar*
Lullero, Dumb. Lld., 107 ; Pasp., *lalóri*

M.

Malleco, False. Bw., Ll., 63 ; ? Pasp., *makló*, stained
Mander, From me. Bw., Ll., 64 ; Pasp., *mándar*
Manrickli, Cake. Bw., 3 L., 52 ; Pasp., *manrikló*
Manro,⎫
     ⎬ Bread. { Bw., 2 L., 167 ; } Pasp., *manró*
Manor,⎭   { Boorde ;   }
Mille, Thousand. Bw., Ll., 154 ; Bw., Span. G., Zinc., *milan*
Mokkado tanengre, Marshall, a Gypsy tribe. Bw., Ll., 232
Mole pis lauena, Wyl you drynke some wine (lit., Pray will
     you drink beer). Boorde ; Pasp., *molisardva;*
     Mikl., i., 24
Mormusti, Midwife. Bw., Ll., 68 ; Lieb., *mamischizza*

Mosco, A fly. Bw., Ll., 68 ; Pasp., *makí;* Lieb., *madzlin*
Muscro, Through. Lld., 232 ; Pasp., *maskaré*, in the middle
Mushipen, Lad. Bw., Ll., 69, 176 ; Pasp., *manushipe*,
    humanity

N.

Nick, To take away, steal. Bw., Ll., 71; Pasp., *nikáva*, to
    go out
Nill, River, etc. Lld., 113 ; Pasp., *len*

O.

Ochto, Eight. Bw., Ll., 154 ; Pasp., *okhtó*
Oitoo, Eight. Bnt. ; Pasp., *ohtó*
Olescro, His. Bw., 2 Z., 145*
Opral, Above. Bw., Ll., 72 (pral) ; Pasp., *oprál*

P.

Pa, For. Bw., 1 L., 325 ; Bw., Span. G., *pa*
Paloo, Cup. Irv. ; Pasp., *báli, pal*
Paningosha, Handkerchief. Roberts, 98 ; Pott, ii., 348, *pand-*
    schoche; Mikl., i., 31
Panschto, Fifth. Bw., Ll., 120; Lieb., *panschto*
Pashall, With. Lld., 225 ; Pasp., *pashál*, near
Pauvero,⎫
Pauveri, ⎬ Poor. Lld., 29, 203, 234 ; French, *pauvre*
Penchava, To think. Bw., Ll., 76, 142, 156, 162 ; Pasp.,
    pintchardva, to understand, know
Peneka, Nut. Bgt. ;   ⎫ 1 Pott, 120, 191, *pennach;*
Penliois, Nuts. Bw., Ll., 77 ;⎭ 108, *pelenda*, Bisch.
Peshota, Bellows. Bw., 3 L., 192 ; Lld., 39 ; Pasp., *pishót;*
    Mikl., i., 33
Phar, Silk. Bnt. ; Lieb., *păr*
Pindro, Hoof. Bw., 3 L., 194 ; Pasp., *pinró*
Pitarre, Basket. Irv. (bedra)

Pitch, To stick. Lld., 116; Mikl., ii., 34 (112), Bukowina
    Vocab., *pisdéas*, er stiess
Plaistra, Pincers. Bw., 3 L., 193; Pasp., *kláshta;* Mikl., i., 16
Poshavaben, False laughter. Smith, 382
Powiskie, Musket. Sim., 314; Bw., Ll., 318, *pushca;* Pasp.,
    pushká; Mikl., i., 33
Prala, To seize. Bw., 3 L., 192
Pral, Up. Lld., 247, sky; Harr.⎫
Praller, Above. Lld., 221;   ⎬ (opral); Pasp., *oprál*
Prosser,⎫
Pross,   ⎬ To ridicule. Lld., 94; Pasp., *prasáva*
Put, Abyss. Bw., Ll., 119; Bw., Span. G., *butron, putar*

R.

Rek of the tarpe, ? the vault of heaven. Bw., Ll., 120
Rin, File. Bw., 3 L., 194; Pasp., *rin*
Romanie, Whisky. Sim., 296, 314, 333; Pott, ii., 274,
    rapánus
Rossarmescro, Herne, a Gypsy tribe. Bw., Ll., 85

S.

Sano, Soft. Lld., 231; Pasp., *sannó*
Selno, Green. Lld., 29; Lieb., *sennélo;* Mikl., i., 47
Shel, Hundred. Bw., Ll., 140, 154, 158, 162; Pasp., *shel*
Sherrafo, *and* Sharrafo, Religious. Bw., Ll., 89, 122
Shovardesh, Sixty. Bw., Ll., 154; Pasp., *shov far desh*
Shukara, Hammer. Bw., 3 L., 193; Pasp., *tchokános*
Surrelo, Strong. Ll., 29, 31, 177, etc.; Lieb., *sorélo;* Pasp.,
    zoraló
Swa, Fear (f for t ?), Bgt.; Pasp., *ásfa, ásva,* tears
Swety, Folk. Bw., 1 R., 84; Ll., 92; 1 Pott, 107, *svaetos,*
    swieto; Mikl., i., 39

T.

Tarpe, Heaven. Bw., Ll., 120; Bw., Span. G., *tarpe*
Teeyakas, Shoes. Sim., 297, 315, 332; ? Pasp., *triák*

Trianda, Thirty. Bw., Ll., 158 ; Pasp., *triánda*
Trito, Third. Bw., 2 Z., 145* ; Lieb., *trinto*
Tschar, Ashes. I.L.N., 1851, Dec., p. 715 ; Pasp., *tchar* (As.)
Tschammedini, A slap on the face. Bgt.; 1 Pott, 173,
    dschamtinya; Lieb., *tschammadini*

V.

Vastro, Hand. Smith, 528; Pasp., *vastoró*, a little hand
Villarminni, It lightens. Bw., 1 L., 338 ; Mikl., ii., 60 (1642),
    villáminel; (1643), *villamo*
Vol, To fly. Bw., Ll., 120, *volélan,* 210 ; Mikl., ii., 33, *volavèl,*
    vuravel, fliegt
Voker, To talk. Hotten, 266 ; Pasp., *vrakeráva*

Y.

Yeckto, First. Bw., Ll., 119; Lieb., *jekkto*

Z.

Zezro, Left (hand). Bgt.; Bw., Span. G., *iesdra;* Lieb.,
    serwes

ENGLISH-GYPSY VOCABULARY;

OR,

Index to the Principal Words and Roots

IN THE GYPSY-ENGLISH VOCABULARY AND ITS APPENDIX.

Note.—Words marked with an asterisk (*) will be found in the Appendix to the Gypsy-English Vocabulary.

A.

About, Troostál

Above, Apré, opré, pré, opral,* praller*

Ache, n. and v., Doóker

Across, Paúdel, párdel

Actions, Káiropen

Active, Sig

Actor, Peiáskro-moosh

Afraid, Tráshlo, atrásh

After, Pálla, palál, tálla

After-birth, Poshbeenimus

Again, Apópli, pópli

Age, Poóroben

Ago, Pálla, ghiás, q.v.

Air, Bával

Alehouse, Kítchema

Alien, Gaújo

Alive, Jívdo, jívo, jído

All, Sor

Allow, Mook

Alone, Akónyo, bikónyo, kókero, kokeró

Along, Talé (o drom)

Already, Kenáw

Also, Tei

Altogether, Sor-ketané, ketané

Always, Sor cheéruses, sorkón cheérus

Am, Shom

Amen, 'Jaw see ta 'jaw see

Anchor, Béresto tíloméngri

Ancient, Poóro, poórokono

And, Ta

Angel, Yek o' midoóvel's tátcho gairé

Anger, Colee*

Angry, Hóino, hóno, haúrino, kórni

Ankle, Píresto-kokálos

Another, Wavér, awóver, ovávo, wóver

Answer, Poóker, del lav káter
Ant, Kreéa
Anus, Jeer
Anvil, Covantza,* kaúlomés-kro-kóva, pétalésto-kóva, wast-hánik
Any, Ványiso, váriso, wóriso
Apple, Póbo
Apple-tree, Póbesko rook
Apprehend, Lel opré
Apron, Járifa, járika, jorjófa, jorjóχa, chárdoka, shárdoka, yárduχa, yárdooka
Are, Shan, see, *q.v.*
Arm, Moóshi, moósho, wást-eni-moosh
Armpit, Moósheno-hev
Army, Koórimóngeri
Artful, Gózvero
As, 'Jaw, sar
Ascend, Jal opré
Ashamed, *A*ládj, ladj
Ashes, Chik, yog-chik, tschar*
Ask, Pootch
Asleep, Soóto
Ass, Méila, móila
Assize, Bauryó, baúri, baúro-poókenyuski-béshopen
Astonish, Trásher
Asylum, Dívio-kair
Attorney. See Lawyer
Auction, Bíkinopen
Aunt, Beébi
Autumn, Pálla lileí
Avoid, Nísser
Awake, *v.*, Jónger, atch opré, hushti*

Away, *A*dróm, avrí
Awful, Trásh*ful*
Axe, Tóver, tobár

B.

Baby, Tíkno chávo, tárno chávo
Back, *n.*, Doómo
Back, *adv.*, Paúli, pálla
Bacon, Bálovás
Bad, Vásavo, wásedo, wáfedo, béngalo, doosh
Badger, *Badj*aárus
Badness, Wáfedopen
Bag, Gúnno
Baker, Mauréngro
Bald, Nóngo
Ball (*dance*), Kélopen
Baptise, Bolla *
Barber, Morméngro, múrav-mángro
Bare, Nóngo
Barefoot, Nóngo-peéro
Bark, *v.*, Bosh
Barley, Lívina-ghiv
Barn, Gránza, gráinsi, loód-open
Basket, Képsi, kípsi, kúshni, túshni, toóshni, troóshni, pitaree *
Bastard, Dadéngro, dádlo, dádoméngro, boshtárdus, bostárdo, bastárdo
Bathe, Jal adré *the* paáni
Battle, Koóroben, koórimus
Be, See, vel, wel

Beads, Mérikios, mériklies

Beak, Chíriklesto nok

Bean, Boóbi

Bearded,. Choóralo

Beat, Koor, del

Beating, Koóroben

Beautiful, Rínkeno

Become, Vel, wel, *q.v.*

Bed, Voódrus, woódrus

Bedfordshire, Woódrus-gav-tem

Bee, Písham, poóshamer, goódlo-písham̃er, goódlo-písham

Beef, Moóshkeno-más, groóvenesko-más

Beer, Lívina, lovína, 'víní

Beerseller, Lívenéngro

Before, Anglo,* aglál, 'glal, agál, 'gal

Beg, Mong

Beggar, Móngaméngro

Begging, Mongamus

Behaviour, Káiropen, kériben, kérimus

Behind, Pálla, palál, paúli

Belief, Pátsaben

Believe, Pátser

Bell, Shoon-*to*-kóngri

Bellows, Peshota,* poódaméngri, poodélas

Below, Beneath, } Talé, alé, 'lé, tálla

Bend, Kair bóngo

Bent, Bóngo

Berry, Dúril

Better, Féterdaíro, féradair

Bible, Mi-doóvelésko-lil

Big, Baúro

Bigger, Baurodár

Billhook, Chínoméngro, kássoni

Bind, Pánder, pand, pan

Bird, Chériklo, chíriklo

Birdcage, Chériklesto kair

Birmingham, Kaúlo-gav

Bit, *n.*, Kótor, koósi

Bitch, Joókli

Bite, Dánder, dan

Bitter, Shoótlo (lit., sour)

Black, Kaúlo

Blackbird, Kaúlo-chériklo

Blackness, Kaúlopen, kaúloben

Blackpool, Kaúlo gav, kaúlopaáni-gav

Blacksmith, Kaúloméskro, kaúloméngro, sástraméskro, pétaléngro

Blanket, Kóppa

Blaze, Yog, hótcher, kátchar

Bless, Párav, párik

Blind, Korédo, kórdi, koró

Blindness, Kórodomus

Blood, Ratt

Bloody, Ráttvalo, ratt*fullo*

Blow, *v.*, Pood

Blow, *n.*, Koor

Boar, Moóshkeno baúlo

Boast, *v.*, Shor

Boat, Béro, paanéngro

Body, Troópus, troópo

Boil, Kérav

Bone, Kokálos, kokoólus

Bonnet, Joóvioko stárdi

Book, Lil

Boot, Skō'ni, *pl.*, skrúnya, chok, chókka

Booty, Loóripen

Born, Beéno

Bosh, Lavines

Bosom, Berk

Boswell, Choomomengro *

Both, Doói

Bother, Kínger, chára

Bottle, Válin, wálin

Bottle-neck, Válinésko-men

Bough, Bei

Bowels, Véndri, wéndraw

Box, Móχto, mókto, moókto, klísi

Boxer, Koóromèngro

Boy, Chávo, moosh-chávi, ráklo

Brandy, Tátto paáni

Bread, Manro,* mauro

Bread and butter, Kil maúro

Break, Póger, pog

Break-wind, Ril

Breast, Berk, toótchi (*nipple*)

Breath, Bával

Breeches. See Trousers

Brick, Chíkino-kóva

Brickfield, Chíkino tan, kaíriko tan

Bride, Rómadi, rómeni, rómni

Bridegroom, Rom

Bridewell, Klísoméngro

Bridge, Poodj

Bridle, Sheréngro, sólivéngro, sólovárdo, sálivárus, shóllovárdo

Bright, Doódeno, doódengi, doódoméngro

Bring, And, hand, rígher

Bristle, *n.*, Baúlesko bal

Broad, Baúro

Broadsheets, Ghílyaws

Broken, Pógado

Broken-kneed horse, Peléngro, póga(do)-chóngaw-grei

Broken-winded horse, Pógado bávaléngro, bavéngro, pógabával-grei

Broken-backed horse, Dooméngro, dooméksno-grei

Brooch, Spíngo

Broom, } Yoósering-kosht
Brush, }

Broth, Zímen

Brother, Pal

Brother-in-law, Stífo-pal

Brow, Kor

Bull, Goóro, grōv, goóroni, moóshkeni-groóvni

Bung, *Bung*árus

Burn, Hótcher, hotch, kátchar

Bury, Poórav, poóras

Business, Káiropen, jívoben, boóti, boótsi·

Butcher, Maséngro

Butter, Kil

Buttermilk, Kaléngri

Button, Kráfni

Buy, Kin

By, *prep.*, Hjr *

By, *adv.*, Pósha, posh

C.

Cabbage, Shok, *pl.*, shókyaw

Cake, Manrickli,* márekli

Caldron, Peéri, kekávi

Call, Kor

Cambridgeshire, Dóva tem kei o shórokoné gairé jivénna

Camp, Tan

Can, Sástis, *vide* Tastís

Cannot, Nastíssa, nestís

Candle, Múmbli

Cannon, Baúro-yógoméngri

Cap, Koófa, hoófa

Captain, Sheréngro, shoréngro, béresto-sheréngro

Cards, Wárdi

Care, Késser, trad

Carpet, Peéresto-kóppa

Carriage, Réiesko-várdo

Carrion, Moólomás

Carry, Rígher, ríker, rig

Cart, Várdo, wárdo

Castle, Králisko-poóro-kair

Cat, Mátchka

Certainly, Our, oúrli, aáva, aávali

Chain, Chítti, vériga, wériga, vériglo, wériglo

Chair, Béshoméngro, boólkoóva, skámin

Chamber, Kamóra

Change, *v.*, Pára, púra

Change, *n.*, Párapen

Chap, *n.*, Chal

Charm, *n.*, Fiz

Cheat, Hoax, chiv opré

Cheater, Kóroméngro

Cheek, Cham

Cheer up, Mántchi too

Cheese, Kal

Cherries, Lálo koóvaw

Cheshire, Kálesko-tém, kalkéling-tém, kal-kélimus-tém

Chief, Shórokno

Child, Chávo, chábo, tárno, tíkno, tíkeno

Chin, Choómbo, chúmba, kúmbo

Choke, Tásser

Chopper, Chínoméskro

Christ, Mi-dúvelesko Chávo

Christmas Day, Bóllesko-dívvus, mi-dúvel's-dívvus, moldívvus

Church, Kóngri

Circus, Síkoméngro

Clean, Yoóso, yoózo

Clean, *v.*, Yoóser, yoósheróva, kósher, kósser

Clean up, Yoóser apré

Clear, *adj.*, Yoósho, doódoméngro, doódeno

Cleaver, Chínoméngro, chínoméskro

Cloak, Plaáshta, plóχta, plóchta

Clock, Óra, yóra

Close, *v.*, Pand apré

Cloth, *adj.* and *n.*, Párno

Cloth, *n.*, Pártan, póktan, póχtan

Clothes, } Eézaw, rívoben,
Clothing, } ródi, ródi-*ing*

Clothes-peg, Gad-kosht-koóva, troósheni

Coals, Ángar, vóngar, wóngar

Coarse, Rúzlo

Coat, Cháho, chóχa, chóka, choóko, choófa, chúka

Cock, Bóshno

Codfish, Moóshkeno-mátcho

Coffin, Múlo móχto

Coïre, Késter, chórda, sōv lása

Cold, *n.*, Shil

Cold, *adj.*, Shílino, shírilo

Collar, Menéngro

Colliers, Wóngaréngri*es*, wóngali-gáiri

Comb, *n.*, Kóngali

Comb, *v.*, Kongl, kónga

Come, Av, avél, awél, 'vel, 'wel, áver

Companions, Mályaw

Confined, Chí*ved to* woódrus, póshli

Constable, Moóshkero

Conversation, Rókeropén, rókerben, rókerobén, rókamus

Convict, *n.*, Bítchaméngro

Cook, *n.*, Hóbenéngro, hóbenéngri

Cook, *v.*, Kérav, kel, kair

Cooper, *n. pr.*, Wardéngro

Copper, *adj.*, Harko,* horkipen,* haúrengo, hólono

Copper, *n.*, Haúro

Coppersmith, Hárkoméskro*

Cord, Shólo, shélo

Corn, Ghiv

Corner, Koónsus, koónshi

Corpse, Troópus, troópo, moólo

Cough, Bósherus, shel

Count, Ghínja, ghínya

Country, } Tem
County, }

Country, *adj.*, Teméskri

Countryman, Teméngro

County-town, Stéripen-gav

Court, *v.*, Kom, píriv

Cousin, Siménsa

Cover, *v.*, Choróva

Cow, Groóvni, groóven

Crab, Heréngro-mátcho

Creám, Smenting, sméntini

Creator, Káiroméngro

Cress, Panéngri shok

Crooked, Bóngo

Cross, *adj.*, Hóïno, hóno, kórni

Crow, Kaúlo chíriklo

Crown (five shillings), Koórona, pansh kóla

Cry, *v.*, Rōv

Cup, Dash, koóri, kóro, kúra, paloo *

Cup and saucer, Doóï-dash, doo-das

Curse, *v.*, Sóverhol, súlverkon, sóvlohol

Curse, *n.*, Sólohólomus, sóvlohóloben, sóverhóloben

Cut, *v.*, Chin

Cut off, Chin talé, chin alé

Cut, *n.*, Chínoben

Cyder, Pobéngro, póbeskopíaméskro

D.

Dance, *v.*, Kel
Dance, *n.*, Kélopen
Dark, Támlo, kaúlo
Daughter, Chei
Day, Dívvus, divéz
Dead, Moólo, múlo
Deaf, 'Shoóko
Deaf person, 'Shoóko kanéngri
Dear, Kómelo
Death, Méripen
Deceit, Hoókaben
Deep, Baúro
Deer, Staáni
Derbyshire, Chúmba-káleskotem
Deserter, Práster-méngro, prástero-móngro
Devil, Bang, beng
Devil's Dyke, Béngesko-hev
Devilish, Béngalo, bengésko
Diamond, Bárvalo-bar
Die, Mer, mel
Dig, Chin *the* poov
Dirt, Chik
Dirty, *adj.*, Chíklo, híndi, moókedo, móχodo
Dirty, *v.*, Móker
Distance, } Door
Distant, }
Divine, Doóvelkanésto, doóvelésko
Do, Kair, kel
Doctor, Tátcho drabéngro, drabéngro

Doer, Kéloméngro
Dog, Joókel, jook, yákel
Doll, Koókelo, kóshno chávi, kóshteno tíkno
Doncaster, *n. pr.*, Meílesto-gav, moílesto-gav
Donkey, Méila, móila
Don't, Maw, ma
Door, Woóda
Down, Talé, alé, 'lé
Dress, *v.*, Rood
Dress, *n.*, Roódopen, rívoben, joóvni-kólaw
Drink, *v.*, Pee, pióva
Drink, *n.*, Píaben, píamus
Drown, Tásser
Drug, Drab
Druggist, Drabéngri
Drum, Krámbrookos, koóroméngri, wásto-bóshoméngro
Drunk, Mótto, peédlo
Drunk, To get, Lel mótti
Drunkard, Móttoméngro, peeméngro, píaméngro
Drunkenness, Móttoben
Dry, Shoóko
Duck, Réṭza
Dumb, Shoóker, kek tátcho adré *the* moo, lúllero *
Dung, Full, chik
Dunghill, Chíkesko-chúmba

E.

Ear, Kan
Earring, Kanéngro, kíli, kánoméngro

Earth, *n.*, Poov, chik
Earth, *adj.*, Poóvesto
Easter, Yórakana koóroko
Easy, Shookár
Eat, Kol, hol, haw
Eatables, Kóben, hóben, hól-
ben
Educate, And apré
Eel, Sap, sápesko-mátcho
Egg, Yóro, yóri
Eight, Oitoo,* ochto,* doóï-
storáw
Eighteen-pence, Déshto-haúri,
désti-kóri
Encamp, Tan
Enchantment, Fiz
Enemy, Wáfedo gáiro
England, Ánghitérra
English, Gaújokones, gaújones
Englishman, Gaújo, Ánitrá-
kero (Ánghiterrákero)
Enough, Doósta, dósta
Entire, Chólo
Entrails, Wéndraw, vénderi
Every, Sórkon
Evil, Doosh
Except, Tálla
Exchange, Púraben
. Excuse, *n.*, Veéna
Eye, Yok
Eyebrow, Kor
Eyeglasses, Yokéngri*es*

F.

Face, Moóï
Fagot, Túshni, toóshni

Fair, *n.*, Fáiros, wagyaúro,
walgaúrus, wélingaúro
Fairies, Mi-doóveléski-bítta-
fólki
Fall, *v.*, Peróva, pel
False, Fóshono, malleco*
False laughter, Poshavaben *
Falsehood, Hoókapen
Famine, Baúro bókalobén
Far, Door
Farmer, Ghivéngro
Farmhouse, Ghívesto kair
Farther, Doórdair
Farthing, Lóli, lúli
Fashion, Drom
Fasten, Pánder, pand, pan
Fast, Pánlo
Fat, *adj.*, Túlo
Fat, *n.*, Túlopen
Father, Dad, dádus
Father-in-law, Stífo-dad
Fear, *n.* and *v.*, Trash
Fearful, Trash*ful*
Feather, Pur, por
Feather-bed, Pórongo-wúdrus
Fellow, Chal
Female, } Joóvni, joóvioko
Feminine, }
Fern, Foozhári
Fetch, Rígher
Fiddle, *v.* and *n.*, Bosh
Fiddle, *n.*, Bóshoméngro, bósh-
oméngri
Fiddler, Bóshero, bóshomén-
gro, bóshoméngri
Field, Poov
Fiery, Yógesko

Fight, v., Koor
Fight, n., Koóroben, koórimus
File, Rin *
Fill, Pórder
Filth, Chik
Find, Latch
Fine, Fíne-o
Finger, Vóngusti, vóngushi, vóngus
Finger-nail, Nei
Fire, n., Yog ; adj., Yógesko
Firearm, Yogéngro, yógoméngro, yogéngri
Firebrand, Dood-yógengikóshter
Fireplace, Yógoméskro, yógongo-tan
First, Fírstadáir
Fish, Mátcho, mátchi
Fisherman, Mátchoméngro, matchéngro
Five, Pansh
Five-pound note, Panshéngro
Five shillings, Koórona, pansh kóla
Flame, Prárchadi
Flea, Poóshamer, písham
Flies, Líkyaw
Florin, Doói kóli
Flour, Váro, vóro, pórno
Flower, Rósali, rósheo
Fly, n., Mosco ;* v., vol *
Foal, Tárno-grei, grei's tíkno
In foal, Adré kaáfni, kávni
Fold, Pándoméngro
Folk, Folki, sweti *

Follow, Av pálla, jal pálla
Food, Kóben, hólben, hóben
Fool, Dínilo, dínvero, dínlo
Foolishly, Dínveres
Foolish, Dínveri
Foot, Peéro, píro, peéri
For, Pa *
Forcibly, Drován
Forget, Bísser
Foreign, Gaújokones
Foreigner, Gaújo, gaúji, wáverteméngro
Forest, Vesh
Forgive, Artav,* fordé, fordél, párdel
Forgiveness, Artapen,* fordéloness
Fork, Pósoméngro
Foretell, Doórik, dúker
Fortune, Bok, dúkeriben
Fortunes, To tell, Doórik, dúker
Fortune-telling, Doórikapen, dúkeropen
Foul, v., Móker
Four, Stor
Fox, Vesh-joókel, o lólo wesh-keno-joókel
Fragment, Kótoréndri
Friday, Pansh dívvuses pálla koóroko, Doói dívvuses 'glal koóroko
Friend, Bor, mal, pal, kómelo gáiro
Friendship, Kómoben
Frightened, Tráshedo
Frock, Shoóba

Frog, O stor heréngro béngesko kóli ta jals adré o paáni so pióva

From, Avrí, fon

Frying-pan, Masáli, tátterméngri

Full, Pórdo

Fun, Péias

Further, Doórdair

G.

Gamekeeper, Kanéngri-moosh, yog-moosh, veshéngro, yogéngri-gaújo

Gaol, Stéripen

Garden, Roózho-poov, bor

Garlic, Póruma

Garments, Rívoben

Gate, Bur, stékas, stígher

Gentile, n., Gaújo, gaúji

Gentile, adv., Gaújokones, gaújones ; adj., Gaújokono

Gentleman, Rei

Gentlemanlike, Reiáli

Genuine, Tátcho

Get, Lel, rígher

Get up, Atch opré

Ghost, Múlo, moólo

Gift, Díno (lit., given)

Gipsy. See Gypsy

Girl, Rákli

Give, Del, dé

Glad, Míshto

Glandered horse, Nokéngro

Gloves, Vongshéngri, fólasé, fólasáw

Glutton, Baúro-hóloméngro

God, Doóvel, dúvel

Go, Jóva, jaw, jal, jil, jol

Go back, Jaw paúli

Go slowly, Jal shookár

Goat, Lávines-bókro

Gold, Soónakei

Goldsmith, Soónako-pétaléngro

Gonorrhœa, Hótcheropen, hótchopen, hódjerpen

Good, Koóshko, koóshto, kúshto, kóshto, míshto, tátcho, tátcheno, látcho

Goodness, Koóshkopen, koóshtiben, koóshtoben, kóshtoben, látchipen

Good health! }
Good luck! } Koóshto bok !

Goose, Pápin, pápini, pápinéngri

Gooseberry, Dúril

Gown, Shoóba

Grandchild, Poóro-dad's chávo

Grandfather, Poóro-dad, paúpus

Grandmother, Poóri-dei, baúri-dei

Grass, Chor

Grassy, Chóresto, chórkeno choréngri

Grasshopper, Chór-óχtaméngro

Grave, n., Hev

Gray, n. pr., Bal (lit., hair)

Grease, n., Túlopen

Great, Baúro

Green, _Greéno_, chor-díking, choréngri, selno*
Greenwood, Bívan-kosht
Greyhound, Kanéngri-joókel, shóshi-joókel
Grieve, Toog
Grieved, Toógno, toógeno, toógnus
Ground, Tan, chik, poov
Grouse, _Nöthe_rénghi chíriklo
Guinea, Kótor
Guineafowl, Atch paúli kánni
Gun. See Musket
Gut, Vénderi
Gypsy, _n._, Rom, Rómani-chal, kaúloméngro; _adj._, Rómani
Gypsy language, Rómanes

H.

Hail, _n._, Baúro bíshno; it hails, grondinni*
Hair, Bal
Hairy, Báleno, bál_ly_
Half, Posh
Half-breed, Dídakéi, póshpeérdo
Halfcrown, Posh-koórona
Halfpenny, Posh-hóri
Hall, Fílisin
Halt, Atch
Halter, Múloméngro
Hammer, Déloméskro, pógeroméskro, pógeromésti, tobár, tóver, shukara *
Hand, Vast, wast, vásti, vas, vastro*

Handbills, Ghílyaw_s_
Handcuffs, Wasténgri_es_
Handkerchief, Díklo, póshneckus, póngdishler
Hang, Násher
Happiness, Koóshko-bók
Hard, _adv._, Drován
Hare, Kanéngro, kanéngri
Hark! Shoónta!
Harlot, Loóbni, loódni, lúbni
Harness, Wárdesko kóla
Harvest, Ghívesto-chaírus
Haste, Héka, yéka
Hasten! Réssi toot, kair héka
Hat, Staádi, stádi
Hatchet, Chínoméngro
Hate, Kek-kom
Have, Si, shan, _q.v._
Hawker, Bíkinoméngro, bíkoméngro, kaúroméngro
Hay, Kas
Hayrick, Kaséngro
He, Ov, yov, yow
Head, Shéro, shóro, shoró, shúro
Hear, Shoon
Heart, Zee
Heat, Táttoben
Heaven, Dúvel, midúvelesko cháirus, midúvelesko-kéri
Heavy, Lóko (_q.v._), pórdo
Hedge, Bor
Hedgehog, Hótchi-wítchi
Hedgestake, Boréngri
Height, Tórropen
Hell, Béngesko-tan
Help, Kair-posh, husker*

Hen, Kánni, káχni
Her, Láki, lóki, lákro, láti
Here, Akéi, 'kei
Herefordshire, Póbesko pía-
　meski tem
Heren,⎫ *n.pr.*, Mátcho, Rossar-
Heron,⎬　mescro;* *pl.*, Baúro-
Herne,⎭　kanéngri - mooshάw,
　Bálaws
Herring, Mátcho, báleno
　mátcho
Hide, Gárav, gára
Hidden, *adv.*, Gárones, gárid-
　nes; *adj.*, gáridno, gárido
High, Tórro
Highway, Baúro drom
Hill, Chong, choong, choónga,
　choómba, kúmbo, dúmbo
Him, Las, les, lésti
His, Lésko, lésti's, olescro*
Hit, Del, koor
Hold, *n.*, Bónek; *v.*, Til
Hole, Kev, hev
Holy, Doóvelkanésto
Home, Keré, kéri
Honey, Písham
Hoof, Greíesto-píro, pindro*
Hop, *v.*, Hok
Hops, Lívenéngries
Horn, Shing
Horse, *n.*, Grei; *adj.*, Greíesto
Horse-dealer, Grei-éngro
Horse-shoe, Pétal, greí-eṣto-
　chok
Horse-race, Prastérimus, prás-
　terméngri, greíesto-práster-
　ing

Horse-fair, Gréiesto-fáiros
Horse-whip, Gréiesto-chúkni
Horse-rug, Gréiesto-kóppa
Horse-collar, Gréiesto-menén-
　gro
Hot, Tátto
Hound, Joókel
Hour, Óra, yóra
House, Kair
House-dweller,⎫ Kairéngro,
Housekeeper, ⎭　kairéngri
How, Sar
How d'ye do? Sar shan?
Humble, Choóro, choóreno,
　choórokno
Humbly, Choóvenes
Hundred, Shel*
Hung, Náshedo
Hunger, Bok
Hungry, Bókalo
Hurt, *n.* and *v.*, Doóka
Husband, Rom

I.

I, Man, mé, mándi, mánghi
Ill, Násfelo, náffelo, doosh
Illness, Náffelopén
Illtempered, Kórni
Imitation, Fóshono
Immediately, Kenáw sig
In, Adré, 'dré, ando,* inna*
Indebted, Pázerous
Inflame, Kátcher
Injure, Doóka
Inn, Kítchema
Innkeeper, Kítcheméngro

Intestine, Vénderi
Into, Andé,* adré, 'dré
Ireland, Híndo-tem, Hindi-teméskro-tem
Irishman, Hindi-teméngro, poovéngri-gaújo
Irish Gypsy, Efage *
Iron, *n.*, Sáster, saásta, saáshta
Iron, *adj.*, Sástera
Is, See
It, Les
Itch, *n.* and *v.*, Honj

J.

Jail, Stéripen
Jews, Midúvelesto-maúroméngri
Jockey, Késterméngro
Judgment, Bítchama
Jump, Hókter, hok, óχta
Jumper, Hóχter*er*
Just now, Kenáw sig
Justice of the peace, Chívlo-gaújo, chúvno-gaújo, pōkén-yus, poókinyus

K.

Keep, Rígher, ríker
Kettle, Kekávvi, 'kávvi
Key, Klérin, klísin
Kick, *v.*, Del, dé
Kill, Maur
Kin, Siménsa
Kind, *adj.*, Kómelo, kómo-muso

King, Krális
Kingdom, Krális*om*, tem
Kiss, *n.* and *v.*, Choóma
Knee, Chong, choong
Knife, Choóri, chivoméngro, chínoméngro
Knock, *v.*, Koor, dé
Know, Jin
Knowing, Yóki, jinoméngro, jínoméskro

L.

Lad, Chab, chábo, chávo, mushipen.* See Boy
Lady, Raúni
Lamb, Bókocho, vákasho
Lame, Long, bóngo
Lancashire, Píro-dél*ing*-tem
Landlord, Hóleno, holéskro
Lantern, Doódoméngro
Lard, Baúleski túlopen
Large, Baúro
Lass, Chei. See Girl
Last, Kóliko
Laugh, *v.*, Sav, sal, sárler
Laugh, *n.*, Sávaben, sávapen
Laughter, *n.*, Sálimus, sál*ing*
False laughter, Poshavaben *
Lawyer, Shanéngro, sheréks-no, chívomengro, rókero-méngro, rókerméngro, sho-réngro, shéroméngro, moóy-éngro, moo-éngro
Lead (metal), Mólus, mólov
Lead, *v.*, Rígher
Leaf, Pátrin

12

Lean, *adj.*, Bíto, bítl
Leather, Cham
Leave, *v.*, Mook
Leaves, Roókenghi chóχas
Lee, *n. pr.*, Poórum
Leek, Poórumi
Left, *adj.*, Bóngo, zezro *
Left, *p. part.*, Moóklo
Leg, Héro
Leggings, Heréngri*es*
Lent, Moóklo
Let, Mook
Letter, Chínoméngro, Chívo-méngro
Liar, Hóχano, hókeno, sha-néngro
Lice, Joové, joóvas
Lick, *v.*, Kósher
Lie, Hóχaben, hóχani, hoók-apen
Life, Méripen, jívoben
Lift, Had, ázer
Light, *n.*, Dood
Light (lucidus), *adj.*, Doódeno
Light (levis), *adj.*, lóko (gene-rally used for *heavy*)
Lightning, Baúro-dood, mi-dúvelesto-dood, mi-doóvel-esko-yog, villarminni *
Like, *v.*, Kom ; *adj.*, Pénsa, pénza, sar
Likeness, Dikoméngri
Lincolnshire, Túlo-mas tem
Lip, Wisht
Listen, Shoon
Little, Tíkno, bíto
A little, Koósi

Live, Jiv
Livelihood,⎫ Jívoben
Living,   ⎭
Lively, Jído
Liver, Boóko
Liverpool, Boóko-paáni, boó-kesto-paáni-gav, béro-gav, baúro-béresto-gav
Loaf of bread, Chólo maúro
Lock, *v.*, Klísin
Lock-up, *n.*, Klísoméngro
Lodge, *v.*, Lod
Lodging-house, Loódopen
London, Lundro, Lónderi, Lúndra, Kaúlo-gav, Baúro-gav
Lonely, Kókero, toógeno
Long, Door
Very long way, Doovorí-doo-vorí
Look ! Dórdi ! hókki !
Look, *v.*, Dik
Looking-glass, Díkoméngro, moóesto-kóva
Loose, Píro
Lose, Násher
Louse, Joóva
Lousy, Joóvli
Love, *v.*, Kom ; *n.*, Kómoben
Lovell, *n. pr.*, Kómoméskro, kómelo
Lover, Pírino, pírini
Lucifer-match, Déloméngro, doódoméskri
Luck, Bok
Lucky, Bókalo

M.

Mad, Dívio

Made, Kaírdo, kédo

Magistrate. See Justice of the peace

Magpie, Kákarátchi, rómani-chal-róker*ing* chíriklo

Maid, Rákli

Make, Kair, kel

Maker, Kéroméngro

Make love, Píriv

Male, Moóshkeno

Man, Gáiro, mánoosh, moosh

Manchester, Poovéngri gav, Moóshkeno gav, Távesto-gav, Póχtan gav

Mangy, Hónji*fied*

Mansion, Fílisin

Many, Doósta, dósta

Mare, Grásni

Market-town, Fórus

Married, Rómedo

Marry, Rómer

Marshall, *n. pr.*, Mokkado tan-engre *

Masculine, Moóshkeno

Master, Shórokno gáiro

Match, Déloméngro, doódo-méskri

Mate, Bor

Mates! Choováli! chawóli! mályaw!

May, Te (preceding verb)

May be, Estist *

Mayor, Grésti

Me, Man, mándi

Meal, Kona*

Meat, Mas, -vas

Meddle, Chálav, chárvo, chára

Mercy, Kómoben

Midnight, Múlo raáti

Midwife, Mormusti,*dívi-gáiri

Mile, Meéä

Milestone, Mcéasto bar, poók-er*ing* bar

Milk, *n.* and *v.*, Tood

Mill, Pornéngri, pógaméngri, bávál-pógaméngri

Miller, Pógeroméngro, pórno-mésti, varéngro, vardéngro-gáiro

Mind! Lel trad! Rak! Lel veéna!

Mine. See My

Miss, Nísser .

Monday, Yek dívvus pálla koóroko

Monkey, Búmbaros, *munk*áros

Money, Lúva, ángar, vóngar, vángar, wóngar

Month, Shoon

Moon, Shoon, shool, chein, choom, síkerméngro, mi-dúvelesko-dood

More, Boótodair, kómi, kómo-dair

Morning, Saúla, saála

This morning, Kesaúla

Mother, Dei

Mother-in-law, Stífi-dei

Mountain, Dúmbo

Mourn, Rōv

Mouse, *Mouse*-us

Mouth, Moói
Much, Boot, boóti, kísi, doósta
Muck,
Mud, } Chik
Muck-cart, Fúll-várdo
Muddy, Chíklo
Mule, Sháni
Mumper, Choórokono moosh, choórodo
Musket, Pushca,* powiskie,* yogéngro
I must, Shom te
Mustard, Dánoméskri
Mutton, Joóvioko-mas
My, Meéro, meíro, míno, mi, mandi's

N.

Nail (finger), Nei
Nail (iron), Kráfni
Naked, Nóngo
Name, Nav, lav
Narrow, Bíto
Naughty, Wáfedo
Near, Pósha
Neck, Men
Necklace, Men-wériga
Needle, Soov
Negatives, Kek, maw, na (see p. 49)
Nettles, Dándiméngri chor
Never, Kek-kómi
New, Névo
Newspaper, Shoónaben, Shoó-naméngri, ghílyaws, ghil-yéngries

Night, Raáti
Nine, Enneah *
Ninety, Enyovardesh *
Nit, Lik
No, Kek, kéker, kékeno, naw, na, nei, naneí, kek-naneí
Nobody, Kek-kómeni
'No road,' Chíchikeno drom
Noise, Gúdli, gódli
None, Kékero, kékeno, kek-kómeni, kek-naneí
Norfolk, Mátchesko-gav-tem, póbesko-gav-tem
Norwich, Póbomuski-gav, pó-bomusti-gav
North, Shílo-tem
Nose, Nok
Not, Kek.   See No
Notice, n., Veéna
Nothing, Chíchi, chi
Now, Kenáw, konáw, kánna, kónna, kon
Nudge, Moónjer
Nuts, Pédliaw, pétliaw, pév-liaw, peneka,* penliois,* nuti

O.

Oak, Poóroder rook, králisko rook
Oath, Sóverhóloben, sóvlohó-loben, sólohólomus
Oats, Job
Oat-stack, Job-pooséngro
Off, Avrí, talé, alé
Ointment, Túlipen
Old, Poóro

Old-fashioned, Poórokono
On, Opré, apré, 'pré
Once, Yékorus
One, Yek
One-year-old horse, Beshén-
gro
Onion, Poórumi, strángli
Only, *adj.*, Yékino
Open, *v.*, Píriv; *adj.*, Píro
Opened, Pírivdo
Opposite, Pósh-aglál, tátcho
'glal
Orange, Póbomus
Order, *n.*, Trad; *v.*, Del trad
Osier, Ran
Other, Wáver, wóver
Our, Móro, méndi's, amandi's*
Out, out of, Avrí
Over, Paúdel, párdel
Owe, Kom
Owl, Wéshni-múlo
Own, *adj.*, Nógo, nágo, névus
Ox, Moóshkeni-groóvni

P.

Pail, bedra*
Pain, *n.* and *v.*, Doóka
Palace, Králisko kair, krális-
késko kair
Pales, palings, Pályaw
Paper, Lil, lílesko kóva
Pardon, *v.*, Artav,* *for*dél,
*for*dé, párdel
Pardon, *n.*, Artapen,* *for*délo-
ness, *párdon*os
Parlour, Beúrus

Parrot, Rómani-chal-róker*ing*
chíriklo, Híndo-kákarátchi
Parson, Ráshei, ráshref, délo-
méngro, mi-dúvel's moosh
Part, Kótor
Partners, Mályaw
Partridge, *Rídji*l
Path, Poovéla, droni
Paunch, Pur
Pauper, Choóredo. See Tramp
Pawn, *v.*, Símmer
Pawnshop, Símmer*ing* boó-
dega
Pay, *v.*, Pésser
Pea, Boóbi
Pear, Ámbrol*
Pedere, Ril
Pedestrian, Peeréngro
Pedlar, Bíkinoméngro, bíko-
méngro
Pen (fold), Pánoméngro
Penny, Kóri, hóro, hóri, hári
People, *Folk*i, sweti*
Pepper, Dánderméskri, tátto-
koóva
Performer, Kéloméngro
Petticoats, Chúffas, shoóva,
shoóba, pállani-chókka
Pheasant, Baúro chériklo, réi-
esko chériklo
Photograph, Díkoméngri
Physician, Drabéngro
Pick, *v.*, Tárder
Pie, Góɪ
Piece, Kótor
Pig, Baúlo
Pig-face, Baúlesko moóɪ

Pig-fair, Baúlesto fóros
Pillow, Woódrus shéroméngro
Pin, Spingl, spínger, spink
Pincers, Tíloméngri, plaistra *
Pinch, v., Moónjer
Pinfold, n. pr., Pánoméngro
Pipe, Swágler, swégler
Piper, Bóshoméngri
Place, v., Chiv ; n. Tan
Placenta, Poshbeénimus
Plate, Chóro, chor, sórsin, skoo-
   dálin
Play, v., Kel ; n., Kélimus, péias
Please! Lel koóshtoben !
Pleasure-grounds, Síkermén-
   gro
Pledge, v., Símmer
Plenty, Doósta, dósta
Plough, Poov-várdo, poóvesto-
   choóri, poóvo-chínoméngri,
   várdo-bavéngro
Plunder, v., Loor ; n., Loóripen
Pocket, Poótsi, pō'chi
Poison, Drab
Policeman, Gavéngro, moósh-
   kero, násherméngro, prás-
   terméngro, chukéngro
Poor, Choóro, chúveno, choó-
   reno, choórokno
Poorer, Choórodár
Pork, Báleno-mas, baúlesko-
   mas
Post, Kosht
Possible, Astis,* sástis, stastís,
   tastís, q.v.
Pot, Koóri, kóro
Potato, Poovéngri, poovyéngri

Potter, Kóroméngro, koréngro
Pothook, Sáster
Pouch, Gúnno
Pound (£1), Bar, bálanser,
   bálans
Pound (for cattle), Pánoméngro
Pour, Chiv
Powerful, Rúslo, rúzino
Power, Rúzlipen
Praise, v., Shor
Pray, Mong, mole *
Predict, Doórik, dúkker
Pregnant, Baúri, shoóbli,
   shoóvli (of women) ; kávni,
   kaáfni (of animals)
Present, n., Del-to-mándi, díno
Pretty, Rínkeno, ríkeno
Prettily, Rínkenes
Prison, Stáriben, stéripen, sté-
   rimus, stárdo, staúri
Prisoner, Stéroméngro, stéro-
   mésti
Privy, Híndi kair
Prognosticate, Doórik
Prostitute, Lúbni
Protect, Rak
Proud, Boóíno
Public-house, Kítchema
Pudding, Góí
Pudding-bag, Góíongo gúnno
Pudendum muliebre, Mindj,
   minsh
Pudendum virile, Kóri, kaúri
Pugilist, Koóroméngro
Pull, Tárder
Purse, Kísi
Put, Chiv

Q.

Quarrel, *v.*, Chíngar

Quarrel, *n.*, Chíngariben, gódli

Quart, Troóshni

Queen, Kralísi, Králisi

Quick, Sig

Be quick, Sígo toot, réssi toot, kair ábba

Quietly, Shookár

R.

Rabbit, Shóshi, mávi

Rabbit-trap, Klísoméngro

Race, *v.*, Práster

Race, *n.*, Prásterméngri

Rails, Pályaw

Railway train, Práster*ing* kóli

Rain, Bríshindo, bíshno

It rains, Bríshinéla

Rainy, Brísheno, bíshavo

Raise, Had, til apré

Raw, Biván, bívano

Razor, Móroméngro

Read, Del apré, Dé apré, del

Reading, *n. pr.*, Lálo-gav

Real, Tátcho, tátcheno

Reckon, Ghínja, ghínya

Reeds, *Rush*ári

Red, Lólo, lálo

Redford, *n. pr.*, Lálo peéro

Red-herring, Lóli mátcho

Reins, Tíloméngri

Relation, Siménsa

Relieve the bowels, Kínder, hínder, híngher, hind

Religious, Mi-dúvelesko

Remember, Chiv *it* adré *your* shéro, shoon léndi, kek bísser, répper toot

Remove, Ránjer

Resurrection, Átch*ing* apré a*p*ópli

Return, *v.*, Av paúli, jaw paúli

Rib, Kokálo

Riband, Dóri

Rich, Bárvalo

Riches, Bárvalopen

Ride, Késter, kíster

Rider, Késterméngro

Ridicule, *v.*, Prosser,* pross*

Right, *adj.*, Tátcho, tátcheno

Right, *adv.*, Tátchnes

Right, *n.*, Tátchopen

Right arm, Kúshto moóshi

Ring, *n.*, Vóngus, vóngustí, vóngushi

River, Dorió'v, Doyáv, nill*

Road, Drom

Roast, Pek

Rob, Loor

Rock, *n.*, Bar

Rod, Ran

Room, Kamóra

Rope, Shélo, shólo

Royal, Králisko

Row (noise), Gúdli, gódli

Rump, Bool

Run, *v.*, Násher, práster

Runner, Násherméngro, Prásterméngro

Rushes, *Rush*ári

S.

Sack, Góno, gúnno, kányo
Saddle, Béshto, bóshto, bóshta
Safe, Tátcho, tátcheno
Sail, *n.*, Béresto plóχta
Sailor, Beréngro, béroméngro, paanéngro-gaújo
Saints, Mi-dúveleski gairé
Sake, *Sáke*-os
Saliva, Choóngarben
Salt, *n.*, Lŏn, lon
Salt, *adj.*, Lóndo, lóndudno
Sand, Chik
Saturday, O dívvus 'glal koóroko
Savage, Haúrini
Say, Pen
Scent, Soóngimus
Scissors, Kátse*rs*, kátsi*es*
Scold, *v.*, Chíngar
Scotland, *Nórther*éngri-tem
Scotchmen, *Norther*éngri gairé
Sea, Doriŏ'v, doyáv, dovál, dovyál, baúro páni, lóndo paáni, lóndudno paáni
Search, *v.*, Rŏd, rŏder
Search, *n.*, Roódopen
Second, Duito*
Secretly, Koónjones, gárones, gáridnes
See! Dórdi! hókki!
See, *v.*, Dik
Seek, Rŏ'der, rŏd
Seize, Til, prala *
Self, Kókero
Sell, Bíkin, bik

Send, Sentence, } Bítcher, *n.*, Bítchama
Serpent, Sap
Servant, Boótiéngro, boótsiéngro
Sessions, Béshopen
Seven, Afta,* eft,* doór trinyáw ta yek, trin ta stor, trínstor
Seventy, Heftwardesh,* doór trinyáw ta yek desháw
Sew, Siv
Shake, Rísser
Shame, *v.*, Ládjer; *n.*, Ladj
Shamefully, Ládj*fully*
Sharp, Jínoméngro
Shave, Mórov
Shawl, Baúro díklo
She, Yói, yoi
Sheep, Bókoro, bókro, mas
Sheffield, *n. pr.*, Choóresto gav
Shepherd, Barséngri, baséngro, bókoroméngro, bókroméngro, bókoméngro, bókoréngro
Shilling, Tringórishi, kólli
Ship, Béro
Shirt, Gad
Shirt-sleeve, Gádesto bei
Shoe, Chok, chóka
Shoemaker, Chokéngro
Shoot, Poóder
Shooting-coat, Yogéngri choóko
Shop, Boódega, boódika, boórika
Shopkeeper, Boódegaméngro, boórikaméngro

Shoulder, Pikó
Shout, v., Kaur
Show, v., Síker
Showman, } Síkerméngro
Show-gardens, }
Shut, v., Pánder
Sick, Násfalo, náffalo
Sickness, Náfflopen
Side, Rig
Sign-post, Poókering-kosht,
  síkeroméngro
Silence! Shoóker, shookár
Silk, Kaish, kaidj, p'har*
Silken, Kaísheno, kaídjino
Silly, Dínveri
Silver,n., Roop; adj., Roópeno
Silversmith, Roópnoméngro
Sing, Ghil, ghiv
Single, Yékino
Sir! Refä!
Sin, Wáfedopen
Sister, Pen
Sister-in-law, Stífi-pen
Sit, Besh
Six, Shov, sho*
Sixpence, Shookaúri
Sixty, Shovardesh*
Skewer, Chúngar, spingárus
Skewer-maker,Spingáro-kélo-
  méngro
Skin, Moótsi
Sky, Dúvel, poodj, midúve-
  lesto-tem
Slap on the face, Tschamme-
  dini*
Slay, Maur, hetavava*
Sleep, v., Sov, soóter

Sleeve, Bei
Slowly, Droóven, shookár
Sly, Gózvero, jínoméskro, yóky
Small, Bíto, tíkno
Smallpox, Boókenyus, boóko
Smell, v., Soon, soom; n.,
  Soóngimus, soónaben
Smith, n. pr., Pétaléngro
Smith, Sásterméngro, pétal-
  éngro, kaúloméskro
Smoke, n. and v., Toov
Smoke tobacco, Pood toóvalo
Snail, Boúri
Snake, Sap
Snaptrap, Klísoméngro, pán-
  doméngro, tíloméngro
Snare, Tíloméngro
Snow, Iv, yiv, ghiv, shiv, hiv
It snows, Yivyéla
Snowball, Iv-bar
Snuff, Nokéngro
So, Ajáw, 'jaw
Soap, Sápanis, sápan
Soft, Sano*
Soldier, Koóroméngro
Something,} Choómoni, kú-
Some, } meni, kómeni
Son, Chor
Song, Ghíli, ghíveli
Soon, Sig
Sorry, Toógeno, toógno, toóg-
  nus
Soul, Zee
Sour, Shoótlo
Sorrel, Shoótlo-chor
Sovereign (£1), Bar, bálans,
  bálanser

Sovereign, Krális, kralísi
Spavined horse, Bóngo grei
Spectacles, Yokéngries
Spirited, See-éngro
Spirits, Tátto paáni
Spit, v., Choóngar, chúngar
Spittle, Choóngarben
Spit, Spingárus
Sport, Peläs
Spree, Kélopen
Spring, Fírstadaír, or bígno-
mus, o' Iílei
Spur, Bísko, poósoméngri
Squirrel, Roókaméngro
Stable, Stánya
Stacks, Stíghi
Staff, Kosht
Staffordshire, Koréngri-tem,
kóroméngro-tem
Stag, Staáni
Stallion, Baréskro-grei, barén-
gro-grei, péleno-grei, pelén-
gro-grei, moóshkeno-grei
Stand,
Stay,   } v., Atch
Stanley, n. pr., Baréngri, Besha-
ley*
Star, Stári, liléngro, dúvel, mi-
doóvelesko-dood
Station, Prástering-wárdesko-
átching-tan
Stays, Troópus
Steal, Chor, loor, nick*
Stick, n., Kosht
Stile, Peéroméngro
Still, adj., Átchlo, shoókar
Stink, v., Kánder, hínder, kan

Stinking, Kánelo, kánlo
Stockings, Olivas, hoólavas,
oúlavers
Stone, Bar
Stop, Atch
Stove, Bo*
Stranger, Gaújo
Straw, n., Poos; adj., Poóskenó,
poóskeni
Straw-stack, Pooséngro
Street, Drom
Stretch, v., Tárder
String, Dóri, doóri
Strong, Rúzlo, rúzino, roózlus,
surrelo*
Such, Jáfri, jáfra
Suffolk, Shoóko-maúromén-
gro-tem
Sugar, Goódlo
Summer, Táttoben, liléí, Iílei
Summons, Goódli
Sun, Kam, tam, sken
Sunny, Támlo (kámlo)
Sunday, Koóroki, Kroókingo-
dívvus, Kúlpho
Supper-time, Hóben-chaírus
Swan, Pórno-raúni
Swear, Sóverhol, súlverkon,
sóvlohol
Sweaty, Kíndo
Sweep, v., Yoóser apré
Sweet, Goódlo
Sweetheart, Pírino, pírini
Sweetmeats, Gúdlopen
Swelled, swollen, Shoóvlo
Sword, Haúro, baúro-choóri

T.

Table, Misáli, mísali, sálamán-
ka, hauméskro, hóbenéskro
Tail, Póri
Tailor, *n.* and *n. pr.*, Sívomén-
gro, suvéngro
Take, Lel, lé
Take care, Lel trad
Take care of, Rak
Take notice, Lel veéna
Take off, Ránjer
Take up, Lel opré
Talk, *v.*, Róker, voker;* *n.*,
Rókeropén. See Conver-
sation
Talker, Rókeroméskro
Tambourine, Koóroméngri
Tart, Gór
Tea, Múterimóngri, mooténgri,
píaméskri
Tea-kettle, Kekávvi
Teapot, Múterimóngri-koóva,
peeméngro,píaméskri-skoo-
dálin, skoodílin
Tear, *v.*, Chíngar
Tease, Kínger, chára
Teeth, Dányaw
Telescope, Door-díkoméngro
Tell, Pen, poóker
Tell fortunes, Doórik, dúkker
Ten, Desh
Tent, Tan
Testicles, Pelé, pélonos
Thank, Párik, párikaróva, pa-
rikráw
That, *conj.*, Te; *pron.*, Ta,
adoóva, adúvel, 'doóva

The, O
Thee, Toot, toóti
Their, theirs, Lénti, lénghi
Them, Len
Then, Kon
There, Adoí, odoí, 'doi
They, Yaun, yon
Thief, Chor, chóroméngro, loó-
roméngro
Thin, Bíto
Thine, Teéro
Thing, Kóva
Think, Penchava,* *thínk*asóva
Third, Trito*
Thirst, Troosh
Thirsty, Troóshlo
Thirty, Trianda*
This, Akóva, 'kóva
Thorn, Kóro
Those, Dúla, dóla
Thou, Too, toóti
Thousand, Mille*
Thread, Tav, taf, tel
Three, Trin
Throat, Kárlo, kaúri, kur, gur,
goóshum
Through, Adrál,'dral, muscro*
Throw, Woóser, woósher
Thunder, Maloóna, koóroko
grommena,*grovena,* grub-
bena,* mi-dúvelésko-gódli
It thunders, D<i>e</i>argínni *
Thursday, Stor dívvus*es* pálla
koóroko
Thus, Ajáw, 'jaw
Thy, Teéro, toóti, toóki, ti
Tie, *v.*, Pánder, pand, pan

Time, Cháirus, *pl.*, koppas *
Tin, Kúri, cham
Tinder, Poótan
Tired, Kíno, kinó
Tiresome, Droóveno, droóven
Tiring, Túgno
To, Ke, katár, kátar, káter
Toad, Jámba, jómbo
Tobacco, Túvlo, toóvlo, túvlo-pen
To-day, Kedívvus, kedivéz, kóva dívvus, tedívvus
Together, Ketané, ketanés, katené, káteni, kátenes
Tollgate, Stígher. See Turn-pike
To-morrow, Ovávo dívvus
To-morrow morning, Kóliko-saúla
Tongs, Yógesto-wástaw
Tongue, Chib, chiv, jib
Too, Tei
Tooth, Dan
Touch, Chárvo, chálav, chára
Towel, Kóssering plóχta
Town, Gav
Trail, Pátrín, páten, troóshel
Train, Prástering-kóli, poodj
Traitor, Poókeroméngro
Tramp,. Choórodo, choóro-méngro, peérdo
Transported, Bítchadi paúdel, paúdel-i-paáni, paúnied
Trap, Pándoméngro
Treadmill, treadywheel, Póge-roméngri
Tree, Rook

Tremble, Rísser
Trickster, Kóroméngro
Tripe, Bókochesto-pur
Trousers, Rokónyus, roχínyes, roχínya, ríknies, rokhámyas, 'hámyas, rokéngries, rokrén-yes, brö'gies, booléngries, booliéngries
Trout, Reíeski-mátcho
True, Tátcho, tátcheno
Trust, *v.*, Pázer; *n.*, pázeroben
Truth, Tátchipen
Tuesday, Doóī dívvuses pálla koóroko
Turkey, Kaúli raúni, pápini
Turnip, Konáfia, konáfni, kraáfni, panéngro
Turnpike, Pósh*free*, stékas, stígher, pésser-stígher
Twenty, Bish, stor-pansh
Two, Doóī
Two shillings, Doóī-kóli

U.

Unable, Nastíssa, nestís
Uncle, Kóko, kok
Under, *prep.*, Talé, alé, 'lé
Under, *adj.*, Tállani
Up, upon, Opré, apré, 'pré
Upper, Pré-éngro
Urine, ⎱
Urinate, ⎰ Múter
Urinal, Mútering kóla
Us, Men, méndi
Used, Síklo

V.

Vagrant, Peérdo
Very, Boot, boóti
Verily, Aáva, our. See Yes
Vessel, Troóshni
Vex, Kínger
Victuals, Kóben, hóben, hól-
ben, hólen
Village, Gav
Vinegar, Shoóto
Vinegry, Shoótlo
The Virgin, Doóveleski-joó-
vel
Vomit, Woóser apré

W.

Wagon, Wárdo, várdo
Waistcoat, Bángeri
Wakefield, *n. pr.*, Choórones-
gav
Wales, Wólsho, Wótchkeni-
tem, Lávines-tem
Walk, Peer, píriv
Warm, *v.*, Tátto
Warmth, Táttopen
Was, Shō'mas, sas, *q.v.*
Wash, Tōv
Watch, *n.*, Óra, yóra, hóra,
poókeroméngro
Watch *v.*, Várter, dik pálla
Water, Paáni, páni, paúni
Watercress, Paánesto-shok,
paáni-shok, paanéngri-shok
Watery, Paánisko
Way, Drom

We, Men, méndi
Wealth, Bárvalopen
Wealthy, Bárvalo
Wear, Riv
Wearing apparel, Rívoben
Wearisome, Droóveno, droó-
ven
Weary, *adj.*, Kíno, kinó
Wednesday, Trin dívvus*es*,
pálla koóroko
Week, Koóroki, kroóko, koóko,
kókerus
Weep, Rōv
Well, *adv.*, Míshto, mistó,
tátcho; *s.*, Hánik, hánikos
Welsh Gypsies, Ingrin*ies*
Welshman, Wótchkenéngro,
Lávinéngro, Lávines-gaújo
Welsh language, Lávines ró-
kerben, Wólshitíkka
Were, Shámas, sas, *q.v.*
Wet, Kíndo
Whale, Baúro-mátcho
What, Sávo, So
Wheat, Ghiv
Wheat, *adj.*, Ghívesto
Wheat-stack, Ghiv-poosén-
gro
Wheedle, Pándjer
Wheel, Héro, wárdesko-prás-
terméngri, wárdesko-heré
When, Kánna, kónna, vónka,
wónka, sávo-cheérus
Where, Kei
Whey, Kaléngri
Whip, Choókni, choópni
Whiskers, Bánga

Whistle, v., Shol, shool
Whistler, Sheléngro
White, Pórno
Who, Ko, kon, sávo
Whole, Chólo
Whore, Lúbni
Why, Sóski
Wicked, Vásavo, wásedo, wáfedo, béngalo
Wickedness, Wáfedopen
Widow, Peévli-gáiri
Widower, Peévlo-gáiro
Widowed, Peévlo
Wife, Rómeni, rómni, rómi
Wild, Dívio
Will-o'-th'-Wisp, Doódeskomoólo
Wind, Bával
Windmill, Bával pógaméngri
Window, Hev, kev
Wine, Mol, mul
Winter, Ven, wen; adj., Vénesto
Wintry, Vénlo
Wise, Jínoméngro
Witch, Choófihóni, choóvikon, chō'vihóni
With, Sar, pashal*
Within, Inna*
Withy, Ran
Wolf, Baúro-hóloméngro-joókel
Woman, Gáiri, joóvel, manoóshni, moóshni, mónoshi
Woman's bonnet, Joóviokostaádi
Woman's clothing, Joóvni kóla
Womb, Doódum

Woo, Píriv
Wood, Vesh, kosht
Woodcutter, Koshténgro
Wooden dishes, Kóshtudno skoodílyaw
Wool, Poósham
Word, Lav
Work, n. and v., Boóti, boótsi
Worker, Boótiéngro
World, Sweti,* doóvelestochaíros
Worm, Kérmo
Worth, Mool, mol
Wound, Chínoben
Wrexham, n. pr., Réltum
Wrong, Bóngo
Wrongly, Bónges

Y.

Ye, Tuméndi
Year, Besh
Yearling, Beshéngro
Yes, Aáva, aávali, our, oúwa, oúrli
Yesterday, Kóliko, kóliko-dívvus, káliko
Yew, Moóleno rook
Yonder, Odói, adói, 'doi
Yorkshire, Bárvalo-tem, Chórkeno-tem, Meílesko-tem
You, Too, toot, toóti
Your, yours, Teéro, toóti's
Young, adj. and n. pr., Tárno, taúno
Younger, Tárnodár
Youth, Tárnomus.

GENUINE ROMANY COMPOSITIONS

REFERRING TO

𝕻eculiar 𝕳abits and 𝕹otions in 𝕧ogue among 𝕰nglish 𝕲ypsies.

IN numerous instances Gypsy customs have been related to us in Rómanes by Gypsies themselves, and it has appeared to us to be of considerable interest and value to take down these communications as we received them, and to preserve the *ipsissima verba* made use of by our informants. It would be beyond the scope of the present work, to which we have set strictly linguistic limits, to enter into details concerning manners and traditional observances which are still to be found among the Gypsies of this country. But, incidentally, it has become necessary to refer to them, in order to explain certain allusions which might otherwise be imperfectly understood. We have therefore introduced, where necessary, in the following pages, a few explanatory notes to render clearer the meaning of particular passages and expressions, but at the same time wish to disclaim any intention of treating comprehensively a subject which has a special interest apart from the language. In spite of the numerous violations of every grammatical rule, these compositions are (as far as our experience goes) written in the "deepest" English Rómanes extant.

PITCHING A TENT.*

Né, chōwóli, kair ti greíaw te jal sig. Raáti see wélin'
sig opré méndi.   Kek tan see méndi kóva raáti te sov talé;
kek bíto shoóko tan méndi latchóva kóva raáti te jaw *to*
soóto opré.

So sig see o praásterméngro jinéla méndi shem akeí, yov
koméla *to* chiv méndi door dósta opré o drom, *or to* lel mén
opré.   Yov see tátcho dósta.   Chivéla men adré o stéripen,
ta bíken sor móri greíaw, ta wárdi, ta sórkon kóvaw sham
mé (mendi).

Konáw, chōwóli, kair sig.   Kair tí tan opré.   Dósta
bríshno wéla talé, ta hiv tei.   Méndi sor meróva *to*-raáti te

---

* The old-fashioned Gypsy encampments, once so frequent in shady
lanes and secluded spots, have almost entirely disappeared from some
parts of England.   Hence it has been too hastily assumed that these
inveterate strollers have forsaken tent-life and become permanent house-
dwellers.   Even Mr. Borrow makes the remark ("Lavo-lil," p. 221,)
that you may "walk from London to Carlisle, but neither by the road-
side nor on heath or common will you see a single Gypsy tent."   This
is certainly a mistake.   Harassed by the rural police, deprived of his
accustomed camping-grounds by Enclosure Acts, the Gypsy, like the
bittern, has been extirpated from many of his old haunts—ancient
commons and wastes from which "the Northern farmer" and other
pioneers of modern agriculture have "raäved an' rembled un oot"—but
he has only shifted his quarters, and not changed his habits.   On our
coasts where holiday-makers congregate, and in the neighbourhood of
popular watering-places, still as heretofore are

"The Gypsies all the summer seen,
Native as poppies to the green,"

their tents having become a permanent feature in many such localities.
Here they ply their traditional vocations, and reap a rich harvest from
the visitors, a seaside flirtation being hardly deemed complete unless a
Gypsy sybil has told the fortune of the amorous couple.

The Gypsy willingly pays a small ground-rent for the patch he occu-
pies, and then his frail tent becomes as much his castle as an Englishman's house, and is as safe from the intrusion of prastermengros,
and other unwelcome visitors.   We know of an instance at Blackpool
where a Gypsy, though living in a tent, has been so long a squatter on
the same spot as to have been assessed for the poor-rate, which he
duly discharges.

shil, ta and choómoni te kair *a* koóshto yog tei. Chiv o
tan talé koóshto.

Dósta bával wéla kóva raáti. Poóderéla men o bával
sor opré kóva raáti. Mi chávi merénna *o'* shil. Chiv sor
o rányaw adré o tan tátcho, *to* hatch míshto, ta spínger o
kóppa opré o rányaw tátcho, *to* kel *it* hatch míshto. O
chóro chávi rovénna tálla lénghi hóben. Mi Doóvel, so
mándi kairóva te lel léndi hóben te hol. Chíchi naneí
mándi te del léndi. Merénna yon tálla hóben.

TRANSLATION.

Now, mates, make your horses go quick. Night is
coming quick upon us. No tent is there for us this night
to sleep under ; no little dry place shall we find this night
to go to sleep on.

As soon as the policeman knows we are here, he will
want to put us very far on the road, or to take us up.
He is fit enough (for that). He will put us in prison, and
sell all our horses and carts, and everything we have.

Now, mates, be quick. Put your tent up—much rain
comes down and snow too. We all shall die to-night of
cold ; and bring something to make a good fire too. Put
the tent down well. Much wind will come this night.
My children will die of cold. Put all the rods in the
ground properly, to stand well, and pin the blanket on
the rods properly to make it stand well. The poor children cry for their food. My God, what shall I do to
get them food to eat? I have nothing to give them.
They will die without food.

CHOOSING A CAMP.

Kei jássa tuméndi, chavóli, tedívvus te sov?

Méndi jaw káter dóva ghivéskro kair. Yov koméla
Rómano-chaláw.

Kei see dóva?

Dóï, kei atchdém yek besh paúli, wónka jáfra iv pedás
talé.

Jinóva konáw sávo tan see. Kei viás o Rei káter méndi te del méndi jaw kíssi kas te del maúri greiáw. Our, jinóva konáw. Jas ménghi odói te atch. Kek yov penéla kek wáfedo *to* méndi. Méndi koméla. Atchás* odói *a* koóroko, te méndi kom*s*. Yov deléla men koshtáw te hótcher. Yov mookéla men chiv maúri greiáw adré lésko pooyyáw. Yon te vel sor tátcho. Kek yon te wel pánlo. Atchás* méndi adré maúri woódrus tátcho te sov. Kek te atch opré *to* dik tálla maúri greiáw adré o múllo raáti.

TRANSLATION.

Where are you going, mates, to-day, to sleep?
We are going to that farmer's house. He likes Gypsies. Where is it?
There, where we stopped a year back, when so much snow fell.
I know now where the place is. Where the gentleman came to us to give us so much hay to feed our horses with. Oh yes, I know now. Let us go and stop there. He will not rate at us. He likes us. Let us (*or*, we will) stay there a week, if it suits us. He will give us some firewood, and let us put our horses in his fields, where they will be safe, and not be put in the pound. We shall rest in bed safe asleep, and not have to get up to look after our horses in the dead of night.

O MOÓLO.

Kei jássa, choowáli, te sōv tedívvus? Mook méndi jal *to* soóto adré dóva gránsa.
Káter dóva tan, kei dóva kóshto Rei, te Raúni, jivéla. Kei o moólo sas diknó.
Kek mándi jal odoí te sōv. Mándi shom trash te dik moolé, te wel tráshedo *o'* mi mériben. Gaujé poókadás mándi dósta chaírus*es*, o moosh, ghivéngro sas-ló, nashadás lésko kókero opré o rook adré o koónsa, kei méndi jál*in'* te atch.

---

* First pers., pl., pres., or fut., indicative, or the Imperative V. Gram., p. 39.

So keréssa kon ?   Jássa too odói, te atchás ?
Kékera mándi.
Kei jássa kon ?
Adré *a* wáver poóro drom, yek mee doóroder.   Döl
méndi atchéssa.*   Kek kómeni charás (*sic*) méndi.

TRANSLATION.
THE GHOST.

Where are you going to sleep to-day, mates? Let us
go to sleep in that barn.

At that place where that kind gentleman and lady live—
where the ghost was seen.

I will not go and sleep *there*. I am afraid of seeing
ghosts, and being frightened to death.   The Gentiles have
told me many a time how the man, he was a farmer,
hanged himself on the tree in the corner where we are
going to stop.

What will you do, then?   Will you go there and stop?

Not I !

Where will you go, then ?

Down another old road, a mile further on. We will stop
there.   No one will dsiturb us.

A CAUTION.

Maw mook teéro greiáw, chawóli, jal talé dóva drom, kei
see dóva kóshto chor.   Yon te vel pandadó.

TRANSLATION.

Do not let your horses, mates, go down that road, where
that good grass is, or they will be put in the pound.

THE HAUNTED CAMP.

"I can just about remember the old times when our old
folk hardly spoke any Gaujines.   They were timid folk.
You might hear them say:—

---

* First pers., pl., pres., or fut., indicative.

"Kon see doóva, dádi?"
Who is that, father?

"Kékena jinóva mé.   Diktás kómeni?"
Not   know I.   Did you see any (thing)?

"Kek mándi.   Shoondóm choómoni.   So shoondóm ghiás
.Not I.   I heard something.   What I heard went
pénsa groóvni."
like (a) cow.

"Jaw opré o drom.   Dik so see."
Go up the road.   See what it is.

"Ghióm justa konáw.   Kek naneí mándi diktóm chíchi,
 I went just now.   No not I   saw   nothing,
na shoondóm chíchi.   O beng see, tátcho dósta."
nor heard nothing.   The devil it is, sure enough.

"Maw trash toóti."
Don't fear thou.

"Trash see mándi."
Fear is to me.

"Mántcha too!   Atch o koósi.   Shoondóm-les popli.
Cheer up!   Wait a bit.   I heard   it again.
Kómeni sas mórdno akéi.   Avéla yov apópli."
Some one was killed here.   Comes he again.

"Wónka 'saula vels, jaw mónghi akéi.   Kek na komóva
 When morning comes, go I hence.   No not I love
jáfri tanáw see kóli, pósha baúro weshaw.   Méripen tanáw
such places as these, near great woods.   Murdering places
see dikéla."
as it looks.

"Ei, dórdi!   Wáfedo díking tan see kóva.   Tátcho
 Eh, look!   Evil   looking place is this.   True
moolesko tan see kóva, patsóva mándi ajáw."
ghost's place is this, believe I   so.

"Kaúlo raáti see.   Sórkon wáfedi kóli see opré méndi.
 Dark night it is.   Every evil   thing is upon us.

Yek wáfedo ková kairs dósta wáver wáfedi kóli."
One evil   thing makes plenty of other evil things.

WESTER BOSWELL.

SUPPER-TIME.

Né, chawóli, kair koósi yog. Shílalo shom mándi. Chiv
o kekávi opré o yog, te kel píaméngri. Bókalo shom.
Dósta hóben see mándi.

Dósta groóveni-mas see mándi. Kindóm-les káter dová
koóshto yoózho maséngro's boódiga. Beshás sor méndi
talé, te porder maúri peráw mishtó. Tálla méndi ghivóva,
te keř o bóshoméngri. Sor méndi kerás méndi. Mook sor
dúla tárno raúnia ker ménsa. Tálla yon déla men lúva, ta
lel méndi koóshto nav.

TRANSLATION.

Now, mates, make up a little fire, for I am cold. Put
the kettle on the fire, and make tea. I am hungry. I
have lots of food, and plenty of beef, which I bought at
that nice clean butcher's shop. Let us all sit down and
satisfy our appetites. Afterwards we will sing, and play
the violin. Let us all set to. Let all those young ladies
dance with us. Afterwards they will give us some money,
and give us a good name.

HEDGEHOG HUNTING AND GYPSY CAKE.*

"Né moóshaw! Kóshto dood-raáti see konáw. Jas
Now men!   Good   light night it is now.   Let
ménghi perdál kóla poovyáw. Dikás méndi pálla doóï-trin
us go   over   these fields.   Let us look after two (or) three
hótchi-wítchi. Koshté see-lé konáw. Toólo see-lé (or léndi).
hedge-hogs.   Good (pl.) are they now.   Fat are they.
Mándi jinóva poovyáw kei *used* to ven dósta. Latchás
I   know   fields   where used to come plenty. Let us find

---

* See also " Dinner Dialogue."

ménghi doói-trin *to*-raáti. Avésa mándi?" "Oúa. Mándi
two (or) three to-night. Will you go (with) me?" "Yes. I
jal túsa." "Nashéna sor konáw párdal o poovyáw kóla
go with you." "They run all now over   the fields   these
dood-raátiä. Kerás ménghi Rómani márikli o' doói.
light-nights.   Let us make (a) Gypsy   cake   or two.
Lóva léndi *to* mándi's hóben adré káliko 'saula.
I will have them to my   breakfast in to-morrow morning.
Keróva mánghi *a* Rómani márikli. (Máriklí see kédo *o*'
I will make for me a Gypsy cake.   (Cake   is   made of
pórno.) Keróva kóshto yog. Chivóva-les adré *a* hev
flour.) I will make (a) good fire. I will put it in   a hole
adré o yog. Choróva-les pardál *o*' yog. Keróva-
in the fire (ash). I will cover it over with fire (ash). I will cook
les. Chinóva les opré. See man dósta kil, chivóva kil
it. I will cut it up. Is me sufficient butter, I will put butter
opré, ta holóva les mónghi sor mi, *or* meéro, kókero."
on,   and I will eat it myself all my-   self."

"You make them of flour and water, and roll them well.
Then you make a hole in the ashes, wood ashes are best,
and put the cake in, and cover it over with ashes, and
when it is cooked you just cut off the burnt part, and it
eats so sweet."*

WESTER BOSWELL.

PATRÉNI.

Kei jássa, choowáli?

Méndi jáls yek gáver té o wáver. Sor mendí jála, ta
mándi jóva mi kókero.

Kek na jináw mé sávo drom ta mándi jála.

---

* Another standard dish among the Gypsies is *moolo-mas*, or the
flesh of animals which have sickened and died unattended in their
last moments by the butcher. They sometimes make a kind of broth
or soup of snails, which they call *bouri-zimmen*, and which is not
unsavoury.

Mook méndi jal káter o Meílesto-gav Praásterimus, ta dikás o gréiaw praáster*in*'.   Door door dósta; doóvorí akeí ; door dósta see pardál odór.

Kek na jinóva o drom.

Mookóva patréni opré o drom te jin sávo drom ghióm mé.

So keréssa o patréni troóstal?   Kek na jinóva.

Poókeróva toot kon.   Keróva-les koósi chor, koósi dándiméngri-chor.   Woóseróva lésti talé opré o drom so jóva:

Mi Doóvel jal toósa.   Atch káter mi Doóvel.

Maw jal talé dóva drom.   See *a* chíchikeni drom.   Kóva drom jála káter bítto gav.   Koóshko dívvus, Bor.

Yon ghiás léndi kétané yek t'o wáver.

TRANSLATION.

TRAILS.

Where are you off to, mates?

Going from one town to the other.   We are all going, and I am going myself.

I do not know which way I shall go.

Let us go to Doncaster Races, and see the horses run.   It is a very long way; a great distance from here; far away over in *that* direction.

I do not know the way.

I will leave a sign on the road by which you will know which way I have gone.

What will you make the sign with?   I do not know.

I will tell you then.   I will make it of a little grass,—a few nettles.   I will throw them down on the road I go.

Goodbye.   God bless you.

Do not go down *that* road.   There is no thoroughfare. *This* road leads to the village.   Good day, mate.

They went away together, both of them. *

---

* The patrin, or Gypsy trail, deserves a few words of explanation. As the Gypsies are a wandering and vagabond race, it has always been necessary for them to have some way of pointing out to stragglers the

LAMENT ON THE DECAY OF THE LANGUAGE.

Kánna sas mándi *a* Tíkno, sor o poóro *fólki* rókerdé tátcho poóro Rómani laváw.   Kek naneí see jaw síklo konáw, see sas béshaw doósta palál.

Konáw o tárno *fólki*, kek yon rókerénna tátcho konáw. Boot gaujé-kani *fólki* see-lé konáw.   Kek né jinénna lénghi kókeri so see tátcho ta wáfedo.   Kánna too pootchés léndi tátcho lávaw, kek yon *can* poóker toot o tátcho drom *o*' léndi.

Meéro kókero rígheróva o tátcho poóro laváw.

Mándi penóva meéro kókero, "Kek Rómani-chals jivénna konáw, pénsa mi kókero adré tátcho poóro Rómani-chal-rókerimus, ta kóshto poóro tátcho laváw.   Sor gaujé see o *fólki* konáw.   Mándi see *a* tátcho poóro Rómano-chal pardál sor móχadé posh-kedó Rómani-chals."

Komóva te róker troóstal jáfri poóri rókeroben.

TRANSLATION.

When I was a lad, all the old folk spoke good old Gypsy words.   They are not so much used now as they were many years ago.

---

direction taken by the rest of the gang.   As, moreover, in civilized countries they must travel more or less along the principal roads and highways, any ordinary spoor or trace would soon be effaced by the subsequent traffic.   Hence arose the patrin-system, the invention of certain recognizable signs, by which the caravan on the march could indicate to loiterers the path it had taken, and guide them safely to the halting-place.   Different kinds of patrins :

(1) Three heaps of grass (or any plant agreed upon) placed on the left-hand side of the road taken (day-patrin).

(2) Pieces of rag, generally three in number, tied to the twigs of the hedge on the left-hand side of the road taken (day-patrin).

(3) Boughs, or cleft sticks, pointing down the road taken (night-patrin).

(4) Marks and signs on the road itself—generally a cross (used in snowy, dusty, or dirty weather).

(5) Stones placed in a certain manner on the left-hand side of the road taken (used in windy weather).

(6) Shoe-prints or foot-marks, etc., etc.

Now the young folk do not talk deep. They are too gaujo-like now. They do not know what is right or wrong. When you ask them deep words they cannot tell you their real meaning. I myself preserve the good old words.

I say to myself, "There are no Gypsies now so well up as myself in real old Gypsy talk, and good old deep words. The people are all English now. I am a pure old Gypsy, above all these dirty half-bred Gypsies."

I like to talk about such ancient speech.

EHEU, FUGACES!

Kánna sas mándi *a* tíkno,—koóshto cheéru*ses* sas,—sor meéro chóro *fólk*i sas jído sor adré koóshtomus, ta míshto sas yon.

Konáw (kenáw) see-lé sor mooló, ta ghilé. Kek nane*í* mándi konáw kei shom moóklo sor kókero. Te wel mándi te mer, kek kómeni pósha mándi te del mándi koósi paáni, te ker mandi kóshto. Sor meéri chávi, ta meéri *fólk*i, dei, ta dad, ta pénaw, sor see moólo.

Kek nane*í* mándi konáw, yek pal, yek pen adré Ánghi-terra. Kek yon wel*s* te dik mándi.

Mándi poótch*es* meéro *dear*o Doóvel te koóshto bo𝜒t. Yov del*s* mándi sor mándi poótch*es* tálla. Nane*í* yov te atch *to* mandi, mándi te wel kerdó sor kétané. Tátcho shom konáw, párik mi-Doóvel. Yov see sor koóshto káter mándi. Yov shoonéla tei meéro mongámus *to* lesti.

TRANSLATION.

When I was a lad,—good times were they,—all my poor people lived in peace, and were at ease.

Now they are all dead, or gone. There is no one here but myself, and I am left all alone. Should I die, there is no one near me to give me a drop of water to relieve me. All my children, and my people, my mother, father, and sisters, all are dead. I have not now one brother, one sister in England. They never come to see me.

I ask my dear God for good luck, and he grants me all I ask for. If he did not stand by me, I should be done for altogether. I am well now, thank God. He is all-merciful to me. He hears, too, my petition.

FUNERAL RITES.

Ei! dórdi! chawáli. So mándi keróva kenáw? Meéro chóro pooro dad see moólo konáw. So shom te keráw te lésti koláw, so yov muktás pálla lesti?

Hótcheróva-len sor. Sórkon koováw tálla saástera kóli. Woóseróva sor dúlla 'dré o baúro paáni.

Delóva meéro lav káter mi Doóvel, yov te jal káter yov te atch odói adré Koóshtoben, sor mi Doóvelésti chaíros.

TRANSLATION.

Alas! alas! my friends. What shall I do? My poor old father is no more. What must I do with all he left behind?

I will burn them all.[*] Everything except those things that are of iron, and those I will cast into the deep.

God grant he may rest in peace with Him for ever.

Cuthbert Bede sent to "Notes and Queries" (2nd Ser., iii., 442), in 1857, an account of a grand funeral of a Gypsy, followed by the destruction of his property, clothes, blankets, fiddle, books, and his *grindstone,*—the last being thrown into the river Severn, and the others burnt.

SOMETHING ABOUT GYPSY BURIALS.—Those who know little about Gypsies would have been astonished had they visited the encampment at Ashton, outside Birmingham, last week. Many who were led by curiosity, or "to have their fortune told," or for some other equally good reason,

---

[*] "Des verstorbenen Zigeuners Kleider, insoweit er sie nicht mit in die Erde genommen, sein Bett oder was sonst ihm zum Lager und zur Decke gedient hat, werden unter freiem Himmel verbrannt."— *Vide* Liebich's Zigeuner, p. 55.

to pay the Gypsy camp a visit last Wednesday, must have thought the demon of destruction possessed the nut-brown people. Men were smashing up a van, such as the Gypsies use for their residence; women were breaking chairs; children tearing up dresses, breaking crockery, and setting fire to whatever of the remains would burn; whilst the Queen of the Gypsies superintended the work. Those whose curiosity led them to inquire the reason, discovered that it is the Gypsies' custom after a funeral to destroy everything that belonged to the deceased member of the fraternity. They had just returned from the burial of a dead sister, and straightway commenced to break up and burn everything that belonged to her. Even the horse that drew her residential van had to be shot; and the husband and children through this folly are left for a time without home comforts.—*Catholic Times*, Dec. 13th, 1873.

One instance came under our notice, not far from Manchester (at Cheadle), where a favourite dog of the deceased was destroyed, and its body added to the funeral pile.

For further particulars concerning Gypsy burials, *vide* Crabb (pp. 29, 30); Borrow's "Lavo-lil," (pp. 299, 300); Hone's Year Book, 1832; Table Book, 1827; Liebich (pp. 52—56); and N. and Q.

HORSE-DEALING.

Né, chowaáll, jóva ménghi káter velgaúro. And sor ti gréiaw apré. Yoózher léndi míshto. Kair léndi *to* dik míshto, *and* del dóva póga-bával grásni koósi báuleskI túlopen. Chívóva-les adré lóki moór *to* atch lóki bával koósi; ta biknóva-les, tastís.

And dóva nokéngro grei akei *to* mándi. Pand asár lésti opré káter rook. And asár mándi *a* koósi paáni. Tovóva-les míshto; ta kósseróva-les yoózho tálla. Dóva kéla. Biknóva-les tei, te vániso lúvva. Yov bíkindás sor lésko greiáw káter dova welgáuro adré o Lávines-tem. Bíkinás améndi sor móro greiáw te chiv léndi adré lóvo.

HORSE-DEALING.

Now, mates, let us be off to the fair.   Bring up all your
horses.   Clean them well, and make them look smart, and
give that broken-winded mare a little lard.   I will put it in
her mouth to ease her breathing a little, and I will sell it,
if I can.

Bring that glandered horse here to me, and tie it up
to the tree, and bring me a little water.   I will wash
it well, and wipe it clean afterwards.   There, that will do.
I will sell it too, at any price.   *He* sold *his* horses at that
fair in Wales.   Let us sell all our horses, and turn them
into cash.*

ZUBA B——.

A GYPSY'S ACCOUNT.

Kóva liléi, shoondóm, Rómani-chal tárno joǫvel adré o
Chúmba-kálesko tem, shoondóm, sas adré o Ghilyéngri.

Yóɪ ghiás káter o baúro kair.   Diktás yóɪ doóɪ trin
raúnya.   Pootchté yóɪ yon, "Mook man doókeróva toot.
Mándi poókeróva too ókki yek rínkeno tárno rei.   Koméssa
toot te lel lesti te rómmer toot?   Yov mol dósta lóvo.
Moók man doóker toot.   Poókeróva toot sor troostál yov,
kánna too lél lésti."

Yóɪ pendás, "Our.   Too doóker mándi.   So dóva toot?"

---

* Instead of lard, some Romani-chals prefer to tie a little aloës
(which they call 'aloways') in a piece of muslin, under the horse's
tongue, 'which will hatch the baval misto.'   Another way of treating
a nokengro is to stuff its nose full of nettles (dandimengri chor) an
hour or two before offering it for sale.   On removing the plug, a great
quantity of purulent and highly offensive discharge comes away.   The
animal's nose is then well washed and syringed with spring water.*
Gypsies display much skill in managing a horse so as to conceal its
defects and show it off to the best advantage.   They have been known
to buy a worthless animal, and after clipping its coat, and manipulating
it in other ways, to sell it again on the same day for a high price to
its former owner.   Their great love for horses—especially for other
people's horses—brought many unlucky Gypsies to the gallows in those
days when horse-stealing was a capital offence.

---

* These customs are but little practised nowadays.

"Yek kótor." O raúni diás yóɩ *a* kótor. Yoɩ pootchtás láti kómoder tálla.

Yóɩ pendás láti te chiv óri te vongushté adré *a* móχto.

O Raúni ándadás sor dúla kóli, yoi pootchté *o*' léndi. Tálla yóɩ chidás láti's wast opré o móχto, sor pardál lésti, akeí *and* odói. Yóɩ pendás káter raúni, "Too mookás mándi lel kóva.   Moók-les káter mándi yek koórokó. Tálla mándi and asár lésti paúli pópli káter too.   Tálla wénna dósta lóvo te soónaka, ta bárvali kóli adré léstiʼ wónka mándi and lésti paúli káter too."

O raúni kedás ajáw. Ghiás yon (yoɩ), o Rómani chei, kéri. Righadé (righadás) o kóli pardál o chaírus.

Tálla diktás o raúni, yoi kek ne viás paúli, yóɩ poókadás opré láti.   Kánna sig bítchadás o prásterméngro pálla láti. Liás láti.   Chidás yóɩ adré stéripen.

Adré o saúla liás láti aglál o Pokényus. O Pokényus pendás káter láti, "So shan too akeí troostál?"

Yóɩ pendás, "O Raúni odóɩ poochtás mándi te doóker láti, te poóker láti kánna yóɩ lela o tárno rei te lati's rom.   Yóɩ pendás, o raúni, 'dóva toot vániso.   Poóker man tátchó.'"

Pendás o Pokényus káter raúni.   "See dóva tátcho?"

"Our."   Raúni pendás.   "Kek yóɩ ándadás meéri kóli paúli see yóɩ pendás."

O Pokényus pendás.   "See toóti teéri kóli paúli konáw?"

"Our."   Hótchi raúni.   "Sor tátcho see konáw.   Kek naneí mándi te ker wáfedo te yóɩ."

"Too liás sor ti kóli paúli.   Kek naneí too koméssa te chiv kóva joóvel adré o stáripen?"

"Naw."   Pendás o raúni.

"Jaw toóki kon."   Pendás o Pokényus.   "Maw mook mándi dik toot adré kóva gav kek kómmi."

O Pokényus pendás káter raúni, "Te baúro dínli shánas too te mook teéri kóli te jáfri kómeni.   Kek na too jindás, too sas o dínli?   Kek naneí o Rómani chei sas dínli.   Jaw toóki.   Maw mook mándi dik toot akeí kek kómmi."   "Kek nanéi mándi nastís doókeróva toot."

TRANSLATION.

I heard this summer (about) a young Gypsy girl in Derbyshire, (and) I heard it was 'in the papers.'

She went to a (the) big house, and saw two or three women. She asked (one of) them, "Let me tell you your fortune. I tell you there is a nice young man; would you like to have him to marry you? He is worth plenty of money. Let me tell you your fortune. I will tell you all about him, (and) when you'll be married."

The woman replied, "Very well, you may tell me my fortune. What shall I give you?" "A guinea" (said the Gypsy). The woman gave her a guinea, (but the Gypsy) afterwards asked her for more. She told her to put (some) watches and rings in a box, (and) the woman fetched all those things that she asked of her. The Gypsy then passed her hand here and there, all over the box, (and) said to the woman, "You will let me take it. Lend it me a week; after (that) I will bring it back again to you, (and) then there'll be lots of money, gold, and precious stones in it, when I bring it back to you."

The woman did so. The Gypsy girl went home, but kept them more than the week.

When the woman saw she did not return, she gave information, and the constable was sent after her at once, and apprehended her, and locked her up.

The next morning he took her before the Justice of the Peace, who asked her what she was there for.

She replied, "That woman asked me to tell her her fortune, and tell her when she would get her young man for a husband. She said she would give me anything to let her know the truth."

The Justice asked the woman if it was correct.

"Yes," said the woman; "(but) she did not bring my things back as she promised she would."

Then the Justice asked if she had recovered her things.

"Yes," said she, "they are all right now. I do not want to do harm to her."

"You have got all your things back, and don't wish to have the girl put in prison?" said the Justice.

" No," replied the woman.

" You can go, then," said the Justice to the Gypsy girl. " Don't let me see you in this town any more."

And he said to the woman, " What a big fool you were to lend your things to one like her.   Don't you know that you were the fool?   The Gypsy girl was no fool.   Get off with you.   Don't let me see you here any more."   And he told the Gypsy girl he could not punish her.

"Manchester Guardian" account, August 13, 1874:—

EXTRAORDINARY CREDULITY.—At the Ashton-under-Lyne County Petty Sessions, yesterday, a Gypsy named Zuba B—— was charged with fortune-telling and obtaining goods under false pretences.   Mary Ann Ellice, a domestic servant at Oldham, said that on Sunday night she went with her sister Hannah to a field at Fitton Hill, in which there was a Gypsy encampment.   The prisoner asked them into a tent, and witness gave her a shilling to tell her fortune. The prisoner told her there was a young man who wore a pen beside his ear who loved the ground she walked upon. (Laughter.)   Witness took off her glove, and prisoner, seeing a ring on her finger, asked to look at it.   Prisoner tried it on her finger, and then got her brooch and cuffs from witness.   She touched the end of witness's finger with the brooch, the ring, and the shilling, and then rolled them up and put them in a cigar-box, and said it would take till Wednesday to "make the charm work."*   She told witness to be sure to come for them on Wednesday night.   She became uneasy on Monday, and went to the field, but the Gypsies had gone.   (Laughter.)—Hannah Ellice said the prisoner also told her there was a young man who loved the ground she walked on.   The prisoner got her watch and guard, and also wanted her brooch and skirt, but she

---

* A well-known trick. See Bw., Zincali, i., 319 ; Lavo-lil, 244.

would not leave them. Prisoner looked at her hand, and said there was luck before her, and all that. (Laughter.) Prisoner told them to go home, and tell no one, not even their parents. Prisoner told them the tribe had taken the field for nine months.—Mr. Mellor, M.P. (one of the magistrates): Have you received any education?—Witness: No, sir, I have not.—Superintendent Ludlam: Perhaps you don't understand. Have you ever been to school? Can you read and write?—Witness: No, sir.—Sergeant Barnett proved that he apprehended the prisoner at Bardsley on Tuesday night, and recovered the property.—Mr. Thomas Harrison, the presiding magistrate, dismissed the case, but counselled the prisoner to be cautious. Addressing the girls, he said it was most extraordinary that silly people should go to such places to have their fortunes told. It served them right if they lost their money.

KOKERI INDIKI.
A DIALOGUE.

So see dóva?

'*Kókeri Indiki*' (Cocculus Indicus) Rei. ¡Chivóva-les adré o paáni.

Sóski, mi pal?

Maw pootch mándi jáfri dínili koováw. Komés too mátcho, Rei?

Ourli, pal. Komóva-les dósta.

'*Kókeri Indiki*' kairéla sor o matcháw posh-mótto. Lióm dósta *and* dósta *wi*' lésti.

THE WHITE DOG.
A DIALOGUE.

Dóva see *a* rínkeno paúno joókel odoí, pal!

Our. Latchadóm-les yek dívvus adré o baúro-gav.

So see lésko nav?

Sebastopol. Poóker mándi o feterdáir drom *to* kair lesti kaúlo.

Nástis poókeróva toot.

ADRÉ STÉRIPEN.

A DIALOGUE.

Sar shan, chei? Toógeno shom mé, *to* dik toot adré stéripen akeí. So see too akeí tálla?

For doókerin' adré o baúro gav.

Sávo cheérus lián, *to* atch akeí?

Trin shoónaw. Mi rom see adré stéripen tei!

Sóski?

For chórin' a grei, mi pal! *The* ráttvalo praásterméngros poóker'd hoókapens troóstal lésti. Yov see tárderin' shélo kótoréndri konáw. Yov's peérin' opré o pógeriméngri.

Toógno shom *to* shoon lésti. Poókeróva kek-kómeni, ta mándi diktás (diktóm) toot akéi adré stéripen.

Párrik mi Doóvel te kék avél akei kek-kómeni *so long as* too jivéssa. Jinéssa too "*The Trumpet*," a tíkeni kítchema adré *de* gav?

Kékera mándi.

Mooktóm mi koóshnies odoí. Poóker móri *fólk*i ajáw, mi pal.

Our. Keróva-les, tastís.

Koóshto dívvus.

Til opré *your* zee. Mántchi too.

TRANSLATION.

IN PRISON.

How are you, my child? I am grieved to see thee here in prison. What are you here for?

For telling fortunes in the city.

How long have you to stop here?

Three months. My husband is in prison too!

What for?

For horse-stealing, mate. The cursed constables committed perjury about it. He is picking oakum now, and working on the treadwheel.

I am sorry to hear it. I will not tell any one I have seen you here in prison.

14

God grant that you may never come here as long as you
live. Do you know "The Trumpet," a small public-house
in the town?

No, I do not.

I left my baskets there. Tell our people so, friend.

Certainly I will do, if I can.

Good day.

Keep up your spirits. Cheer up.

REMARKS SHOWING A GYPSY'S DISLIKE TO MIXED MARRIAGES.

O Rómani-chei kedás kóshto láti-kókeri tall' sor láti's
loóberiben. Kek naneí yói rínkeni. Wáfedo díkomusti
chei sas yói. O moosh, yov sas kórodo, ta loóbni yek sas-ló.
Yov sas baúro dínelo te woóser lésko kókero adré jáfra
wáfedo chei's wastáw.

Yói sas chíchi féterdér te loóbni. Yói sas yek. Yói
atchéla opré dromáw adré o Gav, pósha kítchemáw, te dik
tálla o gairé te del yói trin-górishi, te shau-háuri, te sōv wi'
láti. Bítta gaujé, raklé, vart asár láti dósta chaíruses, te jal
adré wesháw, te mook wárdi-gairé te sōv wi' láti, and dóva
see tátcho. Gaujé penéla jaw troostál láti konáw.

Mándi penóva, wónka yov jivéla láti yek besh, yov
násheréla sor lésko lóvo, ta sor lésko zee, ta wel te jal ta
mong maúro te hol, kánna sas-ló (see-ló) bókalo. Yói sig
keléla dóva lesti.

Yói léla sor lésko wóngur. Yói déla lésti káter láti's dad
ta dei, te wel yóki fólki, tálla sor láti's loóberiben.

Dórdi! dordi!! Sávo baúro Dínelo sas-ló!!!

Tales.

O CHOÓRODO'S GOZVERO KERIMUS.

Yek raáti *a* Choórodo ghiás kater Drabéngro te átch-les opré, te wel káter lésti choóri Rómni. Yót sas poshlé adré woódrus.

Kánna o Drabéngro shoondás lésti, yov róker'*d* *to* lésti, *and* o Choórodo poochtás-les, so yov léia te wel káter lésko Rómni, te dóva cheérus *o*' raáti.

O Choórodo pendás "Meéri Rómni see chiv'*d* káter woódrus. Mándi penóva yót'*ll* mer. Wel, Rei, te dik *at* láti. Mándi delova toot *a* kótor te kair o féterdér *to* láti, tastís."

O Drabéngro ghiás. Kánna sor sas kedó, o Choórodo diás o Drabéngro yek kótor. O Drabéngro diktás yoy sas *a* choórokono moosh. Yov diás-les posh-kótor paúli, ta dóva kótor sas wáfedo yek.

Kánna o Rei diktás o kótor, yov latch'*d* lesti avrí. Wáfedo sas.

Kánna o Drabéngro diktás o kótor wáfedo sas, kenáw-sig o Drabéngro ghiás te dík pálla o Choórodo, te poóker yoy wáfedo kótor sas, yov diás lésti.

Yov ghiás káter tan, kei sas-ló.

O Choórodo kerdás sor léski kóli opré. Ghiás péski. Yov jindás wáfedo kótor sas.

TRANSLATION.

THE MUMPER'S ARTFUL DODGE.

A mumper one night went to a doctor to call him up to attend his poor wife, who was confined to bed.

As soon as the doctor heard him, he answered ; and the mumper asked him what fee he would want to attend his wife at that time of the night. He said to the doctor, "My wife is confined, and I fear she will die. Come and look at her, sir. I will give you a guinea to do the best you can for her."

So the doctor went; and when he had finished, the mumper handed him a guinea. The doctor, however, seeing he was a poor man, returned him half the fee; but the guinea was bad, and the doctor found it out as soon as he examined it. He immediately set off to look for the mumper, and to tell him the guinea he had paid was a bad one. He went to the place where he had been, but the mumper had packed up his goods and taken himself off, for he knew the guinea was bad.

O JÍNOMÉSKRO HÍNDI-TEMÉNGRO.

Yek cháirus a tátcho koóshto Drabéngro jivdás adré o Meflesko-tem. Yek shílalo raáti, yov sas kíno dósta. Shoondás a moosh. Yov sas a Híndi-teméngro. Viás káter lésko kair. Diás drován opré o woóda. Yov pendás káter Drabéngro, "Kair sig, ta wel mánsa. Meéro chóro poóro rómni see 'pré mér-in'. Wel káter yóï. Mándi déla (dóva) toot yek kótor."

O Drabéngro pendás to lésti, "Kek mándi jóva toósa, Jaw wáfedo shílalo raáti see, ta o dromáw see jaw wáfedo ta chíklo."

O Híndi-teméngro pendás káter Drabéngro, "Wel tooti mánsa, mi Doóveléski! Mándi dóva toot yek kótor, te kel láti te jiv te mer."

O Drabéngro ghiás lésti. Kánna yov viás odóï káter yóï, yóï sas boot náfelo te mer. O Drabéngro diás yóï koósi drab te pee. Tálla yov ghiás péski kókero keré pópli.

Adré o saúla, o Drabéngro shoondás yóï sas moólo.

Yov ghiás káter o Híndi-teméngro. Pootchtás-les pálla lésko kótor.

O Híndi-teméngro pendás káter o Drabéngro, "Kek mándi dóva toot 'dóva kótor."

Tálla o Drabéngro liás gódli lésti. Liás-les opré káter o Pookényus te lel lésko lúva. Kánna yov sas aglál o Pookényus, o Pookényus pootchtás-les, "Sar sas kóva. Too kek naneí pésser'*d* o Drabéngro?"

O Pookényus pootch'*d* o Híndi teméngro, "See toót moóïéngro te róker toóki?"

"Kek," hótchi yov, o poóro Híndi-teméngro, "Mándi see meéro nógo rókeroméngro."

O Pookényus pendás káter o Híndi-teméngro, "Too see laváw te pen te pootch lésti vániso?"

"Our, Rei!" pendás káter Pookényus.

"Pootch lésti, kon."

"Drabéngro!" hótchi o Híndi-teméngro, "Too kerdás meéro rómni te jiv?"

"Kek," hotch' o Drabéngro.

"Too kairdás yoï te mer kon?"

"Kek," hótchi o Drabéngro.

"So mándi te del toot lúva troostál kon? Too kek naneí kair'*d* yóï te jiv. Too kek naneí maur'*d* láti. Sávo Koóshtopen kairdás too tálla? Konáw, Rei," pendás o Híndi-teméngro káter Pookényus, "So mándi te kair? Te del yov lúva te kek?"

O Pookényus pendás, "Kek naneí yov ker'*d* lésko boótsi tátcho, ta yov pendás te kel láti te jiv te mer. Yov ker'*d* kek *o'* léndi. Te yov sas te kair o joóvel te jiv, mándi kairóva te del o Drabéngro o kótor so too pendás. Te wel yov te maur láti, mándi chivóva-les paúli káter o Baúri, ta yov véla náshado, kair*in'* mériben."

"So mándi te kair konáw, Rei, kon?" pendás o poóro Híndi-teméngro, "Too jál*in'* te chiv mándi adré stéripen troostál lésti, te mook mándi yoózho?"

Pendás o Pookényus, "Yoózho shan. Too shan tátcho. Jaw toóki kei too koméssa."

TRANSLATION.

THE KNOWING IRISHMAN.

Once upon a time there was a downright clever doctor living in Yorkshire, and one cold night he was very

tired, when he heard a man. It was an Irishman, who had
come to the house. He knocked at the door hard, and
said to the doctor, "Make haste and come with me. My
poor old wife is nearly dead. Come to her, and I will give
you a guinea."

The doctor replied, "I will not go with you; it is such
a wretchedly cold night, and the roads are so bad and
muddy."

The Irishman said to the doctor, "Do come with me, for
God's sake. I will give you a guinea whether you kill or
cure her."

So the doctor went with him, and when he reached the
place she was evidently on her death-bed. The doctor
gave her a little medicine to drink, and then he took himself off home again.

In the morning the doctor heard she was dead.

He went to the Irishman, and asked for his fee.

The Irishman said to the doctor, "I will not pay you
that guinea."

Then the doctor took out a summons against him. He
summoned him before the justice to obtain his money.
When he appeared before the justice, the justice asked
him, "How is this? You have not paid the doctor?" The
magistrate asked the Irishman if he had a lawyer to defend
him.

"No," said the old Irishman; "I am my own lawyer."

The magistrate said to him, "Have you any questions
to ask him?"

"Yes, sir," he said to the magistrate.

"Ask him, then."

"Doctor," said the Irishman, "did you make my wife
live?"

"No!" cried the doctor.

"You made her die, then?"

"No!" cried the doctor.

"What am I to pay you for, then? You did not make
her live. You did not kill her. What good did you do,

then? Now, sir," said the Irishman to the magistrate, "what am I to do—pay him, or not?"

The magistrate said, "He did not do his work properly, for he said he would kill or cure her, and he did neither. If he had made the woman live, I would make you pay the doctor the guinea you promised. If he be the cause of her death, I will remand him to the assizes, and he will be hanged for committing murder."

"What am I to do now, sir, then?" said the old Irishman. "Are you going to put me in gaol for it, or acquit me?"

The magistrate answered, "You are clear. You are all right. Go where you like."*

KING EDWARD AND THE GYPSY.

Dósta dósta besháw ghiás   kondw,   sas a baúro
Many many years gone (by) now, (there) was a great

Krális adré Ánghitérra; Edward*us sas lésko nav—kdóshto*
King in England; Edward was his name—(a) good

kómelo rei   sas-ló.
kind gentleman was he.

Yek dívvus yov késterdás, sor bikónyo, adrál a baúro
One day he rode, all alone, through a great

tdmlo wesh. Wónka yov sas ajdl'in' *talé a bítto rook, a baúro*
dark wood. When he was going under a little tree, a big

*kosht lel'*d *bónnek o' lésti's bal. O ráttvalo grei pradster'*d
bough took hold of his hair. The cursed horse ran

avrí, ta mooktás Edward*us ndshedo opré o rook.*
off, and left Edward hanged on the tree.

A *poóro Rómani-chal, so   sas odol, bésh*in' *pénsa sap*
An old Gypsy man, who was there, lying like (a) snake

adré o chor, diktás-les. Yov ghiás káter o Krális. Yov
in the grass, saw him. He went to the King. He

---

* This is a well-known anecdote.

chindás o kosht talé, ta mooktás Edward*us jal peéro apópli.*
cut the bough down, and let Edward go free again.
O Krális diás-les párikabén, ta pendás lésti, "*Kon shan*
The King gave him thanks, and said to him, "Who art
too?" *Yov róker'd ajáw:* "*A poóro choóro Rómani-chál*
thou?" He spoke thus: "An old poor Gypsy (man)
shom mé." *O Krális pendás,* "*Mookóva toot te jal keï too*
am I." The King said, "I will let thee go where thou
*koméssa, ta sov kei too koméssa, adré sor mi krális*om ; *ta*
likest, and sleep where thou likest, in all my kingdom; and
sor wáver Rómani-chálaw tei see peéro to kel ajáw."
all other Gypsies too are free to do so."*

O CHÓROMÉNGRO.

Mándi diktóm *a* baúro gaíro. Ghiás adré dóva kair.
Liás chómoni avrí pánlo adré *a* baúro jorjáwχa. Chómoni
sas adré, lóko (sas). Kek né jindóm mé so sas adré lésti.

Sar sig yov diktás mándi, praástadás péski pénsa grei.
Ghiás, gáradás léski kókero. Kékera diktóm lésti kĕk-
kómi.

Tálla yov sas ghiló, o raúni káter kair viás adré o kair.
Diktás sor láti's roópeno kóli, ta soónaka óra, ta soónaka
wériga, ta mérikli, ta vongéshtas, sas sor ghilé.

Dóva gaíro liás léndi sor. Ghiás péski sor kóshto yoózho
te léndi.

TRANSLATION.
THE THIEF.

I saw a big man. He went into that house. He took
something out tied in a big apron. Something was inside
heavy (lit., light). I did not know what was in it.

As soon (as) he saw me, he himself ran like (a) horse.
He went; he hid himself. I never saw him any more.

After he was gone, the lady at (the) house came into

---

* Edward VI. reigned 1547—1553, but all histories have ignored
this incident! Perhaps it is based on some New Forest tradition of
the death of Richard, grandson of William I.

the house. She saw all her silver things, and gold watches,
and gold chains, and bracelets, and rings, were all gone.
That man took them all. He himself went all right
clean (off) with them.

MI DOÓVELESKO BÍTTA *FÓLKI*.

Shoondóm yékera, dósta besháw ghilé, sas varéngro.
Jivdás aglál o Králisko poóro kair káter Kellingworth
pósha Warwick. Chúmba see odói, ta o Králisko poóro
kair see opré-les. Kóshto rei sas-ló. Koméla sórkon
kóshto jívomus, te lívena, ta sor wáver píamus.

Yek dívvus adré o saúla ghiás avrí, te lésko várdo, ta
greiáw tei, te jal káter o baúro gav te bíkin lésko váro.
Kékera viás paúli pópli. Kékera diktás yon. O várdo,
ta greiáw viás paúli. Yov kek viás.

Tálla doói besháw yov viás *a*pópli, ta andadás káter
lésko rómni, toóvlo, ta toóvlo choráw, ta baúri swégler.

Poókerdé lésti, "Kei shánas too sor dúla chaírus, sor
dúla doói besháw?"

Pendás yov, "Talé dóva baúro kair odói. Kek naneí see
doói besháw. Káliko raáti mándi sas wel*in*' kéri, ta mi
Dúvelésko bítta *fólk*i viás. Yon atchté sor ketané aglál
mándi, sor troostál. Liás mándi talé adré *a* baúro *fín*o
rinkeno tan odói, talé o králisko poóro kair.

Hodóm sórkon kóshto hólomus, ta peedóm sórkon píamus
ta mándi kom*s*, lívena, ta mol, ta tátto paáni tei. Kek
naneí paáni see odói! Sas léndi dósta dósta toóvlo, ta
baúri swégler. Diás dósta káter mándi. Kelénna, bósher-
vénna, ghivénna tei sor o raáti. Dói see dósta roópni kóli
ta soónaka.

Kánna saúla viás, yon mookté mándi jal, ta mándi ánda-
dóm kóva toóvlo, ta toóvlo koráw, ta baúri swégler. Dik̦
asár *at* léndi. Diktássa jáfri kóli adré teéro mériben?"

"Kékera," pendé yon, "see dóva sor tátcho?"

"Our," pendás yov, "opré meéro kóshto zee."

Dóva see so gaujé pendé káter mándi. Kánna mándi
sas odói, sas kómeni siménsi o' dóva varéngro adré o gav.

TRANSLATION.

THE FAIRIES.

I heard once, many years ago, there was a miller, who lived opposite Kenilworth Castle, near Warwick. There is a hill there, and the castle stands on it. The miller was a jovial sort of fellow, fond of good living, and liquor.

One day, early in the morning, he set off with his cart and horses to go to town and sell his flour.

He never returned. They never saw him again. His cart and horses came back, but he did not.

After two years, he returned, and brought his wife some 'baccy, 'bacca dishes, and long pipes.

They asked him where he had been all those two years.

He replied, " Under the castle, yonder; but it isn't two years. Last night I was coming home, and a whole lot of fairies came and stood in a ring round me, and then they took me off to a splendid place under the castle over there.

" I ate of the best, and had every kind of drink I like —ale and wine, and spirits too. There's no water *there!* They had lots of 'baccy, and great long pipes, and they gave me plenty. They were dancing, and fiddling, and singing too all night long, and there were heaps of gold and silver.

" As soon as it was morning they let me go, and I brought this here tobacco, and 'bacca dishes, and pipes away with me. Just look at 'em. Did you ever see such things in your lives ?"

" Not we," said they. " Is it all true ?"

" Yes," said he ; " upon my honour it is."

That is a story the people told me ; and when I was there, some of the miller's descendants were still living in the village.*

---

* Versions of this story are common to almost all mythologies.

HOW PETALENGRO WENT TO HEAVEN.
OLD DIALECT.

Mandí pookerova toot sar Petalengro ghiás kater mi Doovelesko keri :—

Yek divvus mi Doovel viás adré bitto gav. Kek nanéj kitchema sas adói. Yov ghiás adré Petalengro's kair. Yov sootadás odoi sor doova raati.

Adré o saula o Petalengro's poori romni pendás. "Komova te jal adré mi Doovolesko keri kanna merova."

Mi Doovel diktás adré laki mooi. Yov pendás "Maw trash. Too nastís te jal adré o bengesko tan. Odoi see rovoben ta kairing wafedo mooiáw ta danding ti danáw. Tooti see kek nanéi danáw. Too jasa adré meero keri."

Yov pendás kater laki rom. "Delova tooti stor kola. So bootodáir too komesa te lel?"

O Petalengro pendás "Komova. O moosh so jala opré meero pobesko rook, nastis te wel talé. Doova see yek kova.

"Komova. O moosh so beshela opre o kova so mandi kerova greiesti choχa opré, nastis te atch opré apopli. Dula see dooi kola

"Komova. O moosh so jala adré meero bitto sastera mokto, nastissa te wel avrí. Dula see trin kola

"Komova. Meero hoofa see mandi adré sorkon cheerus, ta kanna beshova opré-les kek moosh nastís te kair mandi te atch opré. Dula see o stor kola so komova feterdáir."

Mi Doovel pendás yov 'Our' kater sor dula kola, so yov pootchdás-les. Yov ghiás opré lesko drom.

Palla doova o Petalengro jivdás dosta dosta besháw.

Yek divvus o Bauro-shorokono-mulo-moosh viás. Yov pendás kater o Petalengro "Av mansa!"

O Petalengro pendás "Atch koosi, Bor! Mook mandi pen 'kooshko divvus' kater meeri poori romni. Too jasa opré meero rook te lel pobé."

Yov ghiás opré o rook. Nastís te wel talé apopli. O Petalengro kedás-les pen "Mookova toot bikonyo bish besháw." Yov pendás doova. Yov viás talé.

Palla bish beshaw, yov viás *a*popli. Yov pendás "Av mansa!"

O Petalengro pendás "Atch koosi, Bor! Too shan kinó. Besh talé opré doova kova." Sas o kova so yov kedás o greiesto choχa opré.

Yov beshtás talé opré lesti. Nastissa te atch opré *a*popli. O Petalengro kedás-les pen "Mookova tootí bikonyo bish beshaw *a*popli." Yov pendás doova. Yov atchdás opré.

Palla bish beshaw *a*popli o BENG viás. Yov pendás "Av mansa."

O Petalengro pendás "Atch koosi, Bor! Kek jaw sig, mi pooro chavo! Mé shom jaw kooshto sar tooti. Mook mandi dik tooti jal adré kova bitto sastera mokto."

Yov ghiás adré-les. Nastissa te wel avrí. O Petalengro chidás o mokto adré o yog. Kanna les sas loħo-tatto yov chidás-les opré o kova so yov kedás o greiesto choχa opré. Yov koordás-les sar sor lesko roozlopen. O Beng rovdás ta kordás avrí sor o cheerus "Mook mandi jal. Mookóva tooti bikonyo adré sor cheerus." Kanna o Petalengro sas sor kino, yov mooktás o Beng jal.

Palla waver doosta dooro cheerus mi Doovel bitchadás yek *o*' mi Doovel*s* tatcho gairé. Yov pendás "Av mansa kater o Bengesko tan."

O Petalengro pendás "Sor tatcho."

Kanna o Beng diktás-les, yov pendás "Jal avrí sig, wafedo gairo. Kek komova tooti akéi."

Jaw o tatcho gairo liás-les kater mi Doovel*s* tem. Mi Doovel pootchdás "Welessa too avrí o Bengesko tan?"

O Petalengro pendás "Kek." Mi Doovel pendás "Jal avrí sig, wafedo gairo. Kek komova tooti akéi."

O Petalengro pendás "Mook mandi dik adré teero kair." Mi Doovel pirivdás o wooda. O Petalengro wooserdás lesko hoofa adré. Prasterdás. Beshtás talé opré-les, ta pendás kater mi Doovel "Nastissa too te kair mandi jal kenáw."

Doova see sar o Petalengro ghiás kater mi Doovel*s* kair.

THE SAME.

NEW DIALECT.

Mandi'*ll* pooker tooti *how the* Petalengro jal'*d* adré mi Doovel'*s* kair.

Yek divvus mi Doovel wel'*d* adré *a* bitti gav, *and* latch'*d* kekeno kitchema odói, *so he* jal'*d* adré *the* Petalengro'*s* kair, *and* sooter'*d* odói sor doova raati.

Adré *the* saula *the* Petalengro'*s* poori romni pen'*d*. "*I'*d kom *to* jál adré mi Doovel'*s* kair *when* mandi mers," so mi Doovel dik'*d* adré lati'*s* mooi, *and* pen'*d* "Maw trash Tooti *can't* jal adré *the* Bengesko tan, '*cause* odói *there's* rovoben *and* dand*ing* o' danyaw, *and* tooti's danyaw *are* sor nasher'*d* avrí *your* mooi. Tooti *shall* jal adré meeri kair."

And he pen'*d to* lati'*s* rom "Mandi'*ll* del tooti stor kova*s*. So *does* tooti kom?"

"*The* Petalengro pen'*d* "Mandi kom*s as any* moosh, *as* jal*s* opré meero rook *to* lel pobo*s*, *can't* wel talé *a*popli. Doova'*s* yek kova.

"Mandi kom*s as any* moosh, *as* besh*es* opré *the* kova mandi kair*s* greiesto choka*s* opre, *can't* atch opré *a*popli. Doova'*s* doo*i* kova*s*.

"Mandi kom*s as any* moosh, *as* jal *s* adré meeri bitto sastera mokto, *can't* wel avrí *a*popli. Doova'*s* trin kova*s*.

"Mandi kom*s as* meeri hoofa *may be mine* adré sor cheerus, *and when* mandi besh*es* apré lesti kek moosh *can* kair mandi atch opré *a*popli. Doova'*s the* stor kova*s as* mandi kom*s*."

Mi Doovel pen'*d*, "Our," *to* sor doova kova*s*, *and* jal'*d* opré lesti'*s* drom.

Palla doova *the* Petalengro jiv'*d* boot adoosta besh*es*.

Yek divvus *the* Bauro-shorokono-moolo-moosh wel'*d and* pen'*d to the* Petalengro, "Av *with* mandi."

The Petalengro pen'*d*, "Atch *a* koosi, Bor! Mook mandi pen 'Kooshto divvus' *to* meeri poori romni. Tooti *can* jal opré meerí rook, *and* lel *some* pobos," *and when he* jal'd opré *the* rook, *he couldn't* wel talé *a*popli, *so the* Petalengro kair'*d him* pen "Mandi '*ll* mook tooti *a*konyo bish besh*es*" *and* sar sig *as he* pen'd doova *he could* wel talé.

Palla bish besh*es he* wel'd *a*popli *and* pen'd, "Av *with* mandi," *and the* Petalengro pen'd, "Atch *a* koosi, Bor! Tooti'*s* kini. Besh talé opré doova kova."

He besh'd talé opré *the* kóvva *he* kair'd grelesto choka*s* opré *and couldn't* atch opré *a*popli, *so the* Petaléngro kair'*d him* pen, "Mandi '*ll* mook tooti *a*konyo bish besh*es a*popli," *and* sar sig *as* he pen'*d* doova *he could* atch opré.

Palla bish besh*es a*popli *the* Beng wel'd *and* pen'd, "Av *with* mandi," *and the* Petalengro pen'd, "Atch *a* koosi, Bor! Kek *so* sig, mi poori chavi. Mandi'*s as* kooshti *as* tooti. Mook mandi dik tooti jal adré kovva bitti sastera mokto asár," He jal'd adré lesti *and couldn't* wel avrí *so the* Petalengro chiv'*d it* adré *the* yog, *and when it was* sor lolo-tatto *he* chiv'd *it* opré *the* kova *he* kair'd greiesto choka*s* opré *and* koor'd lesti *with* sor *his* roozlopen, *and the* Beng rov'*d and* kor'd avrí sor *the* cheerus, "Mook mandi jal. Mandi '*ll* mook tooti *a*konyo 'dré sor cheerus," *and when the* Petalengro *was quite* kíno, *he* mook'd *the* Beng jal.

Palla *a* baúro cheerus mi Doovel bitcher'*d* yek *of his* tatcho gairi*es, who* pen'd to *the* Petalengro, "Av *with* mandi *to the* Bengesko tan," *and the* Petalengro pen'd, "Sor tatcho."

When the Beng dik'd lesti, *he* pen'd, "Jal avrí sig, *you* wáfedo gairo. Mandi *doesn't* kom tooti akei."

So *the* tatcho gairo lel'*d him to* mi Doovel'*s* tem, *and* mi Doovel pootch'*d* lésti, "*Has* tooti wel'd *from the* Bengesko tan?"

And the Petalengro pen'd, "Keker," so mi Doovel pen'd, "Jal avrí sig, *you* wafedo gairo. Mandi *doesn't* kom tooti akei."

And the Petalengro pen'd, "Mook mándi dik adré *your* kair," *and* sar sig *as* mi Doovel piriv'*d the* wooda, *the* Peta-lengro wooser'*d his* hoofa adré, *and* praster'd, *and* besh'*d talé opré lesti, *and* pen'*d* *to* mi Doovel, "Tooti *can't* kair mandi jal kenáw."

Doova'*s* *the* drom *the* Petalengro jal'*d* adré mi Doovel'*s* kair.*

Translations.

THE TARNO BOSHNO *AND THE* BARVALO BAR.

THE YOUNG COCK AND THE DIAMOND.

A tarno boshno *wi'* doo*ı* trin kann*ies,* lesko romn*ies,* sas
A young cock with two (or) three hens, his wives, was
dik*in'* *for* choomoni *to* hol opré *a* chikesko-chumba. Yov
looking for something to eat on a dung-hill.   *He*
latch*ed* odo*ı* *a* barvalo bar *and* pen'*d* ajáw : "Mandi'*d*
found there a diamond, and said thus: "*I'd*
sigadáir latch *a* koosi ghiv te chiv adré mi pur *dan* sor
sooner find a little corn to put into my belly than all
the barvalo bar*s* talé *the* kam."
the diamonds under the sun."

SAR *THE* JOOKEL NASHER*ED HIS* MAS.

HOW THE DOG LOST HIS MEAT.

A chooro dinilo jookel sas peer*in'* posha *the* paani-rig *wi'*
A poor foolish dog was walking near the water-side with
koosi mas adré leski moo*ı.* Dik*tás* kumeni kova pensa
a little meat in his mouth. He saw some thing like

---

* This story is taken from "Hone's Every Day Book," ed. 1857, vol. i., p. 447. The translations were originally my own, but have been so altered, amended, and criticised by Gypsy auditors, that we have included them here, as examples of the two dialects.— H. T. C.

waver mas adré o paani. Yov piriv*ed* lesko danyaw *to
other meat in the water. He opened his teeth to*
lel o waver mas, ta mooktás o tatcho kova pel talé
get the other meat, and   let   the   real   thing fall down
adré o paani. Jaw sor lesko hoben sas nashedo. Yek
into the water. So all   his   food   was   lost.   One
shosho adré o kóro see mol dooɪ adré o wesh.
rabbit   in   the pot   is worth two   in   the wood.

THE LOLO-WESHKENO JOOKEL *AND* LESKO
PORI.

THE FOX AND HIS TAIL.

Yek divvus *a* lolo-wéshkeno-jookel sas lino *by* lesko pori
One   day   a red-wood-dog (fox)   was caught by   his   tail
adré *a* tilomengro. Yov pendás kater *his* kokero, "So
in   a   trap.   He   said   to   himself,   "What
kerova mandi kenáw? Nastís lova lesti avrí *a*popli."
shall   I do   now?   I cannot get   it   out   again."
Tardadás-les ta mooktás-les palla lesti adré o weshkeni-
He pulled it and   left   it behind him   in the   wood-
tilomengro. Palla doova yov sas *a*ládj *tó* sikker *his*
holder (-trap). After that   he was ashamed to show him-
kokero kater leski palaw. Kordás-len *to*ketané, ta pendás
self   to   his   mates.   He called them together, and said
ajáw: "Mook sor mendi chin moro poryáw talé. Kek naneɪ
thus: "Let all of us   cut   our   tails   off.   No
kooshto jafri koli *to* mendi." Talla *a* pooro jinomeskro
good (are) such things to   us."   But an   old   knowing
jookel pendás, "Kanna meero nogo pori see lino adré yek,
dog said,   "When   my   own tail is taken in   one,
kerova ajáw, tastís, talla righerova-les kenáw."
I will   do so, if I can, but I will keep it   now."

THE BAURO HOLOMENGRO JOOKEL *AND THE* TIKNO BOKOCHO.

THE WOLF AND THE LITTLE LAMB.

Yek divvus *a* bauro holomengro jookel ghiás kater *the*
One   day   a   big   ravenous dog (wolf) went   to   the
paani-rig *to* pee, *and a* tikno bokocho sas odoí tei,
water-side to drink, and a   little   lamb   was there too,
pee*in'* kek door *from* lesti.   *And the* bauro holomengro
drinking not far   from him.   And the   wolf
jookel sas doosta bokalo, *and* dik'd *the* tikno bokocho, *and*
was very hungry, and saw   the little   lamb, and
pen'*d*, "Horno shom mé tusa.   Kairessa sor o paani
said,   "Angry am I with thee.   Thou makest all the water
mokado."   Pendás o tikno bokocho, "Kek mandi see.
dirty."   Said the little   lamb,   "Not I   is it.
O   paani nasher*s* talé *from* tooti *to* mandi, 'jaw nastissa
The water   runs   down from thee to   me,   so   cannot
mandi kair o paani mokado."   Pendás o bauro holomengro
I   make the water dirty."   Said the   wolf,
jookel, "Tooti's jaw wafedo sar teero dad   ta   dei ;
*   "Thou art as   bad   as thy father and mother ;*
mandi maurdóm lendi dooí.   Mandi maurova tooti."   Yov
I   killed   them both.   I   will kill thee."   He
hodás lesti opré.
ate   it   up.

PATER NOSTER.

(Compare six versions, Pott, ii., 472, *et seq.*; also those
     in the Appendices to Borrow's "Zincali," and in his
     "Lavo-lil.")

Moro Dad, so see adré mi Duvelesko keri, te wel teero
kraliso*m ;* Too zee *be* kedo adré chik, jaw see adré mi
Duvelesko keri.   Del mendi kova divvus moro divvus*ly*

mauro; ta *for*del mendi moro wafedo-kerimus, pensa mendi *for*del*s* yon ta kair*s* wafedo *a*posh mendi, ta lel mendi kek adré wafedo-kerimus. Jaw keressa te righer mendi avrí wafedo. Jaw see ta jaw see.

> WESTER BOSWELL, with a little help
> in paraphrasing the English.

CREED.

(Compare two versions, Pott, ii., 470, 471 ; and those in
Borrow's " Lavo-lil.")

Mandi patser * adré mi Duvel, o Dad sor-ruzlo, kon kedás mi Duvelesko keri, ta chik ;

Ta 'dré Duvelesko Chavo, lesko yekino tikno, moro Duvel, kon o Tatcho Mulo lino. Beeno palla o Tatchi Tarni Duveleski Juvel, so'*s* nav sas Mary, ta kedás wafedo talé Pontius Pilate, jaw sas mordno opré o rook, moolo ta poorosto. Yov jal'*d* talé adré o Bengesko Tan. Trin divvus*es* palla doova yov wel'*d* opré *a*popli avrí o Mulo Tan. Yov jal'*d* opré adré mi Duvelesko keri, beshtás opré o tatcho wast *of* mi Duvel, o Dad sor ruzlo. Avrí doova tan yov avesa † *a*popli, pensa pookinyus, te bitcher o jido ta o mulo.

Mandi patser * adré o Tatcho Mulo, o tatcho Hinditemengro'*s* Kongri, o rokeri*n*' *of* koshto *fol*k*i, o *for*delo*ness* *of* wafedopen*s*, o atchi*n*' opré *a*popli *of* o troopus, ta o meriben kedo *for* sor chairus. Jaw see ta jaw see.

> WESTER BOSWELL, with a little help
> in paraphrasing the English.

THE TEN COMMANDMENTS.

(Compare Pott, ii., 488.)

I.

Mandi shom teero tatcho Doovel. Kek komeni Doovel'*s* see tooti talla mandi.

---

* Patsova.   † Avela.

II.

Maw kair tooti kek komeni foshono kookelo, na kek
pensa waver kova palla lesti ta see adré Duvelesko keri
opré, adré o chik talé, *or* 'dré o paani talé o chik. Maw
pel talé kater lendi. Maw pootch lendi te del tooti variso.
Maw pen teero lavyaw kater léndi, 'jaw mandi teero tatcho
Doovel shom tatcho Doovel, ta kairova o chavé dooker *for*
o dad's wafedo-pens 'jaw door sar o pooro dad's chavé, ta
lenghi chavé tei, so kek nanei komela (komenna) mandi,
ta siker komoben kater lendi so komesa (komenna) mandi
ta kairesa (kairenna) meero tatcho trad.

III.

Maw lel teero Doovel's nav bonges, jaw mi Doovel kek
tilesa (tilela) lesti sor tatcho so lels lesko nav bonges.

IV.

Maw bisser te righer tatcho o Kooroko divvus. Shov
divvusaw too bootiesa ta kair sor so see tooti te kair, talla o
trin ta stor divvus see o tatcho doovel's kooroko. 'Dré lesti
maw kair komeni booti, too, ta teero chavo, ta teeri chei,
ta teero mooshkeni bootiengro, ta teero joovni bootiengro,
teeri groovné, ta o gaújo so see adré teero tan. Jaw 'dré
shov divvusáw mi Doovel kedás mi Doovelesko keri, ta o
chik, o bauro londo paani, ta sor so see adré lesti, ta beshtás
talé o trin ta stor divvus ta kedás chichi. Jaw mi Doovel
pendás kooshto o trin ta stor divvus ta kedás-les tatcho.

V.

Kair kooshtoben kater teero dad ta teeri dei, 'jaw too
jivesa bauro cheerus adré o tem so teero tatcho Doovel dels
tooti.

VI.

Maw too maur.

VII.

Maw sōv sar gairies talla teero nogo romni. Kek nanei
too sōv troostal waver moosh's romni.

VIII.

Maw too chor.

IX.

Maw sovlohol bonges *a*posh o gairé so see posha tooti.

X.

Maw too pootch troostal vaniso kova ta naneí see teero.
Maw kom o moosh'*s* kair so see posha tooti. Maw kom
lesko romni, na lesko bootiengro, ta lesko bootiengri rakli,
na lesko mooshkeni groovni, na lesko meila, na variso kova
so see lesti.

WESTER BOSWELL, with a little help
in paraphrasing the English.

THE LORD IS MY SHEPHERD.

(Psalm xxiii. 1—6, Bible Version.)

1. O Doovel see meero bokorengro *so* odoi mandi nastís
*want*asova chichi ; *or*, Meero Doovel see meero bokorengro
kek nanneí wantasova.

2. Yov kair*s* (kairela) mandi te sov telé adré o chorengri
poovyaw. Yov lel*eth* mandi posh-rig o shookár paani ; *or*,
o atchlo paani.

3. Kairela tatcho *to* mandi'*s* meripen, kanna shom mullo.
Yov siker*eth* mandi adré o tatcho drom ajáw lesko nav'*s*
sake-os.

4. Our. *Though* mandi peer*eth* adrál o kaulo meripen-
drom, mandi'*s* kek *a*trásh *of* kek wáfedo, *for* too shan posha
mandi. Teero ran, ta teero kosht kairenna yon mandi
kooshtoben.

5. Too kairéss *a* misalli 'glal mandi, aglál meero wafedo-
*fol*ki. Too chivéss tulipen opré meero shoro, ta meero koro
nash*eth* párdal.

6. Tatcho kooshtoben, ta tatcho komoben, wel palla
mandi sor o divvus*es* te meero meriben ; ta mandi jivova
adré mi Doovelesko kair sor mi meriben.

WESTER BOSWELL, without any help.

THE SEVEN LOAVES MIRACLE.

(Mark viii. 1—8.)

1. Adré kola divvusáw, kanna sas dosta komeni odoí lel*in*' chichi sor kova cheerus, mi Doovel pootchtás lesko *folk*i, ta pendás kater lendi.

2. Mandi shom toogno talla sor o *folk*i. Yon sas mandi trin divvusáw, ta kek naneí lendi sas yon te hol sor kova cheerus.

3. Te wel mandi te bitcherova-len avrí kater lenghi kairáw, yon penna [perenna] talé o' bok. Dosta lendi vién door dosta.

4. Lesko nogo *folk*i pendás *to* yov. "Sar sastís te yek moosh del jaw kisi mooshaw mauro dosta te hol te porder lenghi peráw adré kova wafedo-dik*in*' tan?"

5. Yov pootchtás lendi. "Sar kisi chelé mauré see toot?" Yon pen'*d*, "Dooí trinyáw ta yek."

6. Yov pendás lendi te besh talé o poov (*or*, chik). Yov liás o dooí trinyáw ta yek chelé mauré. Yov del'*d* parikabén kater mi Doovel. Yov pogadás o mauro, diás-les kater leski *folk*i te besh aglál lendi sor. Yon kair'*d* ajáw.

7. (Ta) yon lián dooí trin bitta matchi. Yov del'*d* lesko kooshto lav, ta pookadás yon te besh lesti talé aglál lendi.

8. Jaw yon hodé ta lenghi peráw sor lendi pordé sas. Yon lel'*d* opré, talla yon hodé, dooí trinyáw ta yek kooshné pordo o' pogado hoben, so sas mooklo talla yon porder'*d* sor lendi peráw.

WESTER BOSWELL, without any help.

LOVE YOUR ENEMIES.

(Luke vi. 27—31.)

27. Mandi pooker kater too, "Kom asár teero wafedo *folk*i. Kair koshto kater dula te kair*s* wafedo kater toot.

28. Kom too dola *folk*i kanna yon pen wafedo laváw kater tooki. Mong asár mi Duvel kanna yon kel*s* bonges kater tooki.

29. Kanna yon del toot pré yek rig o' ti mooï, chiv o waver kater lendi. Yov te lela teero plashta, maw penaw te yov lela teero choχa tei.

30. Del kater sorkon moosh ta pootchela vaniso kova toti. Dova komeni lela teero koli pootch lesti kek komi.

31. Kair too kater waver mooshἀw, jaw too komessa lendi te kel tooti.

THE WIDOW'S SON.
(Luke vii. 11—15.)

11. Ta wel'd ajἀw o divvus palla, yov jal'd adré a shorokono gav. O nav sas Nain. Dosta o' lesti shorokono mooshaw ghién lesti, ta dosta waver *folk*i.

12. Talla yov viἀs kater o stigher o bauro shorokono gav, yov diktἀs a moolo moosh and'd avrí o stigher. Yov sas o tatcho yek o' lesko dei. Yoï sas a peevli gairi, ta dosta *folk*i sas posha yoï.

13. Kanna mi Doovel diktἀs yoï, yov kom'd lati. Pendἀs mi Doovel kater lati. "Maw rōv too."

14. Yov viἀs. Chivdἀs lesko vast opré o kova so yon righer'd o moolo gairo opré. Yon (ta) rigadἀs-les atchté lendi (*or* yon atch'd). Pendἀs mi Doovel, "Tarno moosh, (ta) sas moolo, atch opré jído."

15. Yov, ta sas moolo, atchtἀs lesko kokero opré. Talla atchtἀs opré, rokadἀs. Meero Doovel talla dél'd kova tarno moosh *to* lesko dei.

WESTER BOSWELL, without any help.

THE SUPPER.
(Luke xiv. 16—24.)

16. Yek raati gairo kedἀs bauro holomus, ta poochdἀs boot doosta *folk*i te wel, ta hol lesti.

17. Ta yov bitchadἀs lesko bootsiengro, *at* hoben-chairos, te pen lendi, kon sas poochlo, "Av. Sor kola see tatcho k'naw. Wel adré."

18. Ta yon sor, *with* yek zee, welessa (vién) te kel veena. O *first*adér pendás kater lesti, "Mandi kindóm kotor poov, ta jova te dik lesti. Mongova tooti kair mandi veenlo."

19. Ta yek waver pendás, "Mandi kindóm pansh *yoke* mooshkeni groovni, ta jova te dik palla lendi. Mandl mongova tooti kair mandi veenlo."

20. Ta yek waver pendás, "Mandi romedóm kedivvus kater joovel, mandi nastissa te wel."

21. Palla doova o bootsiengro welassa (viás) ta sikadás kater lesko Rei dula kola. Ta kanna o Shorokno-pardal-o-kair shoondás, yov sas hoïno, ta pendás kater o bootsiengro, "Jal avrí sig adré o bauré-gavesti-dromaw, ta adré o bitté-gavesti-dromaw, ta and adré kova tan dula mooshaw ta joovel*s* so see choorokné, ta o kek-mooshengri, ta o longé, ta o korodé."

22. Ta o bootsiengro kedás ajáw, ta yov wel'*d* *a*poplì, ta pendás kater lesko Rei. "Rei! mandi kedóm sor too pendás, ta sor o skaminé kek nanéi pordo."

23. Ta o Rei pendás kater o bootsiengro, "Jal avrí ta dik adré o bauré dromaw, ta talé o boryaw, ta kair lendi wel adré, sar meero kair *be* pordo.

24. Mandi pookerova tumendi kek nanéi dula gairé so sas poochlé holessa (holenna) yek koosi meero hoben."

WESTER BOSWELL, with a little help
in paraphrasing the English.

THE PRODIGAL SON.

(Luke xv. 11—32.)

11. Yekorus yek gairo sas dooï chavé.

12. Ta o tarnodaír pendás kater lesko dad. "Dad! Dé mandi o kotor *o'* kóli ta peréla mandi." Ta yov diás lendi lesko jivoben.

13. Ta, kek dósta divusáw palla, o tarnodaír chavo chidás sor ketané ta yov liás lesko drom adré dooro tem, ta odoi yov nashedás sor lesko kola 'dré wáfedo jivoben.

14. Ta kanna yov nashedás sor, odói sas bauro bokaloben adré doova tem ta yov viás te kom kumeni te hol.

15. Ta yov ghiás ta pandás lesti kokero kater gavengro *of* doova tem, ta o moosh bitchadás-les adré o poovyaw te del hoben kater baulé.

16. Ta komessa (komdás) te porder lesko pur *with* o kola so o baulé hodé. Ta kek gairo diás leski vaniso.

17. Ta kanna yov diktás lesti kokero yov pendás, "Sar kisi mi dadeski pessadé bootsiengri si mauro dosta ta dosta, ta mandi merova bokalo.

18. Mandi atchova opré ta jova kater meero Dad, *and* penova lesti, Meero Dad! Kedóm wafedo *a*posh mi Doovel ta tooti.

19. Ta mandi shom kek komi mol *to be* kordo teero chavo. Kair mandi sar yek *o'* teero pessado bootsiengri."

20. Ta yov atchdás ta viás kater lesko Dad. Ta kanna yov sas ajáw *a* bauro door avrí, lesko dad diktás-les ta yov sas dosta toogno, ta nashdás, ta pedás opré lesko men ta choomadás-les.

21. Ta o chavo pendás kater lesti dad, "Mandi kedóm wafedo *a*pósh mi Doovel ta 'dré teero dikimus ta mandi shom kek komi mol *to be* kordo teero chavo."

22. Ta o dad pendás kater lesko bootsiengri, "And avrí o feterdaír ploχta ta chiv-les opré lesti, ta chiv wongusti opré lesko wast, ta choχáw opré lesko peeré.

23. Ta and akeí o tikno groovni so see kedo tullo, ta maur lesti, ta mook mendi hol ta *be* mishto adré moro zeeáw.

24. Jaw mi chavo sas mulo ta see jido *a*popli. Yov sas nashedo talla see yov latchno *a*popli." Ta yon vián (viás) *to be* mishto adré lenghi zeeáw.

25. Lesko poorodaír chavo sas adré o poov. Jaw yov viás ta sas posha o kair yov shoondás o boshomengri ta o kelopen.

26. Ta yov kordás bootsiengro ta pootchdás, "So see?"

27. O bootsiengro pendás, "Teero pal viás ta teero dad mordás o tullo tikno groovni, jaw yov liás-les sor kooshto *a*popli."

28. O poorodáir chavo sas hoïno ta pendás yov'd kek jal adré. Jaw lesko dad viás avrí ta pootchdás-les te wel adré.

29. Ta yov diás lav ta pendás kater lesko dad, "Dordi! So kisi beshaw mandi kedóm sorkon kola too pootchdás (pootchdán) mandi? Kekeno cheerus mandi pogadóm teero trad. Kekeno cheerus too diás man bokoro te kel peias sar meero komyáw.

30. Jaw sig meero pal avela, maurdás too lesti o tullo tikno groovni, ta yov nashedás sor teero jivoben sar loobniáw."

31. Lesko dad pendás, "Mi chavo! Too shan mansa sorkon cheerus ta sor meero kola see tooti.

32. Tatcho sas mendi te kel peias. Teero pal sas mulo. Yov see jido apopli. Yov sas nashedo ta see latchno apopli."

WESTER BOSWELL, with a little help
in paraphrasing the English.

THE RICH MAN AND LAZARUS.

(Luke xvi. 19—31.)

19. Yekorus sas barvalo moosh kon sas rido adré lolo poχtan ta yoki rivoben ta hodás kooshko hoben sórkon divusáw.

20. Sas mongamengro tei. O nav see lesti *Lázarus*. Yov sas chido kater o wooda sor naflo ta pordo o' wafedo tanaw.

21. Yov pootchdás o barvalo gairo *to* mook yov lel o bito kotoré o' mauro so pedás talé o barvalo gairo's misali. Jookels vián tei ta kossadé lesko wafedo tanáw opré lesti.

22. O mongamengro merdás, ta yek o' mi Doovel's tatcho gairé liás-les adré *Abraham's* berk adré mi Duvelesko tem. O barvalo moosh merdás tei, ta yov sas poorasto.

23. Kanna yov sas adré o Bengesko tan, yov sas dookadno ta diktás Abraham doovorí adré mi Duvelesko tem, ta diktás Lazarus adré lesko berk.

24. O Barvalo moosh rovdás ta pendás, "Méero dad, Abraham! Te wel tooti komoben opré mandi ta bitcher Lazarus te chiv lesko nei adré paani ta kel meero chib shilalo. Shom dosta dookadno adré kova yog."

25. Abraham pendás, "Chor! Kek bisser too? Adré teero meripen ta liás (lián) kooshti kola, pensa Lazarus liás wafedo kola. Kenáw yov see kedo mishto ta too shan dookadno.

26. Ta, poshrig sor dula kola, bauro hev see chido posh drom o' mendi ta tooti, jaw dula gairé so komena te jal avrí mi Duvelesko tem kater tooti odoi nastissa, ta dula gairé so komena te wel avrí o bengesko tan akéi nastissa."

27. O barvalo moosh pendás, "Kair mandi dova koshto, Dad, te bitcher Lazarus kater meero dadesko kair.

28. Pansh palaw see mandi. Mook Lazarus pooker lendi. Trashova yon wena akéi adré kova wafedo bengesko tan."

29. Abraham penela kater lesti, "Moses ta waveré bauro rokeromengri see lendi. Mook ti palaw shoon kater lendi."

30. O barvalo moosh pendás, "Kek, dad Abraham. Sar yek moosh ghiás kater lendi avrí o mulo tem yon kerena mishto."

31. Abraham pendás. "Sar kek shoonena Moses ta o waveré bauro rokeromengri, yon kek nanéi patserena sar yek moosh avela kater lendi avrí o mulo tem."

WESTER BOSWELL, with a little help
in paraphrasing the English.

ZACCHÆUS.

(Luke xix. 1—6.)

1. Ta Jesus viás adré ta ghiás adrál Jericho.

2. Ta dordi sas odoi a Moosh, lesko nav Zacchæus. Yov sas a shorokono Moosh, ta barvalo sas-ló.

3. Ta yov kedás o feterdaír te dik Jesus kon yov sas, ta nastís kel ajaw. A bito moosh sas yov.

4. Ta yov nashedás ta ghiás opré adré *a* rook te dik lesti, *for* yov sas te peer talé dová drom.

5. *And* kanna Jesus viás kater tan, yov diktás opré ta diktás-les odoi, ta pendás lesti. "Zacchæus, kair yeka ta av talé, atchova ke-divvus kater teero kair."

6. Yov kedás yeka, vias talé ta liás-les keré *wi'* tatcho zee.

THE GOOD SHEPHERD.
(Luke x. 11—18.)

11. Mandi shom o kooshto bokromengro (*or* Basengro). O kooshto Basengro dela lesko meripen *for* o bokré.

12. *But* yov kon see pessado te dik palla o bokré, ta kon's see kek nanéi o bokré, kanna dikela o bauro-holomengro-jookel wel*in'*, mukela o bokré ta prasterela, ta o bauro-holomengro-jookel lela len, ta kairela o bokré praster sor paudel o tem.

13. O gairo, kon see pessado te dik palla o bokré, prasterela sar sig yov see pessado, ta yov kesserela kek *for* o bokré.

14. Mandi shom o kooshto Basengro, ta mandi jinova meeri bokré, ta mandi shom jinlo *of* meero.

15. Sar o Dad jinela mandi, ajáw mandi jinova o Dad, ta mandi chivova talé meero meeripen *for* o bokré.

16. Ta mandi shan waver bokré, kon shan (*or* so see) kek *of* meero pandomengro. Yon tei mandi andova dula tastís, ta yon shoonessa (shoonenna) mandi, kanna mandi kaurova lendi, ta mandi kelova yek pandomengro, ta kek nanéi *but* yek basengro pardel o bokré.

17. Meero Dad komessa (komela) mandi, 'jaw see mandi chivova talé meero meripen, ta lelova lesti *a*popli.

18. Kek moosh lel*s* lesti *a*mandi, mandi chivova lesti talé mi-kokero. Mandi kerova te chiv lesti talé, ta lel lesti apré *a*popli. Meero Dad diás mandi kovva kova te kair.

WESTER BOSWELL, with a little help
in paraphrasing the English.

𝔐𝔦𝔰𝔠𝔢𝔩𝔩𝔞𝔫𝔢𝔬𝔲𝔰.

TEMPORA MUTANTUR.

Sor o Lundra Romani chalé mookté Lundra konáw.*
Sor vién talé kova *Noth*erengri tem. Komela lesti feterdér
konáw, kei yon *used* asár te ven yek chairus. ˙Sor adré
waver dromáw righerén lendi kokeré, *for* sor jal*s* kater
paaneska gaváw konáw. Bita kerimus kek naneí kelela
lendi konáw. Yon venna sor reiaw ta raunia konáw.
Naneí yon konáw sas yon beshaw dosta paulé. Trashenna
te atch adré o bauro gaváw yek cheerus. Konáw yon
atchenna 'dré o feterdér gaváw te yon latchenna. Konáw
choorokono hoben kek kela lendi konáw. Yon lela o feterdér masáw, ta cheriklé, ta kanya, ta papinyaw, ta shoshé,
ta kanengré, ta goïa. Jivenna konáw opré o feterdér hoben
see adré o tem.

All the London Gypsies have left London now.* All
come down to these northern parts. They like it better
now, (than) where they used to go once. They all keep
themselves in other ways, for all go to watering-places
now. Small sport does not do for them now. They are
all become gentlemen and ladies now. They are not now
as they were many years ago. They used to be afraid to
stop in the big towns once. Now they stop in the best
towns they can find. Poor victuals won't do for them now.
They get the best meat, birds, hens, geese, rabbits, hares,
and puddings. They live now on the best food there is in
the land.

SPEED THE PARTING GUEST.

Chairus see konáw te jal te keri. Too atchessa bootodér
akei, too nasherela teero praster*in'* kister kater Mooshkeni-

---

* This is not the case.

gav. Kair sig kerí, ta maw nasher teero chairus. Talla too nasher ti chairus, too atchessa adré kova gav sor raati ti kokeró. Kek ti cheiáw jinela (jinenna) kei shan too. You bitcherenna prastermengri palla tooki te latch tooki popli. Ajáw kair sig, jaw tooki. Kair o feterdér tooki keri, ta mi Doovel jaw tusa. Kair sig, wel *a*popli kater mandi popli. And mandi choomoni koshtó. Ta pooker o waver rei te and mandi dosta tovlo te toov monghi kanna shom kokeró a' raati.

It is time now to go home. If you stop longer here, you will lose your train to Manchester. Make haste home, and don't waste your time. If you waste your time, you will stop in this town all night (by) yourself. Your servants don't know where you are. They will send policemen after you to find you again. So make haste, be off. Make the best of your way home, and God be with you. Make haste, come again to me. Bring me something nice. And tell the other gentleman to bring me plenty of tobacco for me to smoke when I am alone at night.

THE CHILD'S CAUL.

And mandi kova so see tikno beeno troostál paudel lenghi mooráw. Lel mandi *a* mootsi talé o tikno, kanna see beeno. Mootsi see pardál lenghi mooráw, kanna see yon beené.

NAUSEA.

Savo wafedo soong see akeí. So see? Soongela jaw wafedo. Mandi soongova kand akeí, boot dosta te kair mandi te charer opré. Mook mendi jas talé o bauro drom.

What a bad smell there is here. What is it? It smells so bad. I smell a something here, sufficient to make me vomit. Let us go down the main road.

STAG-HUNT.

Dikás mendi kater dulla staani. Yon pooderenna lendi
te lendi yogomengri.

Let us watch these stags. They are shooting them with
their guns.

AN ASSAULT.

Yon tardadé dova chookní avrí meero wast. Yon dié
man pardál o shoro lesti. Yon sovlohol'*d* kater mandi.
Pendás kater mandi, " Too rattfullo pooro jookel. Maurova
toot."

They wrenched that whip out of my hand. They hit
me on the head with it. They swore at me. They said
to me, "You cursed old hound. I will kill you."

HIDING.

Dik odoi! Hokki!! Moosh wela palla mendi. Praster
tooki! Hoχter tooki pardál dova bar, ta kair sig te garav
toot. O gairo dikela kater mandi. Yon kair'*d* godli. Yon
kordé avrí. You rovdé, shooldé tei. Kek yon shoondé
lendi. Te wel sor mendi mordené. O Beng sas adré
lenghi kannáw, kek nanéi shoondé mendi.

Look there! See! A man is coming after us. Run!
Jump over that hedge, and be quick and hide yourself.
The man is watching me. They made a noise. They
called out. They bawled, and whistled too. They did not
hear them. We shall all be killed. The devil was in their
ears, that they did not hear us.

WASHING, SHOPPING, ETC.

Mook mendi tōv mauro koli adré kova nashin' paani.
Kosser lesti avrí. Ghióm kater masengro boodika. Mandi
diktóm o feterdér kotor o' mas. Lióm-les talé. Lióm o

choori. Chindóm-les, sar mandi komova. Kek o rei pardál
o boodika pen'*d* chichi kater mandi.   Chichi nanei pendás.
Sadás mandi.   Pendás mandi, "Too jinessa—teero *folk*i
jinenna—so see o feterdér mas.   Too komessa sorkon
chairus te lé o gróvneski bool.

Let us wash our clothes in this stream.   Clean it out.
I went to the butcher's shop.   I saw the best piece of
meat.   I took it down.   I took the knife.   I cut it, as I
like.   The shopman said nothing to me.   He said nothing;
he laughed at me.   He said to me, "You know—your
people know—which is the best meat.   You like always
to take the beefsteak."

STEALING A WIFE.

Rinkené see-lé?   Te wel mandi kater teero kair, chorova
monghi yek o' teero rinkenodér raklia te lel yek mandi.
Righerova lati te wel meero romni, te wel yoɪ rinkenés, ta
koshtó, ta kek loobni.   Kek né too wela palla mandi te lel
yoɪ pauli popli.   Maw lel mandi opré troostál chor*in*' teero
bootsi-*in*' rakli.

Are they pretty?   If I come to your house, I will steal
one of your prettiest girls, that I may have one.   I will
keep her to be my wife, if she is pretty, and good, and not
loose.   Don't come after me to take her back again.
Don't take me up for stealing your servant girl.

SICKNESS AND RECOVERY.

Mandi kaliko kooroko shō'mas jaw nafelo adré meero
chooro pur.   Wafedo dosta sas mandi te mer.   Kek komeni
sas posha mandi te del mandi koosi paani.   Shō'mas te
meróva.

Troostál meero koshto komomusti Doovel ker'*d* mandi
koshto, ta sor tátcho popli, ta tatcho shom konáw.   Parik

meero koshto Doovel. Kek komeni sas ker'*d* man kooshto te yov.

Last week I was very ill (in my poor stomach). I felt as if I was going to die (lit., bad enough was I to die). No one was near me to give me a drop of water. I must die.

But my good merciful God cured me and made me right again, and now I am well. Thank God. No one cured me but He Himself.

PAZEROBEN.

Mandi see adré pazeroben. Mandi pazerova dova kova. Pazerova monghi dova kova tastís. Kek naneí kek lovo adré meero pootsi konáw. Pesserova lesti waver chairos.

' CREDIT,

I am in debt. I will get that thing on trust. I will get that thing on trust, if I can. I have no money in my pocket now. I will pay for it another time.

IPSE DIXIT.

Jinessa too Westaarus? Jinessa too o pooro Romano chal? Lesko nav see Westaarus.

Kooshto jinomeskro see yov. Yov jin*s* bootodér talla sor tumendi. Kekera shoondóm jafra moosh see yov. Yov see kooshto dosta jinomengro te kel *a* shorokono Pookenyus, ta moolengro. Kekera shoondóm vaniso Romani-chal talla yov te roker pensa yov rokerela. Meero waver gairo ta jal*s* *wi'* mandi see *a* moolengro. Mandi see *a* tatcho Drabeñgro. Yov, ta mandi, pens yek *to a*waver, "Mendi jal*in'* te kel *a* moolengro *of* yov te dik palla mendi, te besh adré o Bauri, kanna o shorokoné rokerenna te o sterimengri. Yov *will* pooker mendi sorkon laváw te wel Romani-chaláw adré steripen ta jal aglál o Pookenyus. Yov see koshto dosta lesti, te kel ajáw."

Kekera shoondóm jafra jinomeskro moosh see yov adré mi meriben.

Do you know Sylvester Boswell? Do you know the old Gypsy? His name is Sylvester. He is a capital scholar. He knows more than all the rest of you. I never heard such another. He is sharp enough to be a Lord Chief Justice, or a lawyer. I never heard any Gypsy but him to talk as he talks. My friend (lit., my other man that goes with me) is a lawyer. I am a doctor. He and I say one to another, "We (are) going to make a lawyer of him to look after us, and sit at the Assizes, when the bigwigs plead for the prisoners. He will always send us word if any Gypsies come to prison to go before the Justice. He is quite fit to do so."

I never heard such a clever man as he in all my life.

A REMINDER.

Maw bisser, rei, meeri poori staadia, too pendás too andessa mandi. Parikeráw toot, rei. Too shan koshto reiáw kater mandi. Mandi komova tumendi, reiaw. Ta maw bisser dova poori ploχta too pendás te and *to* mandi. Kair sig tei, rei, tastís. Mandi komova te lel lesti sig, jaw kisi brishno wela talé konáw, kova wen cheerus.

Dosta brishno, ta hiv, ta shilalo divvusáw, ta raatia wela (wenna) sig. Dova kelela man koshto. Kela mandi te sōv shooko, ta tatto kova wen.

Do not forget, sir, my old hats which you promised you would bring me. Thank you, sir. You are good friends to me. I like you, sirs. And do not forget that old tarpaulin you promised to bring to me. Make haste too, sir, if you can. I would like to have it soon, so much rain comes down now, this winter time.

Much rain, and snow, and chilly days and nights will come soon. That (tarpaulin) will make me snug, and make me sleep dry and warm this winter.

16

A PROUD MAN.

Yov tildás leski shoro opré, pensa shorokono rei sas-ló.
Boomus sas-ló adré lesti, so yov ker'*d.*

He carried his head high, as if he were a lord.   He was
conceited about everything he did.

A PEDESTRIAN.

Dik *at* doova moosh.   Peerela opré o drom sig.   Yov
jala pensi *a* shoshi-jookel.   Yov kel*s* lesti te gaujé*s* te dik
-*at* lesti.   Talla kedás-les, yov jal*s* pootch*es* sorkon reiáw ta
raunyaw te lel luva *o'* lendi, te lel lesko jivoben.

TRANSLATION.

Look at that fellow.   He races along the road on foot as
fleet as a greyhound.   He does it to attract the Gentiles'
attention.   When he has finished, he asks all the gentlemen
and ladies, and gets money from them, and gets his living
in that way.

THE LICENCE.

See man *a* chinomengri, o pokenyus diás mandi.   Pessa-
dóm lesti.   Yon, yekera, sas doo**ı** kotoráw.   Konáw see-lé
pansh koli.   Mandi see yek pansh kolenghi yek, te bikin
vaniso kova.   Kek trash.'pré mandi te jal te bikin koli, so
komova.   Kek mandi te wel lino opré troostal lesti.

TRANSLATION.

I have a licence, which the magistrate gave me.   I paid
for it.   Once, they were two guineas; now they cost five
shillings.   Mine is a five shilling one, and is a general
hawker's licence.   I am not afraid to go and sell anything
I choose.   I shall not be taken up for it.

THE GREYHOUND.

Shool palla o jookel, chawoli!   O yogomengri see akei
Whistle after the dog, mates!   The gamekeeper is here

adré kova vesh.   Maurela o choro jookel, ta yov dikela
in   this wood.   He will kill the poor dog, if he   sees
lesti nash*ing* talla o kanengri.
it   running after the hares.

THE FROG.

We have often asked Gypsies for the *Romani lav* for a
frog. Charlie Boswell told us it was the "*tikeni koli* as *jal*s
adré de *paani*, and *lel*s de *drab avri*" [little thing that goes
into the water and takes the poison out].   Wester Boswell
told us it was "*O stor-herengro bengesko koli ta jal*s *adré o
paani so piova*" [the four-legged diabolic thing that swims
in the water which I drink].   The Gypsies in general
consider any water, into which a frog goes, is fit to drink.
Although they appear to have forgotten the *word* for frog,
they use for toad the word which means frog in other
dialects, vide *jamba, jomba* (Vocab.), but are confused when
questioned about it, and say 'it is no *tatcho lav* (true word),
but means *jumper*.'

THE GYPSY'S CAT.

Dik   *at* o matchka.   Kelela peias ta lesti nogo pori.
Look at the   cat.   It is making fun with it own tail.
Avela   kanna shoolova.
It will come when I whistle.

A SQUABBLE.

Dordi, dordi, choovali.   Te wafedo moosh see yov.
Pookerdás wafedo hoχaben opré mendi, o rattvalo jookel.
Maurova lesti wonka mandi til bonnek *o'* lesti.   Jaw see
lesko loobni romni.   Yoï see wafedodér te yov.   Koorás
amendi yon dooï, avrí morro *folki's* drom, kek yon te wel
posha mensa, jaw meriben *folki* ta pookeromengri see yon.
Chichi nanei lendi te meriben *folki*.   Pookeromengri see-
lé.   Nasherela sor mendi bonges palla lenghi nogo wafedo-
kerimus.

Just see, mates, what a blackguard he is. He has been telling wicked lies about us, the cursed dog, I will murder him when I get hold of him. That creature his wife is just as bad. She is worse than he. Let us thrash them both, and drive them out of our society, and not let them come near us, such cut-throats and informers as they are. They are nothing but murderers. They are informers. We shall all come to grief through their misdoings.

THE APPLE-TREE.

Dordi, te goodlo pobé see odoí, chowali! Maw poger o rook, chowali, mi Doovelenghi. Sor mendi te wel linó.

See, mates, what ripe apples are over there! Do not break the tree, for God's sake, mates, or we shall all be caught.

POLITE INQUIRIES.

"Sar shan, pal?" "Kek mishto, bor. Sar shan tooti? Too shanas naflo waver divvus, hor?" "Ourli; sor mendi shŏ'mas (shumas) wafedo dosta, waver divvus viém pardel lesti. Meero chei sas romedo o waver kooroko. Sor mendi sas motto. Koordém menghi, ta saldova (sadóm) mandi. So sas o vaveré a-kairin' sor o cheerus? Kairenna; Boshervenna, ta ghivenna tei, sor o cheerus, wonka saula viás adré.

"How are you, mate?" "Not very well, friend. How are *you*? You were ill the other day, eh?" "Yes, I was; we were all ill enough the other day we came here over it. My daughter was married the other week, and we all were drunk, and fought with one another, and I laughed." "What were the others doing all the time?" "They dance, and fiddle, and sing too, all the while, till daybreak."

THE JINOMESKRO GREI-ENGRO.

NEW DIALECT.

Mandi'*ll* pen tooti, rei, *a* kooshto drom *to* kair *a* nokengro *to* dik sor tatcho. *When you're* jal*in' to* bikin yek, lel koosi dandermengri chor, chiv *it* adré *the* grei'*s* nok, *and* mook *it* atch odoí *till you* wel*s to the* Walgaurus, *then* tarder *it* avrí, *and* sor *the* wafedo kanipen *will* av avrí tei. *And* mandi'*ll* pen tooti konáw *how to* kel *a* bavengro. Jaw *to the* drabengro boodiga, *and* kin koosi *Alowës.* Kel *it* opré adré *a bit o' crape.* Chiv *it* adré *the* grei'*s* mooí. *When you* avs *to the* Walgaurus, *do you* dik, *you'll* lel *it* avrí popli, *and* dova'*ll* hatch *the* grei'*s* baval mishto. *A* moosh, *as* mandi jin*s*, bikin'*d a* bavengri grasni *for* bish bar *by* kel*in'* ajáw, *and* kin'*d it* popli *for* desh bar. *Some* Romani-chal*s* chiv*s* kil adré *the* grei'*s* mooí, *but the* waver drom'*s the* feterdair*est*.

THE KNOWING HORSE-DEALER.

I will tell (say) you, sir, a good way to make a glandered horse look all right. When you are going to sell one, take a few nettles (lit., a little biting-grass, put them (it) into the horse's nostrils, and let them stay there till you come to the fair ; then pull them out, and all the bad matter will come out too. And I will tell you now, how to 'cook' a broken-winded horse. Go to the druggist's shop, and buy a little aloes. Do it up in a bit of crape. Put it in the horse's mouth. When you come to the fair, do you see, you will take it out again, and that will stop the horse's wind well.* A man that I know sold a broken-winded mare for twenty pounds by doing so, and bought it again for ten pounds. Some Gypsies put butter in the horse's mouth, but the other way is the best.

---

* Some Gypsies adminster butter scrapings and brown paper, worked up into a ball. Our friend Louis L—— declares it to be the "fetterdair*est* drom."—*Vide* p. 204.

Relating to Wester and his Family.

AUTOBIOGRAPHY.

Mandi sas beeno kater Dovár. Kooromongro sas meero Dad. Beeno shō'mas adré o Kooromongri. Meero Dad, kanna shō'mas beeno, yov sas dik*in'* pardál o bauro yogomengri. Talla yov viás keré, ta mooktás sor kooromongri kerimus. Yov wel*'d* talé o Meilesko-tem, ta 'doi yov atch*'d for* beshaw dosta, *and* sor morro tikné sas anlo apré adré dova tem, *and* 'doi atch*'d* sor mendi talla yov sas mord'nó adré o Lincoln-tem. Yov merdás kanna mandi shō'mas *a* tikno chor.

Mi-Dooveleskо yog pedás talé apré lesti, *and* maur*'d* lesti, *a*waver yek tei, dooï ketané. Dooï simensa sas yon. Lenghi *folk*i chiv*'d* lendi dooï adré yek hev. 'Doï mooktóm lendi, choori *folk*i. Toogno sas mé dosta talla. Yov rivdás lesko kokero adré kooshto eezáw sorkon chairus.

Kanna yov sas poorosto, mandi lióm Romni, ta ghióm sor pardal o tem. Mandi ghióm sor pardal Ánghiterra, *Nöthe*rengri-tem, *and* o Lavines-tem, wonka mandi vióm akeï.

TRANSLATION.

I was born at Dover. My father was a soldier, and I was born in the army. My father, when I was born, was in charge of the great gun (Queen Anne's pocket-piece). After a while he came home, and left the army. He came down into Yorkshire, and there he stayed for many years, and all our family were brought up in that county, and there we all stayed after he was killed in Lincolnshire. He died when I was a lad.

The lightning struck him, and killed him and another, both together. They were cousins. Our people put them both in one grave. There I left them, poor fellows. I was much grieved at it. He always dressed well.

When he was buried, I took a wife, and went all over the country. I went all over England, Scotland, and Wales, until I came here.

HIS RESIDENCE AT CODLING GAP.

Mandi jivela konáw adré o poov, kei o gaujé kel*s* dola kola, so yon ker kairáw te jiv adré, avrí o chik.

Te wel kova koosi poov, kei atchova mé konáw, morro nogo. Kelcla man Rei sor meero meriben.

Mandi komova te jiv kater o bauro londo paani. Mandi komova te jiv akeí, kei shom konáw, besháw dosta. Kek mandi te vel kino *o'* lesti, jafra rinkeno tan see.

Kanna shom adré meero woodrus, te dikóv avrí, mandi dikova sor o Bauro Gav, o Bookesko Gav, ta sor o paani, ta bairé jala kater sorkon temáw.

Diktóm dova bauro yog sas hotcherela. Kanna shom (shŏ'mas) mandi adré meero woodrus, diktóm sor.

Yeka kova besh, adré kova lileí, diktóm bauro bairo sor dood, ta kolé sas hotchadé, ta sor o paani sor sas pardál *o'* dood. Sor o koli sas atch*in'* opré o paani. Sor dood sas. Diktás mishto, ta rinkenes diktás.

TRANSLATION.

I live now in the field, where the Gentiles make those things of clay with which they build houses to live in.

Would that this little field, where I am stopping now, were mine. It would make me a gentleman for life.

I like to live by the seaside. I would like to live here, where I am now, for many a long year. I should never be tired of it ; it is such a pretty place.

When I am in bed, if I look out, I see all the city of Liverpool, and the river, and the ships going to every land.

I saw that great fire [at the landing-stage] when it was burning. When I was in bed I could see it all.

Once this year, this very summer, I saw a large vessel all

on fire, and the cotton bales were burnt, and the whole river was in flames. All the bales were floating in the river blazing. It looked well; 'twas a pretty sight indeed.

VERSES AS WRITTEN BY WESTER.	AND HIS OWN TRANSLATION.

I.

After many roming years,
How sweet it is to be,
In love, and peace, and kindness,
With all you see.

I.

Talla boot peeromus besháw,
Te goodlo see te atch
Adré Komomus, ta Kooshtoben,
Te sor mendi dik.

II.

So let all injoy the mind of me,
And that you will plainly see,
That love to God, and peace with man,
Will bring you to a Happy Land.

II.

Jaw mook sorkon ti zee *o'* mandi,
Te too'*ll* tatcheni dik,
Te Komomus kater mi *dear* o Duvel,
    te koshtomus te sor moosháw.
Dova and'a tooti kater tatcho poov,

III.

The rite way. First to love your Christ
First, and obey His Holy Word,
Then you will find that you will be rite,
And make your road quite Strat, in Heaven to dwell,

For ever and ever. Amen.

III.

O tatcho drom te ker aglál té kom
    teero Duvelesko Chavo,
Kom lesti ta lesti heveski lavaw,
Talla too'*ll* latch te too'*ll* atch tatcho,
Ta kerav teero drom tatcho
Opré, adré mi Duvelesko Tem te jiv,
Besháw ta besháw. Amen.

Written by SILVESTER BOSWELL, in the 1874th year of our dear Lord.

LETTERS *written by* WESTER—(1) *Reply to ours inquiring whether he knew anything respecting* MATILDA BOSWELL, *aged* 40, *and* LUCRETIA SMITH, *Queen of the Gypsies, aged* 72, *both of whom were buried at Beighton, in Derbyshire, in* 1844. (See N. and Q., 5 S., vol. ii., p. 76.)

Seacombe, Aug. the 1s, 1874. Comlow Rei kec manday Jin Doler temeskey Ronnichel mandy Ached Jaw kissey Beshaw ovre Dover tem keckeno Jin Chichey trustal a

Lendy keck yoye sas keck Cralacy pardal o Romenaychell
keck mandey Jinover Joffero Nave Rrie Komena sas youne
yoye sas keck Cralacy.

Patcer mandy mandy sea terowe poorow Romineychill,

SILVESTER BOSWELL.

IN OUR ORTHOGRAPHY.

Komelo Rei,—Kek mandi jin dola temeski Romani-chal.
Mandi atch*ed* jaw kisi besháw avrí dova tem, kekeno jin
chichi troostál lendi.

Kek yoї sas kek Kralisi pardál o Romani-chal. Kek
mandi jinova jafri nav, Rei, komeni sas yon. Yoї sas kek
Kralisi.

Patser mandi, mandi see teero pooro Romani-chal.

TRANSLATION.

Dear Sir,—I do not know the Gypsies of that county. I
(have) stayed so many years out of that county, (that) I
know nothing about them.

She was no Queen of the Gypsies.* I do not know such
a name, sir, (or that) there (lit. they) were any (of that
name.) She was no Queen.

Believe me, (that) I am, thy old Gypsy.

(2.)

Seacombe Aug. the 4th 1874   Costo Rieo mandy bisad
mearo cocrow pockerer to trustal merro burrow Dadesco
tacho nave.   Shedrich Boswell sas lesco nave to Richard
Matcho sas mearrow Dieesco purrow Dadesco tacho nave
Dover se tacho—the grandfather of me on the Boswell side
Was shedrich Boswell and the farther of my mother Richard
Harring and the name Emanuel Was his brother   You
Will Plese to tell Mr Smart the same as he has got it Rong

---

* Aged Gypsies are styled Kings and Queens after death, or on
visiting new places, to gain respect and profit from the *gaujos*.

By my forgetfullness. Plese To returne me answer from this

    Mandy shom tearrow tacho porrow Romnichel

                          S. BOS. WESTER.

    Cere sig ta Bicher catter mandy porley.

IN OUR ORTHOGRAPHY.

Koshto Reiä. Mandi bisser'*d* meero kokero pookerer too troostal meero pooro-Dadesko tatcho nav. Shadrach Boswell sas lesko nav, ta Richard Matcho sas meero Def-esko pooro-dadesko tatcho nav. Dova see tatcho. . . . Mandi shom teero tatcho pooro Romani-chal. . . . Kair sig ta bitcher kater mandi pauli.

TRANSLATION.

Good Sir,—I forgot to tell you about my grandfather's proper name. Shadrach B. was his name, and R. Herne was my mother's grandfather's proper name. That is true. . . . I am thy true old Gypsy. . . . Be quick and send me an answer.

(3.)

Seacombe, Oct. 4, 1874. romno rye so se to trustal kec nanni to bicher Eser to Catter manday ta pocker Esa mandy ta to shanush molo o jido mandy shomos togno paller tote kec nini to mucesr mandy o jor Cova Drome Bicher ta mandy a chinamongry Cer sig paller lesty ta muck mandy gin o toty mandy pucker Eser to ta to Cer mandy Wafodo to Ceresa te cockero Wafodo Catter te cockero jor mandy shounomos toty sig.

    Mandy shanous totys coshto poorey Ry Romenichel.

                          WESTEROUS.

IN OUR ORTHOGRAPHY.

Romano Rei. So see too troostal, kek nanei too bitcher-essa too kater mandi, te pookeressa mandi te too shanas moolo *o'* jido.

seacombe oct 4 th 1874
romno Rye so se to trustal lec te
nanni to Ficher Eser to Catter monday
ta Focher Esa mandy ta to shanash
molo o jido mandy shomos
togno praller tote lec nini to
mucesr mandy o jor bour drome
Ficher ta mandy a China mongry
ler sig praller Lesty ta ta
mush mundy jin o toty
mandy praher Eser to ta ta
ler mandy Wafodo to beresa
te Cockero Wafodo Catter te
Cockero jor mandy shounomos
toty sig
          mandy shanous
          totys Coshto
          footey Ry Romenichel
Mesterous

Mandi shōmas toogno palla tooti.   Kek nanei too mookessa mandi ajaw, kova drom.

Bitcher te mandi *a* chinomongri.   Ker sig palla lesti, ta muk mandi jin *o'* tooti.

Mandi pookeressa too, ta too ker mandi wafedo.   Too keressa ti kokero wafedo kater ti kokero; jaw mandi shoonomus tooti sig.   Mandi shanas (shom) tooti's koshto poori Rei Romanichal

WESTÁRUS.

TRANSLATION.

Gypsy Gentleman,—What art thou about, that thou dost not send to me, to tell me if thou wert dead or alive?

I was grieved about thee.   Thou wilt not leave me so, in this way.

Send me a letter.   Make haste about it, and let me know about thee.

I tell thee that thou art doing me harm.   Thou art doing harm to thyself; so (send) me news from thyself soon.

I was thy good old gentleman,

GYPSY SYLVESTER.

(4.)

Merow Commlow Rie maw Cesser trustal o Dover trustal mandy Jin overe tearrow Zea Jaw Coshto Catter mandy Bicher so Comesa ta mandy vanaso Dinow Cearra mandy saw se tacho trustal Dover Pucher youne ta Cack Bissea mearrow Plockter ta stardycar and Lendy a Dray o Bicher Lendy a Draye a Borrow Cusheney so youne Chivener o Canyowre or Canneys a Dray mearrow Chocha tye to penas mandy ta Cusey tovelow ta sweggler Coshto yeck ty Patsea mandy Rie tacho se mandy Catter ta mendy Duye coshto Rieo mandy shom to mendys tacho Beano Romenichel ta Ceck gorgoconness much.

WESTER BOSWELL, sicker Cover
Catter o Drabengro Rie tye.

IN OUR ORTHOGRAPHY.

Meero komelo rei.   Maw kesser troostal adova troostal.

Mandi jinova teero zee jaw koshto kater mandi.   Bitcher
so komessa *to* mandi.   Vaniso dino kair'a mandi.   Sor see
tatcho troostal dova.   Pooker yon te kek bisser meero
ploχta, ta staadia; and lendi adré, *o'* bitcher lendi adré, *a*
bauro kushni, so yon chivenna o kanyaw, *or* kannies adré.
Meero choka tei, too pen(d)as mandi, ta koosi toovlo, ta
swegler, koshto yek tei.   Patser mandi, rei, tatcho see mandi
kater tumendi dooï koshto reiaw.   Mandi shom tumendi's
tatcho beeno Romani-chal, ta kek gaujikanes moosh.

W.B., Siker kova kater o drabengro rei tei.

(5.)

Mearo Comlo rye mandy se velover ta totoes Care ta
Dickover tut Dickavree ta Dickesa mandy o pray o Due-
yeney Dives trustal Corroco Dives mandy veller to tuty o
pray Dover Dives tacho ta Comesa mearro Dovel.

IN OUR ORTHOGRAPHY.

Meero komelo rei.   Mandi see velova *to* tooti's kair te
dikova toot.   Dik avrí, ta dikessa mandi opré o dooïeni
divvus troostal (palla) Kooroko-divvus.   Mandi vela *to*
tooti, opré dova divvus, tatcho, te komessa (komela) meero
Doovel.

TRANSLATION.

My dear sir.   I am coming to your house that I may see
you.   Look out, and you will see me on the second day
after Sunday.   I will come to you, on that day, safe, if my
God be willing.

HIS GENEALOGY IN HIS OWN WORDS.

Sophia Herne was born at Pirton, and was the mother of
Sylvester Boswell.   Teiso (Tasso) Boswell was his father.
Teiso Boswell was killed, and one of his own cousins, two
aged men, by lightning and thunder at Tetford in Lincoln-
shire, near Horncastle.   His cousin's name was called
No Name, because he was not christened till he was an

old man, and then they called him Edward. This occurred on August 5th, 1831.

Sarah Herne, the daughter of No Name, was the mother of my eldest son, Simpronius Bohemia Boswell. He was born on the 8th of July, 1832. She was a beautiful woman. Her face was darker than mine, and hair black as a raven, which hung in curls all down her shoulders,* and eyes like two plums.

Sophia and Teiso's children were—1, Maria; 2, Lucy; 3, Sage; 4, Betsy; 5, Dorēlia; 6, Edward; 7, Delāta; 8, Sylvester.

The father of Sophia was Richard Herne; and Bonny was her mother. Richard Herne was buried at Haslingfield, near Cambridge. Bonny died twenty-three years ago, above a hundred years old. Richard Herne's brother was Emanuel.

Sophia's sisters were Lucy, Ally, Sage, Margaret, Ann, and Sarah. Sarah was the mother of Mantis Buckland. Nan married Jasper Smith.

The father of Teiso was Shadrach Boswell, and Cinderella Wood was the mother of Teiso. Shadrach was a soldier, and died in Holland, and was buried there. Both my grandfathers used to fight on stages.

Maria, my sister, married John Grey, a fiddler.

Lucy, my sister, married Riley Boswell, who died at Harrow-on-the-Hill. She is now in America.

Sage, my sister, married Joseph Smith. She died in America, and left a large family.

Betsy (Elizabeth), my sister, married Job Williams, the son of Jim of the Lávines-tem. He is dead. She is in America. Her daughter married Jasper Gray.

Dorēlia, my sister, married Kaleí Herne. His sons are Yoben, Edward, Minnie, and Nelson.

Edward, my brother, married Sīári Draper, of the

---

* A not uncommon mode of tiring the hair among the older female Gypsies is to tie it in four knotted loops, something after the style of a horse's tail.

Lávines-tem. They live at Blackpool. Their children's names are Dorēlia, and Emma, Alma (a boy), Tobias, and William.

Delāta, my sister, married Allen Boswell, and died in childbed in Lincolnshire.

Sylvester married Florence Chilcott at Yarmouth. He was born at Dover, in 1811, in the army. Florence was born at Norwich, in January 1820, and died in the forty-third year of her age, and was buried at East Ham, near London. One of her sisters married Tom Lee, who has a daughter named Ada, and three sons—Walter, Edgar, and Bendigo.

This is the family of Sylvester and Florence Chilcott :—

1. Byron, born at Benwick, Cambridgeshire, in 1839. He is a fiddler, and now lives in Wales.
2. M'Kenzie, born on Ascot racecourse, on the Derby day, 1842.
3. Oscar, born at Bray, near Windsor, in 1844.
4. Bruce, born at Stisted, near Braintree, Essex, in 1847.
5. Julia, born at Litherland, Sefton, near Liverpool, in 1850.
6. Wallace, born at Sutton, in Cambs, in 1853.
7. Trafalgar, born at Plaistow, Newtown, Essex, in 1856.
8. Laura, born at Burrow, near Woodbridge, Suffolk, in 1859, and since dead.

NOTE.—Isaac Herne (*vide* "The Chase") is the son of Neabei, or Nearboy Herne, and Sinfi, commonly called 'The Crow,' who is said to have instructed Mr. Borrow in 'deep' Romanes; and Neabei was the son of Richard Herne, Sylvester's maternal grandfather. Isaac married a daughter of .Pyramus Gray, and his children are 'Eza, Trainit, 'Lenda, and Collia.

Dialogues.

I.

Kooshko divvus, nogo pal. Sar shan, *my* pal?
'*Tis a* shilino divvus.

Ourli, yivyela.
Kei see tooti koko ghilo *to*-divvus?
Yov ghiás koliko-divvus *to* Lalo peero wagyaura.
Kei see tooti rinkeni pen?
Meiri pen'*s* adré adoova gav *a*-doorik*in*.
Shoon, pal! Boshela jookel.
Dik savo see! *A* gaujo?
De nashermengro.
Maw poger adoova bor, dinelo!
Keker, pal, '*tis a* bauro rei.
Yov'*s a* kooshto kestermengro.
Our, *and* yov'*s* koshto roodo.
Dik! Adoova sce lesti filisin.
Ranjer tooti staadi.
Mook'*s* jal adré akova kitchema *for* choomoni *to* pee.
Besh tooki 'lé, pal.
Akova see wasedo livena.
Kooshto *for* chichi.
Mook'*s* pee *a* wover trooshni livena.
Kooshto bok *to* tooti, pal.
Adoova Hindi-temengro'*s* posh-motto.
Kova moosh *is a* grei-engro.
Atch apré, pal! Mook'*s* jal avrí popli.
Our, meiri tano'*s a* kooshto door fon akéi.
Savo see *de* tatcho drom.
Talé adoova chikli drom.
Dik! Akéi'*s de* patrin apré *de* bongo vas'.

TRANSLATION.

I.

Good day, my own brother. How do you do, brother?
It is a cold day.
Indeed it is. It is snowing.
Where has your uncle gone to-day?
He went yesterday to Redford fair.
Where is your pretty sister?
My sister's in the town there telling fortunes.

Listen, mate ! The dog is barking.
Look who it is ! A stranger?
The policeman.
Do not break the hedge, you fool !
No, brother. It's a gentleman.
He is a good rider.
That he is, and well dressed.
Look. That's his house.
Touch your hat.
Let us go into the inn there for something to drink.
Sit down, brother.
This is bad beer.
Good for nothing.
Let us drink another quart of beer.
Good luck to you, brother.
That Irishman is half drunk.
This fellow is a horse-dealer.
Get up, brother. Let us go out again.
Certainly. My camp is a good distance from here.
Which is the right way ?
Down that dirty lane.
Look ! Here's the trail on the left hand.

II.

'*Tis a* kooshto door *to the* forus.
Ourli. Kiní shom.
Besh tooki 'le, Dei, *and* mook mandi jaw *to* mong *a bit of* hoben.
Keker, *my* Pal. '*Tis* doosh *to* jaw odoi.
The bauro rei, *as* jivs odoi, *is a* Pokenyus.
He'll bitcher *the* nashermengro *to* lel tooti *to* steripen.
Mook'*s* jaw *a* wover drom.
My beebi'*s a* steromeskri kenáw *at the* bauro gav *for* chor*in' at the* moilesto-gav.
She'll be bitchadi paudel.
Dik ! *The* nashermengro *is* lel*in' a* mongamengro *to* steripen.

The Beng *has* chiv'*d* wastengri*es* apré lesti.
Riserela gairo.
Mantchi too, pal.
Til apré *your* zee!   Maw *be a*-ladj!
Lesti nok *is* sor rat.
Yov'*s a* kooshto kooromengro.
Pooker *the* tatchipen!   Maw roker hookapen*s*!
A bairengro del'*d the* moosh *a* kaulo yok, *and a* pogado shero.
Hok 'doova bor, pal!
Chor dooï trin poovengri*es*, *and some* shokyaw.
Chiv '*em* adré *the* gono.
The ghivengro awél akei.
Wooser *de* gono adoi, *and* garav *your* kokero.
Maw roker!
Lel trad!   Lel veena!
He's jaw'*d*.
Tatcho see 'doova.

II.

It is a long way to the city.
Yes.   I am downright tired.
Sit down, mother, and let me go to beg a little food.
No, my brother.   It is no good to go there.
The gentleman that lives there is a magistrate.
He will send the policeman to take you to prison.
Let us go another way.
My aunt is a prisoner now at the town for stealing at Doncaster.
She will be sent to penal servitude.
Look! the policeman is taking a beggar to prison.
The devil has put handcuffs on him.
The man is trembling.
Cheer up, brother.
Keep up your spirits!   Don't be ashamed!
His nose is covered with blood.

17

He is a capital boxer.
Tell the truth! Don't tell lies!
A sailor gave the man a black eye, and a broken head.
Jump that hedge, brother.
Steal two or three potatoes, and some cabbages.
Put them into the sack.
The farmer is coming this way.
Throw the sack there, and hide yourself.
Don't speak.
Take care! Look out!
He has gone.
That's right.

III.

Mé shom bokalo.
Del mandi choomoni *to* hol.
Lel mandi *a* tuli hotchiwitchi.
Hol 'doova bokochesto pur.
Del mandi *a* choori *to* chin *my* mauro.
Del mandi *a* poosomengro.
Bitcher *the* chavi *to the* boodega *for a* koosi balo-vas.
Chiv paani adré *the* kekavi.
Our, *I'll* kel woriso *for* tooti.
Kair *a* kooshko yog.
Chiv wongur opré, *and* lel mandi *the* poodomengro.
Kei's *the* saashter?
The paani see tatto.   Lel mandi *the* peemengro.
Maw pee *the* muterimongeri *without* goodlo.
Mé shom traslo.
Pee *a* koosi livena, tood, kalengri, mool.
There's chichi adré *the* valin.
Meiri pur see pordo kenáw.   Pordo see meiri pur.
Lel mandi *my* swagler.
Meiri swagler see pogado.
Kova tuvlo *is* kek mool *a* full.
Riley! Jaw *to the* boodega *for some* feterdairo.
Del *the* moosh tring hauri.

Riley! *You* bauro dinelo! *You* wasedo bang!
kooshto *for* chichi.

Maw chinger, palaw.

Maw! Maw kel ajáw!

Besh talé *a*popli *by the* yog.

Our! Pootch Pyramus *to* lel lesti boshamengro.

Keker! Mook's jal *to* woodrus.

Kooshko raati.

III.

I am hungry.

Give me something to eat.

Get me a fat hedgehog.

Eat that tripe.

Give me a knife to cut my bread.

Give me a fork.

Send the lad to the shop for a little bacon.

Pour (some) water into the kettle.

Yes, I'll do anything for you.

Make a good fire.

Put (some) coal on, and get me the bellows.

Where's the pot-hook?

The water boils. Get me the teapot.

Don't drink the tea without sugar.

I am thirsty.

Drink a little beer, milk, whey, wine.

The bottle is empty.

I have had enough now. I am satisfied.

Give me my pipe.

My pipe is broken.

This tobacco is perfectly worthless.

Riley! go to the shop for some better.

Give the fellow threepence.

Riley! You great fool! You blackguard! It's
for nothing.

Don't quarrel, brothers.

Pray don't do so.

Sit down again by the fire.
Yes. Ask Pyramus to get his fiddle.
No. Let us go to bed.
Good night.

DINNER DIALOGUE WITH WESTER.

Wester. Bokalo shan too?
Self. Ourli. Shom dosta.
W. Mandi merova *o'* bok, jaw bokalo shom. Mandi see
posh mulo.
S. Kei jivela o masengro?
W. Yov jivela adré o gav. Kek door see, mi Rei.
S. Lel kova posh-koorona, ta jal kater boodega, *and* kin
mandi koosi grooveneesko-mas, *and a* chollo mauro.
W. Parikráw toot, Rei.

> [WESTER *goes, and returns with the provisions.*
> *Conversation continued:*

Jalova *to* lel dooı trin koshtaw, ta koosi wongur . . . . del
mandi *a* delomengri.
S. Dova see *a* kooshto yog.
W. Kek nanéi. Kenáw-sig te wel *a* koshto yog
Yoosherova o tatermengri mishto, ta chivova koosi tulopen
adré-les. Komess too balovás, Rei?
S. Our.

> [*While he is busy cutting the bacon, his cat comes
> and smells at the meat. He addresses her
> thus:*

W. Jaw tooki choovihoneski matchka. Chichi nanéi
dova toot. Jaw adré o shushenghi hevyaw. Maur lendi
ta hol lendi ti kokero. Porder ti pur ajáw.

> [*After a bit, the dog watches his opportunity, and
> runs off with half our dinner.* WESTER *no
> sooner sees this than he gives vent to his rage
> in the following terms:*

Dik odói asár, mi Doovelenghi! O rattvalo jookel!

> [*He takes a stout stick, and rushes out of the tent.*

The bauro holomengro. Maurova lesti konáw-sig. Jinova kei see ghilo.

> [*A great row ensues, and soon after* WESTER *re-appears with the meat in triumph. He washes it in the bucket, and proclaims it as good as ever; we however object to it, so another steak is cooked. A day or two after this occurred, we visited him again, when he informed us :*

Dióm o bito jookel so hodás o mas o waver divvus too kindás. Dióm-les kater bito tarno rei akeí ta jivela posha mandi, ta yov liás-les kater Booko-paani-gav.]

W. Del mandi *the* mauro, Rei. Komés, too *the* avrí-rig ?

S. So see dova ?

W. The hotchedo kotor o' *the* mauro, Rei. . . . Mook mandi del tooti koosi dandimengri.

S. Parikráw toot.

W. Lon see tooti ?

S. Our.

W. And mandi o lon, ta tatto kova, ta hindi kova. Parikráw toot. Kenáw lon see mandi tei. Kova lon see kek moχodo. Chidóm tatto-kova *wi'* lesti. Komés too hotchiwitchi ? Our, kooshto see dova. Poorokono holoben see *a* koshto hotchi-witchi, ta *a* kooshto marikli.* Dova see pooro Romani-chal's holomus. Yon sas jaw yoozho adré lenghi peráw. Yon (hotchi-witchi) see kek kooshto adré o lileí. Yon see bauri konáw.

> [*He added :*

Jaw monghi. Dikova talla o hotchi-witchi. Mandi latch-ova yek. Andova lesti keré. Maurova lesti, ta morrov lesti. Yoosherova lesti. Chivova lesti talé o yog, ta kerav lesti, ta hova-les monghi.]

Mé shom trooshlo. Del mandi choomoni *to* pee. Akei see kooshto paani. Mandi's del'*d* apré sor piamus o' livena. Çhiv les avrí. Parikráw toot. Kooshto see dova. Del mandi koosi *ginger*-livena. Lel o *bung*arus avrí valinesko men.

---

* See p. 197, " Hedgehog Hunting and Gypsy Cake."

TRANSLATION. ·

Wester. Are you hungry ?

Self. Certainly, I am very hungry.

W. I am dying of hunger, I am so hungry.　I am half dead with it.

S. Where does the butcher live ?

W. He lives in the town, not far off, sir.

S. Take this half-crown, and go to the shop, and buy me a little beef, and a loaf of bread.

W. Thank you, sir.

[WESTER *goes and returns.*

I will go for two or three sticks and a little coal. . . . Give me a match.

S. That is a good fire.

W. Not it, but it will be soon a capital one.　I will clean the frying-pan well, and put a little grease in it.　Do you like bacon, sir ?

S. Yes.

[*The cat comes, and smells at the meat.　He says to it,*

Get off with you, you bewitched cat.　There is nothing there for you.　Go to the rabbit-holes, and kill some for yourself, and have a good meal in that way.

[*The dog steals the meat.*

W. Just look there, for God's sake.　The cursed dog! the glutton!　I will kill it this instant.　I know where he is gone.

[*The dog was thrashed, and the meat rescued, and on our next visit :*

W. I gave away the little dog which ate the meat you bought the other day.　I gave it to a young fellow here who lives near me, and he took it to Liverpool.

[*Dialogue continued :*

Give me the bread, sir.　Do you like the avrí-rig ?

S. What is that ?

W. The burnt part of the loaf, sir.　Let me give you some mustard.

S. Thank you.

W. Have you any salt?

S. Yes.

W. Hand me the salt, pepper, and mustard. Thanks. Now I have some salt too. This salt is not dirty. I have mixed pepper with it. Do you like hedgehog? That I do; is not it good? Old-fashioned food is a good hedgehog and potatoes, and a nice cake. That is what the old Gypsies used to eat. They were rather dainty about their food. Hedgehogs are not good to eat in summer. They are with young now. I will go and look for a hedgehog. I will find one, and bring it home. I will kill it, and shave it. I will clean it, and put it in the ashes, and bake it, and eat it myself. I am thirsty. Give me something to drink. Here is good water. I have become a teetotaler. Pour it out. Thank you. That is good. Give me a little ginger-beer, and draw the cork.

Extracts from our Notebooks,

Illustrating peculiar Modes of Expression, and points of Grammar.

Yon rokerela lenghi Romanes, sor adré Romanes. Chivena yon kek gaujikanes adré lesti.

Adré *the Noth*erenghi tem sor o Romani chaláw see korengri, *besom*aari, chorodé, kekavi-Petalengré, roiengré.

O Lavines gairé, ta o *No(r)th*erengri gairé, ta Hinditem-engri gairé, yon roker*s* lenghi lavaw sor katené adré lenghi rokerben so see kordo sar o poruma rokerben.

Rokerela Lavines rokerobén. Adré o Lavines tem o Romani*es*, see *Woods, Roberts, Williams,* and *Jones.*

Yov rokerela misto kenáw. Mandi rokerasár misto kenáw sig. Too roker asár sar see doova chido talé. Kek nanéi jinessa too so penova mandi, tooti tatcho Romani-chal tei? Keker mandi, mandi lova meero soover-holoben. Kek mandi pookerova toot vaniso koovaw talla

sor tatcho. Kek naneí mandi pookasova toot chichi so see
wafedo. Jinova, pal, sorkon koovaw too pookerás mandi see
tatcho. Wonka yon righerenna lesti adré *to* lendi kokeri, talla
chiv*s* lesti adré tatcho wastaw, *to* waver reiaw, jinomeskri
troostal lesti, doova koova kairela lendi mol dosta luvva.

They (Welsh Gypsies) talk their Gypsy all in Gypsy.
They mix no English with it.

In Scotland all the Gypsies are potters, besom-makers,
mumpers, tinkers, or spoon-makers.

The Welsh, and Scotch, and Irish pronounce their words
all together in their language, which is called the Gaelic
tongue.

He talks the Welsh language. In Wales the Gypsies
are Woods, Roberts, etc.

He talks well now. I shall speak well directly. Just
you speak as it is put down. Don't you understand
what I say, and you a real Gypsy too? Not I, I'll take
my oath. I won't tell you anything but what is true. I
will not tell you anything that is wrong. I know everything, my brother, that you tell me is right. When they
keep it to themselves, and afterwards put it in right hands
(or give it) to other gentlemen, who are learned about it, it
will make them worth much money.

Continued.

Pookerova toot, Rei, tastís.

Kek shoonessa too; kona shom mandi rokeri*n*' troostal
dulla kolla.

Doova, see *a* choorokonó lav. Kek ne jinenna yon o
tatcho Romani lav, pensa moro lavaw. Rokerenna posh
dinveres posh gaujikanes.

Soski too nanéi roker *to* mandi? Roker tooti, tastis.

Kek na mandi rokerova, nastís mandi jinova-les.

Savo motto moosh see yov. Yov see motto sor divvus,
lesko pal tei, motto sas-ló. Doova see dooï lavaw ¢hidé
ketané.

Yov pootchtás mandi, "Too diktás (diktán) *a* moosh jal kova drom?"

Nanei too kek dad ta dei?   Merdé yon besh ghiás konáw.   Kon'*s* chavo shan too?   Maw rōv, tikno!

Doova see meeri deieski pen, meeri beebi.

Nanei pookerova toot avrí meero nogo mooí.

Lel kova tringorishi.   Maw nasher lesti.

Komova reiakana ta gaujikana jinomus.

I will tell you, sir, if I can.

Don't you hear, when I am speaking about those things?

That is a mumper's word.   They do not know the right Gypsy word, like our words.   They talk half bosh and half English.

Why do not you speak to me?   Speak, if you can.

I do not speak; I cannot understand it.

What a drunken man he is.   He is drunk all day long; his brother too was a drunkard.   That is two words joined together.

He asked me, "Did you see a man go this way?"

Have you no father or mother?   They died a year ago now.   Whose child art thou?   Don't cry, child.

That is my mother's sister, my aunt.

I will not tell you with my own lips (*lit.*, out of my own mouth).

Take this shilling.   Don't waste it.

I like aristocratic English learning.

Continued.

Kei jivela yov?   Yov jiv*s* tatch' aglál dova reiesko kair Yov jivdás mansa.

Sar door see doova tan?   Doovorí, doovorí.

Dik *folk*i, savo kisi starni 'glal dooveski kair.   Kon'*s* kair see doova?   See *a* bauro rei'*s* filisin.

Kova tan see pordo rookáw.

Besh tooki 'lé kon.

Jaw kater sooto, sar komessa.   O kam see besh'*d*.

Mook les bikonyo.

Diktassa too dova koova?   Our, diktóm dulla kola.

Te jinessa too dulla kola?   Our, pal, jinova sorkon kolli.
Doova moosh jindás-les.

Mook mendi jal, ta maur kanengré!   So dikessa palla?
Dikova o yogomengro; awela akei.

Nastís yov te latch lati.

Del lesti kater o grei.   Del lesti koosi kas te hol.

Mendi dióm o greiaw kas.

Maw kair toot jaw chorikanes.   Kek luva naneí lesti;
kek naneí mandi tei.   Kek naneí yov mauro.   So see yov
te kair?

Kanna meeri romni see shoovli, nastís yoi peerela.   Komova a divi gairi, ta o drabengro, te wel ta dik lati.

So mandi dova toot dova yek papin?   Dova toot trin
posh-kooroni lesti.

Mendi bikindás o grei kater dova yek moosh.

Lel ti jib, ta yoozher lesti (o roï).   Kosher ti wishtáw
konáw.

Kon kerdé-les.   Too shanas?   Kek mandi, lova meero
çovloholoben.

Where does he live?   He lives right opposite that
gentleman's house.   He lived with me.

How far is that place?   Very far indeed.

Look! what a lot of stags (there are) before that house.
Whose house is it?   It is a great gentleman's mansion.

This place is full of trees.

Sit down then.

Go to sleep, if you like.   The sun is set.

Leave it alone.

Did you see that?   Yes, I saw those things.

Do you know those things?   Yes, brother, I know
everything.   That man knew it.

Let us go and kill hares.   What are you watching?   I
see the gamekeeper; he is coming here.

He cannot find her.

Give it to the horse.   Give it a little hay to eat.
We gave the horses hay.
Don't make yourself so humble.   He has no money ; I
have none either.   He has no bread.   What is he to do ?
When my wife is *enceinte*, she cannot walk.   I want a
midwife and the doctor to come and see her.
What shall I give you (for) that single goose ?   I will
give you 7*s*. 6*d*. for it.
Take your tongue, and lick it (the spoon).   Lick your
lips now.
Who did it ?   Was it you ?   Not I, I will take my oath.

Continued.

Mi Doovelenghi, Chowali, maw kel ajáw.   Too trashela
mandi.
Maw kel ajáw.   Keressa too dova *a*popli, moonjerova
toot.
Moonjadóm lati's wast.   Jindás yoï so mandi ker'*d*.
Maw atch aglál mandi ajáw.   Mook man dikás.   Atch
pauli.
Choomerova toot te wel toot rinkeni.
Te wel yov akeí konáw, yov pooker asár mendi, so yon
penenna.
Yov peldás adré o paani kei o bairé jal*s*.
Hotcher o poryáw, adré o yog, talé o papin.
O poori joovel diás o wooda, ta o chei adré o kair pendás ,
" So komessa too, poori gairi ?"   Yoï pendás, " Choori poori
joovel shom mé."   (*Vide* Pasp., p. 582.)
Hokki, doosta gaujé wen akei *to* mendi.
Gaujé shoonenna men.   O gaujé see wel*in*'.   So mandi
kerova konáw.
Rak asár ti toovlo.   Righerova lesti, pensa mi yokaw*s*
adré mi shoro.
Diktóm leski yokaw pordo paani.
Keker mi yokaw te dikova yoï *a*popli.
Bissadás too doova biti lil, so pooker*s* toot o tatcho
laváw ?

Mandi bissadóm lesti.

Yon chivenna lesti opré o misali.

For God's sake, mates, don't do so. You frighten me.

Don't do so. (If) you do that again, I will pinch you.

I squeezed her hand. She knew what I meant (lit., did).

Don't stand in the front of me like that. Let me see.
Stand back.

I will kiss you if you are pretty.

If he were to come here now, he would tell us what they
say.

He fell into the river (lit., the water where the ships
sail).

Singe the feathers, in the fire, off the goose.

The old woman knocked (at) the door, and the girl in
the house said, "What do you want, old woman?" She
said, "I am a poor old woman." *Cf.* Pasp., 582.

Look out! A lot of strangers are coming here to us.

The Gentiles hear us. The Gentiles are coming. What
shall I do now?

Take care of your tobacco. I will keep it, like my eyes
in my head.

I saw his eyes full of tears.

May my eyes never see her again.

Did you forget that little book which tells you the right
words (*i.e., an English Dictionary*)?

I forgot it.

They put it on the table.

Continued.

Roker too avrí, jaw mandi *can* shoonova toot.

Roker shookés.

O ven see boot shilalo.

Mook mendi jal, *or* jalóm (*sic*) mendi, kater sooto.

Mendi dióm yon (*for* lendi,) kil ta mauro.

Dordi, doova's *a* tarno rei piriv*in'* *a* tarni rauni.

Yov see bitadér ta mandi,

O kam kedás mandi kaulo.   O kam see jaw tatto.

Yoï kek na kedás-les.   Yov pendás lati kek nanéi te kel ajáw.

Mandi shom kino.   Mandi besh'*d* alé, mandi shōmas jaw kino.   Mandi chor'*d* mandi adré o koppa, jaw shilalo sas mandi.

Soskí kedás-les talla?

Kei mendi jal *to* lel paani te pee?   Mandi jinova. Pardel kova stigher, talé dova poov, posh *o' a* bauro rook, 'doi see *a* rinkeno tan *o'* paani.   O paani vel avrí o hev odoi.

Kek naneí mandi *can* chiv meero wast jaw door see too.

Kei see mendi te jal te atch tedivvus?

Kanna vián tumendi akeí?

Viém akeí o waver Kooroko.

Kedé *a* bauro godli o waver divvus.

Kon sas doova?   Kek na jináw mé.

Pooker mandi choomoni te and tooti.

And mandi kon *a* koshto bauro matcho.   Kerova-les monghi *o'* kooroko divvus *to* mi hoben.

Yov kom'*d* asár lendi dooï sar yekera.

Yon ghién avri dooï ta dooï ketané.

Tardadóm-les talé.

Speak out, so that I can hear you.

Speak low.

The winter is very cold.

Let us go to sleep.

We gave them bread and butter.

Look, there is a young gentleman courting a young lady.

He is less than I.

The sun made me black.   The sun is so hot.

She did not do it.   He told her not to do so.

I am tired.   I sat down, I was so tired.   I wrapped myself in the blanket, I was so cold.

What did he do it for?

Where shall we go to get water to drink?   I know.

Over this gate, down that field, by the side of a big tree, there is a pretty spring. The water comes out of the hole there.

I cannot reach as far as you.

Where shall we go to stop to-day ?

When came ye here ?

We came here the other Sunday.

They made a great noise the other day.

Who was that ? I do not know.

Tell me something to bring you.

Bring me then a good big fish. I will cook it on Sunday for dinner.

He loved them both equally.

They went out two and two together.

I pulled him down.

Continued.

Kek yov mook mandi jal avrí. Kek yov komela man te roker *to* waver moosháw, jaw wafedo see-ló 'dré lesko zee. Yov pendás ta mandi jal*s* palla waver moosháw.

Maw wooser baryáw !

Rak tooti. Maw ker *a* hev adré o kooshni. Sor o koli pelela adrál lesti, tastís.

Yon hotchadé lenghi koli.

Yon bikindé o jookel kater dova rei.

Yon yoozhadé lenghi skrunya.

Yon rodé palla lenghi dei.

Yon merdé troostál o bogenya.

Yon ridadé lenghi kokeré tatcho mishto.

Yon pidé pensa matché.

Yon vién sor koordené mishto.

Yon atchté trin divvusáw adré dova tan.

Mendi shoondás sor yon pendé.

Yon pandadás opré dova trooshni *o*' koshtáw.

Yon andás mendi opré mishtó, pensa reiáw ta raunia.

Mookás mendi pootchás sor dulla *fol*ki.

Mookás sor mendi kerás opré o boshomengri.

Yon lié o moosh, talla yon chidé-les 'dré o steripen.

Chidé-len sor adré o steripen.

Yov azadás lesti opré.

Mendi shom sorkon cheerus kair*in' a* godli yek te waver.

Mendi see sorkon chairus chingerenna kater yek te waver.

He will not let me go out. He does not like me to speak to other men, he is so jealous. He said that I go after other men.

Don't throw stones.

Take care. Don't make a hole in the basket. All the things will fall through it, if they can.

They burnt their things.

They sold the dog to that gentleman.

They cleaned their boots.

They cried for their mother.

They died of the smallpox.

They dressed right well.

They drank like fishes.

They all got well beaten.

They stayed three days in that place.

We heard all they said.

They tied up that bundle of sticks.

They brought us up well, like gentlemen and ladies.

Let us ask all those people.

Let us all play on the fiddle.

They arrested the man, afterwards they put him in prison.

They put them all into the prison.

He lifted it up.

We are always making a row with one another. We are always quarrelling with one another.

To test the resemblance between the Turkish and English Gypsy dialects, we asked in English the following sentences taken at random from Dr. Paspati's book. The parallelism could be drawn much closer by carefully selecting corresponding English Gypsy words, but, on principle, we have preferred a Gypsy's own-language, even when unnecessarily discordant.

TURKISH-GYPSY.

Savó mas kaména [pl.]? (p. 75)

Asavké manushénde te na biknés. (75)

Me yaká na diklé asavké sukár romniá. (75)

Isí ohtó divés k' alióm avatiá. (74)

Sostar marghiás tut? (74)

Djanén so khuyazghióm tumén? [pl.] (74)

Sostar utchardán i khaníng? (74)

Terávas do pralén. (76)

Dinómas toot, ta na linánas len. (100)

Astardó i tchirikliá, ta tchindó la, pekló la, khaló la. (100)—[*Singular used.*]

Tavdé mas, khalé, pelé, sutté péske. (100)

Me, sar t' astaráv avaklé tchirikliá [*sg.*]? (104)

Leskere bal baré isás, ta umblavdó les opré ko karadjfl. (157)

Kamáma yek báli pái te piáv. (159)

Tu nána djanés, mo gadjó ka bandél man andré ko ker. (160)

O grast paravghiás po bandipé. (160)

Nánasti panlióm me yáka. (160)

ENGLISH-GYPSY.

Sávo mas too koméssa [*sg.*]?

Kek too bikin te jafra moosháw.

Meeri yokáw kekera dikté jafra rinkeno joovel

Dooï-stor divvus*es* (see) kanna mandi vióm akei.

So diás toot troostál?

Too jinessa so mandi kordóm toot troostál? [*sg.*]

Soski chordán too o hanik?

Mandi sas dooï paláw.

Mandi dióm lendi toot, ta kek naneí too lián len.

Yon tildás o chiriklo, chindás les shoro talé, chidé-les adré o koro, ta hodé-les.—[*Plural used.*]

Yon kerdé o mas, hodé-les, ghién talla kater woodrus, ghién lendi sor *to* sooto.

Sar see mandi te lel kolla chiriklé [*pl.*]?

Dosta balaw 'sas opré lesko shoro, ta yon pandadás-les opré o rook ta lesti.

Komova koro paani te pee.

Kek na jinessa too, meero rom pand*s* asár mandi opré adré o kair

O grei pogadás lesko shelo.

Kek mandi pandadóm m yokáw.

I raklí, ta sar ghelé péske, panliás pi vudár. (160)

Ovoklé divesénde, isás yek manúsh, ta terélas trinén raklién, penghiás, me kamadjáv polinàte, putcháva tuméndar, so kaméla tumar' oghí, t' anáv tuménghe. [*pl.*] (394.)

O rakli pandadás o wooda, kanna yon sor ghilé avrí. Adré kola divvusáw 'sas a moosh. Trin rakliaw sas yov. Yov pendás lendi. "Jalova kater o bauro gav. So komessa toot mandi te and pauli tooti [*sg.*]?"

New or Broken Dialect.

[*It is scarcely necessary to observe that there is no precise line of demarcation between the old and new dialects.*]

THE BENGAULER.

Mandi *never* dik'd a gaujo *to* roker Romanes, pensa *a Bengauler* mandi *once met in Derbyshire. We were* jal*in' along the* drom *with our* vardos, *and I was the* shorengro *and* mandi dik'd a moosh besh*in'* apré *a* stigher, *and his* mooī *was* kaulo pensa Romani-chal, *and he* pen'd *to* mandi, " Sar shan, pal?" *and I* dik'd *at* lesti, *and* yov kek pen'd variso *till some* gaujo*s* sar lenghi*'s* wardos *had* jal'd *past, and then I said, "Are you a* Romani-chal?" *and he* pen'd, "Kek, mandi shom *a* Bengauler. Mandi *didn't* kom *to* roker aglál dula gairi," *and then we* roker'd a bauro cheerus, *and* mandi jin'd sor yov pen'd. *So you* dik *the Bengaulers can* roker Romanes.

TRANSLATION.

I never saw a Gentile (able) to talk Gypsy like a Bengal man that I once met in Derbyshire. We were going along the road with our waggons, and I was the chief, and saw a man sitting on a gate, and his face was dark like a Gypsy. He said to me, " How are you, mate?" I looked at him, but he said nothing till some Gentiles with their

18

carts had gone past, and then I said, "Are you a Gypsy?"
He said, "No; I am from Bengal. I did not like to talk
before those men;" and then we talked a long time. I
understood all he said, so you see the Bengalese can talk
Gypsy.

THE THREE WORDS.

BY ISAAC M——.

Look here, Koko! *If* tooti '*ll* del mandi pansh koli,
mandi '*ll* pooker tooti trin lavyaw tooti *doesn't* jin.

"Keker, *my* pal. Kek *if* mandi jins lesti. Pooker
mandi so see *the* lavyaw adré Gaujines, *and* mandi '*ll bet
the five shillings* mandi jins Romanes *for* lendi."

"Ourli. Doova sec tatcho, *Ike.* Pooker *the* Rei 'dré
Gaujines *and* dik *if he doesn't* jin *the* Romanes."

"*Well,* Koko. Pooker mandi sar tooti'*d* pen, '*Put the
saddle and bridle on the horse, and go to the fair.*'"

"Chiv *the* boshto *and* solivardo 'pré *the* grei *and* jal *to the*
welgaurus."

"Doova '*s* kek sor tatcho, Koko. Mandi '*d* pen ' Dordi,
chawoli; jal *and* lel *the* boshto *and* solivardo. And *the*
vardo akei, *and* chiv *the* grei adré lesti *and* mook '*s* jal *to
the* welingaurus, *and have some* peiäs.' Doova '*s the* tatcho
drom *to* pen so mandi pootch'*d* tooti."

"*All right, Mr. H——; I see,* ' *six of one and half a dozen
of the other.' And what are the other words?*"

"Pooker mandi, Koko, so see *the Sun* adré Romanes."

"*The Sun. Well, I call that* Kam."

"Keker, Pal. *It's* Tam, *not* Kam. *And what's a
signpost?*"

"*A* siker-dromengro, *or a* sikermengro."

"*Well, a* sikermengro *might do, but that's a show. We
calls a signpost a* pookerin'-kosht, *but I see* tooti jins
doosta Romanes, *and (getting up to leave the tent) I dare
say as how you* jins *more* lavs *than any of* mendi, *but* ' *the
great secret' you'll never* jin. *Only* tatcheno Roman*ies* jin
DOOVA, *and they'll never* pooker TOOTI."

*[And off he went, leaving us to conceal our dis-
comfiture by cracking with the rest an old joke
on Freemasonry and red-hot pokers. After a
while, the moth returned to singe its wings a
little more in the candle, and was asked if there
were any more five-shillingworths of words we
did not know, and in reply we were asked,*

" Pooker mandi so see *a* beurus?"

"*A brewery ?*"

"*No ; a* beurus."

"*A* Livena-kel*in'* kair *?*"

"Keker ; *that's a brew-house. I said a* beurus.

"*Well, I don't know that word at all.*"

"*It's a parlour,* Koko. *The* shorokono tan *of the* kair,
I thought mandi'*d* latch choomoni tooti *didn't* jin, *besides*
' *the great secret,' and* tooti'*ll never get to* jin DOOVA."

TRANSLATION.

" Look here, old fellow (lit., Uncle) ! If you'll give me
five shillings, I'll tell you three words you do not know."

"Not I, my friend ; not if I know it. Tell me what are
the words in English, and I'll bet the five shillings I know
Gypsy for them."

"Yes, that's fair, Ike. Tell the gentleman in English,
and see if he does not know the Gypsy."

"Well, old boy. Tell me how you would say, ' Put the
saddle and bridle on the horse, and go to the fair.''

" *Chiv* the *boshto,* and *solivardo 'pré* the *grei,* and *jal* to
the *welgaurus.*" (Put the saddle and bridle on the horse,
and go to the fair.)

"That is not quite right, old cock. I would say, ' *Dordi,
chawóli, jal* and *lel* the *boshto* and *solivardo. And* the
vardo akei, and *chiv* the *grei adré lesti,* and *mook*'s *jal* to
the *welingaurus,* and have some *peias.*' (Hi, mates, go and
get the saddle and bridle. Bring the cart here, and put the
horse to, and let us go to the fair, and have some fun.)
That's the right way to say what I asked you."

" All right, Mr. H——; I see : six of one, and half a dozen of the other. And what are the other words ? "

" Tell me, old fellow, what the sun is in Gypsy."

" The sun. Well, I call that *Kam* (Sun).

" No, friend. It's *Tam*, not *Kam*. And what is a Signpost ? "

A *Siker-droméngro* (Show-road-thing), or a *Sikerméngro* (Shower)."

" Well, a *Sikerméngro* might do, but that is a Show. We call a Signpost a *Pookering-kosht* (a Telling-post), but I see you know plenty of Gypsy, and I dare say you know more words than any of us, but 'the great secret' you will never know. Only real Gypsies know *that*, and they will never tell *you*."

He went out, but returned not long after, and said,—

" Tell me, what is a *beurus* ? "

" A brewery ? "

" No, a *beurus*."

" A *Livena-kei*in'-*kair* (beer-making house) ? "

" No, that's a brew-house. I said a *beurus*."

" Well, I don't know that word at all."

" It's a parlour, old cock. The best room of the house. I thought I would find something you did not know, besides the 'great secret,' and you will never get to know *that*."

THE CHASE.

BY IKE M——.

You jin *Wester*, Koko. Lesko dad *was a* kooroméngro adré *the* kooromongri, *and he was killed by lightning*. Lesko dei *was a* Matcho. Romani-chals *used to* chin alé lenghi wongusht*ies then, so they wouldn't* 'press' *them. And they chased my* dad. A Kooromengro opré *a* grei wel'*d, and my* dad praster'd avrí, *and the* kooromengro kister'*d* palla lesti, *and my* dad lel'*d* talé *his* choχas, *and* hokter'*d* adré *the* paani, *and* jal'*d to the* wover rig, *and the* Kooromengro *had a* yogomeskro adré *his* wast, *and he*

hokter'*d* pardal *the* paani opré *his* grei, *and* wel'*d to my* dad
and pen'*d* 'Atch, *or* tooti '*s a* moolo moosh.'   *And some
used to* pander lenghi wongusht*ies with* dori, *and lime, and
soft soap, to* kair *them* bongo, *so they wouldn't* lel *them for
the* Kooromongri.

<h2 style="text-align:center">TRANSLATION.</h2>

You know Sylvester, mate.   His father was a soldier in
the army, and he was killed by lightning.   His mother
was a Herne.   Gypsies used to cut off their fingers then,
so that they would not 'press' them.   And they chased
my father.   A soldier on a horse came, and my father ran
off, and the soldier rode after him, and my father took off
his shoes, and jumped into the river, and swam to the opposite bank.   The soldier had a gun in his hand, and he
jumped over the stream on his horse, and came up with my
father, and said, "Stop, or you're a dead man."   Some used
to tie their fingers with string, and lime, and soft-soap, to
make them crooked, so that they would not take them for
the army.

<h2 style="text-align:center">IKE'S DOG.</h2>

BY IKE M——.

The Bauro Steripen'*s the Bailey* [the New Bailey,
Salford], Koko.   *And they* bitcher'*d me a* godli *for a*
jookel, *as they* pen'*d* mandi'*d* chor'*d*.   *But I didn't* chor
lesti.   *It was my* nogo jookel.   Mandi jin'*d* lesti *when it
was born*.   *And I* lel'*d* Mr. R——*s, the* rokeromengro, *to*
roker *for* mandi.   *And they* kair'*d* mandi pesser pansh bar
for the jookel, *and* lel'*d* lesti *from* mandi, *and* del'*d* lesti *to
the* Rei.   *And* mandi pesser'*d the* rokeromengro stor bar
more.   *And* yek divvus, *when* mandi *was* atch*in' over* odoí
by Belle Vue [pleasure-grounds near Manchester], *the* jookel
wel'*d to my* tan *a*popli.   *And when they* wel'*d, and* pen'*d
as* mandi *must* del *it* opré *a*popli, mandi pen'*d* 'Keker.
Mandi'*s* pesser'*d nearly* desh bar *for* lesti, *and* mandi'*ll*
kek del *it* opré.'   *And I* jal'*d to the* rokeromengro, *and* he

pen'*d they couldn't* lel *the* jookel, '*cause* mandi'*d* pesser'*d
the* pansh bar. *And* mandi righer'*d* doova jookel *a* bauro
cheerus, *and called it ' Bailey.'*

TRANSLATION.

The big prison is the New Bailey at Salford, mate.
They sent me a summons about a dog, which they said I
had stolen; but I had not stolen it. It was my own. I
had known it from a pup. I got Mr. R——s, the attorney,
to speak for me. They fined me five pounds for the dog,
and took it from me, and gave it to the gentleman. I
paid the attorney four pounds more.

One day when I was stopping yonder by Belle Vue
pleasure-grounds, near Manchester, the dog came back
again to my tent. They came, and said I must give it up
again. I said, " No; I have paid nearly ten pounds for it,
and I will not give it up." I went to the attorney, and he
said they could not take the dog, because I had paid the
ten pounds. And I kept that dog a long while, and called
it ' Bailey.'

' PUMPING.'

BY PHILIP M——.

Koliko raati, rei, door trin *o'* mendi'*s folki were* adré *the*
kitchema odof pardal *the* drom. *And a* rei *was* odoi *as
had* doosta luva *wi'* lesti, *and he was* posh motto, *and*
pootch'*d* mendi'*s folki to* dik lesti keri, *as he was* trash *he'd
be* loordo opré *the* drom. *And as they were* jalin' keri *wi'*
lesti *a* praastermengro wel'*d and* pen'*d, they was* kairin' *a*
bauro godli, *and were* sor motto. *And the* rei pen'*d they
were* kek motto, *and* pooker'*d* lesti *to* jal avrí lesti'*s* drom,
and mook *him* akonyo. *And the* praastermengro *wouldn't*
jal avrí *the* drom. Ajáw *the* rei lel'*d* lesti *by the* pikio,
and kair'*d* lesti jal avrí *the* drom. *And the* praastermengro
lel'*d him* opré *for* lesti, *and* pen'*d as he'd* 'assulted' *him.
But they* mook'*d the* rei jal keri, *and* pen'*d as they'd* bitcher

him a godli.   *And* mandi'*d* kom *to* jin, rei, *if the* pookinyus
will mook lesti roker *for his* kokero, *or must* lesti lel *a*
rokeromengro *to* roker *for* lesti.

TRANSLATION.

Last night, sir, two or three of us were in the inn there
across the road. A gentleman was there that had a good
deal of money with him; and he was half drunk, and asked
us to see him home, as he was afraid he would be robbed
on the road. As they were going home with him, a policeman came, and said they were making a great noise, and
were all drunk. The gentleman said they were not drunk,
and asked him to get out of his way, and leave him alone.
The policeman would not get out of the way, so the gentleman took him by the shoulder and made him get out of
the way. The policeman took him up for it, and said that
he had assaulted him; but they let the gentleman go
home, and said they would send him a summons. I want
to know, sir, if the magistrate will let him defend himself,
or must he get an attorney to defend him?

WAVER-TEMENGRI ROMANIES.

BY FENNIK P——.

Did mandi *ever* dik *any* waver temengri Roman*ies*, rei?
Our. Yekorus See *a* doosta besh*es* kenáw. Mandi sas *at*
Bury (*Lanc.*,) welgaurus, *and Wester Bossel, and Ike H——,*
and boot adoosta waver Roman*ies* tei. *And some* waver
Romani *folk*i sas odoi *as* mendi *didn't* jin. Yon atch'*d*
talé *a* bitto drom sor *by* lendi kokero*s*. *They were more*
copper like adré lendi mooľaw *dan* mendi *and* kek *as you*
might pen tatchi kauli *folki*. *They were* doosta barvali
folki—sor *with* roopni kolli*es and* sonakei—*wi'* bauri roopni
wangusht*ers* apré lendi vongushi*es and* adré lendi kanyáw
tei, *and* roopni kolli*es*, peemengri*es*, Koro*s*, shoodilaw, *and*
bauro vardo*s*, *and fin*o grei*s*, *and* roodo sor adré kaish,
*and wi' fin*o rivoben opré lendi dummos. Kavakei *folki*

were waver temengri Roman*ies, don't you* jin*é*ss, rei, *and had* lel'*d* sor kavodoi roopni koll*ies and* jaw kissi luva *by* panjer*in' the* gaujos. *They was a* waver *breed*open to mendi.

We were sor adr*é a* kitchema palla *the* welgaurus yek raati roker*in' about* kavakei *folki, don't you* jin*é*ss, *and Wester* kom'*d to* lel lendi *to* jal mensa. Yov *was beseen wi'* lendi roopni koll*ies, and* sonakei, *don't you* dikess, rei. *He* kom'*d to* roker *wi'* lendi, *but bless you,* rei, *he couldn't* jin posh *o*' sor lendi rokeropen. *They* roker'*d so deep, don't you* dik*é*ss. Yov jin'*d* dosta, *but* kek sor *o'* lesti, komod*á*ir *dan* sor mendi.

'*It'd be* mishto *to* lel lendi *to* jal mensa,' hotchov, '*they're such* barvali *folk*i' hotchov.

And mandi pen'*d to* lesti, 'Maw chiv *your* p*í*ko avr*í, they'll none* jal mensa—*they'll* kek *demean their* kokero*s to the likes o'* mendi—*they're* komodair *to* jal *wi'* kralis*ies, and* bauri rei*á*w, patsova toot,' hotchov.

Me*é*ro chor—kavake*í* tarno moosh ake*í met a* tarno *French*i Romani-chal yek cheerus *at Newcastle.* Yov'*d* kekeni romni, *or* vardo, *or* chav*ies wi'* lesti. Yov sas *a* tarno *un*romedo moosh—*a wild sort of a* tarno moosh. Yov roker'*d* dosta Romanes yov *didn't* jin.

And a waver cheerus mandi *was* adr*é the* Korengi-t*é*m, *and a* kaulo moosh sas odoi adr*é a* kitchema mendi atch'*d at. He was* hol*in*' kal-mauro *and* pee*in*' pobesko-livena. Kavake*í* moosh dik'*d at* mendi *a* bauro cheerus. 'Sarshan, pal?' hotchov—*as it might be your* kokero, rei, *to*-raati. "Sarshan, bor?" hotchov, "shan tooti Romani?"

"Kek, *I'm an Injun,*" hotchov.

"*Does* tooti jiness Romanes?" hotchov.

"Our, pal, doova'*s* mandi'*s* nogo chib," hotchov. *And we* roker'*d* ketnes *a* bauro cheerus; *and he didn't*·jin sor mandi pen'*d to* lesti, *don't yon* dik*é*ss, rei, *and* mandi *didn't* jin' sor leski'*s* lavy*á*w, *but* mandi jin'*d* dosta.

Mandi shoon'*d there were some* waver temengri Roman*ies* wel'*d to Epping Forest* doo*í* trin beshaw *ago, but* mandi

didn't dik *'em* mi kokero; *I only heared on 'em, don't you*
dikéss, rei.

Kavakeí moosh *has* wel'*d* adré *the French* tem. Yov'*s a*
Petalengro. *He* dik'*d the* Roman*ies* odoí, *but they don't*
roker *their* lav*s* tatcho pensa mendi *does; and when they*
wel*s to a* bauro gav *they* jal*s to the* shorokono praastermengro, *and* pen*s* ' mendi kom*s to* atch akeí *a* cheerus,' *and
the* moosh del*s* lendi trin stor divvus*es or a* kooroko *to* atch
and pooker*s* lendi kei *they're to* atch, *and* doova'*s* mishti*er
dan* akeí. *The* praastermengro*s* akeí kair mendi jal sar sig
as we atch *and* mandi'*s too* naflo *and* pooro *to* jal opré *the*
drom*s* sor *the* raati *when* mandi'*s* kino *and the* vardo'*s too*
bauro *to* jal opré *the* drom adré *the* kaulo raati*s, so* mandi
atch*es* akei opré *the* Kaulo.

Doova moosh odoí *as* mandi *was* rokeri*n' about* jivs adré
the gav akeí. Yov romer'*d a* gaují, *and* yov'*s a* barvalo
moosh ken*áw*, *and* leski'*s* romni kek jin*s a* lav *o'* Romanes
as ever I heared on.

FOREIGN GYPSIES.

BY PHŒNIX S——.

Did I ever see any foreign Gypsies, sir? Yes, once. It
is a good many years ago. I was at Bury Fair; and
Sylvester Boswell, and Isaac H., and a lot of other Gypsies
too. Some other Gypsies were there that we did not know.
They camped down a lane quite by themselves. They
were more copper-like in their countenances than we, and
not, so to speak, real black people. They were rather rich
folk, with all sort of gold and silver things, and big silver
rings on their fingers and in their ears too; and silver
articles—teapots, cups, and dishes; and large waggons, and
splendid horses; and they were dressed in silk from head
to foot, and had fine clothes on their backs. These people
were foreign Gypsies, don't you know, sir, and had got all
those silver articles and so much money by wheedling the
Gentiles. They were of another breed to us. We were all

in an inn after the fair one night, talking about these people, don't you know, and Sylvester wanted to get them to join us. He was dazzled by their gold and silver, don't you see, sir. He wanted to talk with them; but bless you, sir, he could not understand half of all their talk. They spoke so deep, don't you see. He understood a good deal, but not all; more, however, than any of us. "It would be a good thing to get them to join us," he said; "they are so rich," said he. I answered, "Don't put your shoulder out; they will never agree to join us. They will not condescend to join such as us. They are more likely to join kings, and lords, I believe you," said I.

My son, this young man, met a French Gypsy once at Newcastle. He had no wife, or waggon, or family with him. He was a young bachelor—a wild sort of a young fellow. He talked plenty of Gypsy my son did not understand.

And another time I was in Staffordshire, and a black man was there in an inn at which we halted. He was eating bread and cheese, and drinking cyder. This fellow stared at us a long while. "Sarshan, pal," (How do you do, friend?) said he, just as you might have done to-night, sir. "Sarshan, bor?" (How do you do, mate?) said I; "Are you a Gypsy?" "No, I am an Indian," said he. "Do you know Gypsy?" said I. "Yes, friend, that is my own language," he answered. We talked together for some time, and he did not understand all I said to him, don't you see, sir; and I did not understand all his words; but I understood sufficiently.

I heard there were some foreign Gypsies who came to Epping Forest two or three years ago; but I did not see them myself. I only heard about them, don't you see, sir.

This man has travelled in France. He is a Smith. He saw the Gypsies there; but they do not pronounce their words properly, like we do. When they arrive at a town, they go to the chief constable, and say, "We want to stop here for a time," and the man grants them leave to stay three or four days, or it may be a week, and tells them

where they must camp, and that is better than here. The
policemen here make us go as soon as we stop; and I am
too ill and old to travel all night when I am tired; and
my waggon is too big to travel during dark nights, so I
stay here on the Common.

That man that I was talking about lives in the town here.
He married a Gentile, and he is a well-to-do man now;
and his wife does not know a single Gypsy word, so far as
I ever heard.

THE POGADO SHERO.

BY ISRAEL P——.

Ourli! mandi's *bin to the* welgaurus *at* ——. *I* lel*ed* mi
shero poger'*d* odoi. *You can feel the* hev akei adré mi bal
still. It kair'*d me* divio *and I was* chiv'*d* adré *the* divio
kair. *It* dooker*s* mandi *still sometimes. How was it done?*
Why, a ratvalo gaujo opré *a* grei wel'*d* kester*in'* adrál *the*
welgaurus, *and I was* atchi*n'* odoi, *and he* pen'*d to* mandi,
"*You* ratvalo jookel, jal avrí *the* drom." (*He* roker'*d* lesti
adré gaujines *you* jin.) *And, without more ado, he up with a*
bauro chookni *he had* adré *his* wast, *and* del'*d* mandi *a*
knock with it opré mi shero. *It knocked* mi staadi *off, and*
poger'*d* mi shero, *and I* pel'*d* talé opré *the* poov, *and I was*
nasfalo *for a* bauro chairus, *and* jal'*d* divio, *and was* chiv'*d*
adré *a* divio kair, *and the* gaujo *never did nothing for* mandi.
The Beng te lel lesti. *He* kester'*d away, and* mandi *never*
dik'*d him* apopli."

TRANSLATION.

THE BROKEN HEAD.

Yes, I've been to the fair at ——. I got my head
broken there. You can feel the hole here in my hair still.
It made me mad, and I was put in the asylum. It hurts
me still sometimes. How was it done? Why a cursed
Gentile on a horse came riding through the fair, and I was
standing there; and he said to me, "You cursed dog, get
out of the way." He said it in English, you know. And,

without more ado, he up with a big whip he had in his hand, and gave me a knock with it on my head. It knocked my hat off, and cracked my skull, and I fell down on the ground, and I was ill for a long time, and went mad, and was put in an asylum, and the Gentile never did anything for me. The devil take him. He rode away, and I never saw him again.

INNOCENCE.

BY ISRAEL P——.

Keker, pal! mandi *didn't* jin *as they was* chordi kova*s*. *You* dik, *me and* mandi'*s* romni akéi jin'*d Bill, and* lesti'*s* romni wel'*d to* lati, *and* pen'*d, " Will you pawn these* koppa*s for* mandi?" *So she pawned 'em, you* dik, *and she* del'*d her a* trin-gorishi, *and then she* wel'*d* apopli, *and* pootch'*d her to* kin *the tickets, and she* kin'*d em, you* dik, *but she didn't* jin' *as the* koppa*s was* chor'*d. They wanted to make us ' fences,' you* jin, *without our* jin*ing it.*

TRANSLATION.

No, mate, I didn't know that they were stolen property. You see, I and my wife here knew Bill, and his wife came to *her*, and said, "Will you pawn these blankets for me?" So she pawned them, you see, and she gave her a shilling; and then she came again, and asked her to buy the tickets, and she bought them, you see; but she didn't know that the blankets were stolen. They wanted to make us ' fences,' you know, without our knowing it.

AN INQUIRY.

BY ISRAEL P——.

Keker, mandi *doesn't* jin —— *Sherratt.* Doova'*s* kek *a* Romani nav. *She must be a* choorodi. (To his wife)— *Mary,* av akei. Kova rei pens *as there's a* monoshi adré *the* divio kair *at* P—— *as he thinks is* 'posh *and* posh,'

and kek *a* moosh *has been to* dik lati *for a* besh kenáw.
He pen*s as* lati *was* beeno adré *Gloucester. Does* tooti jin
lati ?   Mandi jin*s Glossop, but* kek *Gloucester.*   Mandi
doesn't jin booti *about* kova *part of the* tem, *you* dik, rei.
Mandi wel*s from Yorkshire.* . . . Ourli, pal, mandi'*s* jiv*in'*
adré *a* kair kenáw, *'cause it's winter, you* dik.

TRANSLATION.

No, I don't know —— Sherratt.   That's not a Gypsy
name.   She must be a mumper.   (To his wife)—Mary, come
here.   This gentleman says that there is a woman in the
asylum at P——, whom he thinks is a half-breed, and not a
single person has been to see her for a year now.   He says
that she was born in Gloucester.   Do you know her ?   I
know Glossop, but not Gloucester.   I don't know much
about this part of the country, you see, sir.   I come from
Yorkshire. . . .   Yes, mate, I am living in a house now,
because it is winter, you see.

WELSH GYPSIES.

In September 1874 I met with a Welsh Gypsy, Oliver
Lee, at Bettws-y-Coed, North Wales.   His father was an
English Gypsy from the Midland Counties ; his mother
was one of the Woods, patricians amongst Welsh Gypsies.
He was born, and had always lived, in Wales ; was about
twenty-two years old, but, unlike most of the rising generation in England, he could converse in both deep and
broken Romanes, as well as Welsh and English.

He and his wife had just been joined by some of her
relatives, natives of Worcestershire, but Welsh by adoption ;
whose children spoke English with a Welsh accent, and
some of whom had married amongst the Welsh.

I gathered from Oliver that his two aunts, Mary Wood,
nicknamed Taw (W., silent), and Caroline Wood, both aged
about forty, spoke Romanes habitually, and only used
English or Welsh when talking to gaujos.

After satisfying myself of Oliver's knowledge of the old forms, I read to him "The Widow's Son," "The Licence,'' "Zuba B——," and "The Fairies," all of which he interpreted correctly to his companions, the eldest of whom seemed to have a hazy recollection of several of the verbal inflections, and kept exclaiming, "It's just as I used to hear the old folk talking when I were a lad." A reference to the stories themselves will indicate how far the deep Anglo-Romanes corresponds with the current Welsh-Romanes. We did not, however, think we were warranted in concluding that the dialects were so far distinct that we must exclude my notes from the vocabularies, and we therefore incorporated the following, as far as the advanced state of the printing of our dictionary was then practicable.

Gypsies are called in Welsh '*Gyptians, Gipsiaid,* and *Teulu Abram Hood* (A. H.'s family). The origin of the last term is obscure; possibly, *Hood* is *Wood* inflected. H. T. C.

Anitrákero (Anghiterrakero), *n.*, Englishman. A feminine genitive form.

Ker abba, Make haste.

*Bign*omus *o'* lilei, Spring (lit., *begin*ning of summer).

Bor, *n.*, Garden. Bourus, *n.*, Snail. *Bull*us, *n.*, Bull.

Kek chalavár mandi, Don't bother me.

Cham odoí, Halt ! ? From *atch ;* the termination seems anomalous.

Chinomongri, *n.*, One pound sterling ; cf., *chinda,* shilling, silver, Sim., 305, 333. A £1 *note* (now abolished).

Choro gono ; boot choro *for* mandi *to* righer *it.* A heavy sack ; too heavy for me to carry it.

Cherikléski por, Bird's tail. Dei-eski folki, Mother's people. Joovieski chuχa, Petticoat.

Desh*in'*, Praying.

Kek latcho see. Bishavo divéz see ke-divéz. It is not fine. It's a rainy day, to-day.

Dikóm o Beng ; diás opré adré o raati, I saw a ghost (lit., the devil) ; it appeared in the night.

Didás-les manghi, He gave it to me. Dino sas manghi, It
was given to me.

Eiävéla, *n.*, Understanding. Volunteered, in answer to my
inquiry for the Romanes of " I do not understand
you." ? 'Hi! he's coming!' (used as a signal.)

Yon ghiävenna, They are singing.

Godlieskro, *n.*, Bell.

Hev = minsh. *Hill*aarus, *n.*, Hill. Hingher = Hinder.

Hoχtamangro, *n.*, Toad. Holon, *n.*, Landlord.

Jinova monghi, I know. Mé jinova sor, I know everything.
Too jinessa sor, Thou knowest everything.

Jas amenghi, *or*, Jas asár menghi, *or*, Jolta, Let us go.

Lensa jas'*d* yoï, She went with them. Janna ti oχtén, They
will jump (lit., They are going to jump). Jom
odoï mi kokero, I went there alone. Yoï ghiás,
She went.

Kandela, It stinks.

Ke-divéz, To-day. Kaliko divéz, Yesterday. Ke-raati,
To-night. Kaliko raati, Last night. Ke-saula,
This morning. Kaliko saula, To-morrow morning.

Kerav o mas, Boil the meat. O mas see kedó, The meat
is boiled.

Komás (? komova) ti lá-les, I would like to have it.

Kesserova kek, *or* Kek kesserova monghi, I don't care.

Lakro, Hers. Jom lása, I went with her. Sōv lasa, coïre.
Jom lensa, I went with them.

'Doï see mauro, ta mas, ta lovína ; ta so see doï popli,
There is bread, and meat, and what is there besides.

Ladjer o moosh, Shame the man. Várter *how he* lullers,
Look! how he blushes. Lullerova, I am blushing.

Koro, Blind. Kurri, Tin. Mootska, Skin.

Nei-les kek lovo, He has no money.

Oχtenna, They jump. Janna ti oχtén, They will jump.

Kek pandóm okáw sor o raati, I never closed my eyes all
night.

Pardel mandi *for* yeka, Forgive me for once.

Pek o mas, Roast the meat. Pekova mas, I will roast the
    meat. O mas see pekó, The meat is roasted.
Poordas, Stairs. Stor-peerengro, Frog.
Repper toot, Remember.
Sastermangro, An iron-grey horse. *Slug*us, *n.*, Slug.
Shomas kino, I was tired. Shanas kinó, Were you tired?
    Sor kino shamas, We were all tired. Sor lendi
    sas kino tei, They were all tired too.
Sōv, *v.*, Coïre. Sooter, *v.*, To sleep.
Strangli, *n.*, Onion = poorumi.
Tarder, *v.*, To stretch. Tré o saula, In the morning.
Vartínimi, They are watching us.
Vissa *wi'* mandi talé koo kitchema? Will you go with me
    down to the inn?
Yov viás, He came. Sor mendi viám, We all came.
Kek mandi *can* roker Wolshitikka, I cannot talk Welsh.
    Wolsho, *n. pr.*, Wales. Wolshenengro, *n.*, Welsh-
    man.

Money.

Loli,	Farthing.
Posh-hori,	Halfpenny.
Hori, hauri,	Penny.
Door-, trin-, stor-, hori,	Twopence, threepence, four pence.
Pandj hori,	Fivepence.
Shōhauri, shookori,	Sixpence.
Trin-gorishi, koli,	Shilling.
Deshto-kori,	Eighteenpence.
Pansh-kolaw, koorona,	Crown, five shillings.
Posh-koorona,	Half-crown.
Balans, bar,	Sovereign, pound.
Posh balans,	Half-sovereign.
Kótor,	Guinea.
Posh-kótor,	Half-guinea.
Panshengro,	Five-pound note.

APPENDIX.

Bibliography.

After 19th line, insert,—1547, Boorde, Dr. Andrewe, "The first Boke of the Introduction of Knowledge, made by Andrew Boorde of Physyche Doctor," reprinted 1870, edited by F. J. Furnivall, M.A., Trinity Hall, Cambridge, and published for Early English Text Society, by Trübner and Co., London; p. 218. See also "The Academy," July 25th, 1874, p. 100. "The earliest known Specimen of the Gypsy Language," by F. J. Furnivall.

NOTE.—The specimen referred to occurs in Chapter xxxviii., which "treteth of Egypt, and of theyr mony and of theyr speche," and comprises thirteen sentences in all, which we insert here *in extenso*:—

Good morrow! *Lach ittur ydyues!*
How farre is it to the next towne? *Cater myla barforas?*
You be welcome to the towne. *Maysta ves barforas.*
Wyl you drynke some wine? *Mole pis lauena?*
I wyl go wyth you. *A vauatosa.*
Sit you downe, and dryncke. *Hyste len pee.*
Drynke, drynke, for God sake! *Pe, pe, deue lasse!*
Mayde, geue me bread and wyne! *Achae, da mai manor la veue!*
Geue me fleshe! *Da mai masse!*
Mayde, come hyther! harke a worde! *Achae, a wordey susse!*
Geue me aples and peeres! *Da mai paba la ambrell!*
Much good do it you! *Iche misto!*
Good nyght! *Lachira tut!*   (Pp. 217, 218.)

That Boorde collected these phrases from Gypsies, and not from "Egipcions," no one who knows anything about the language can have the slightest doubt. His description, moreover, of the people is very graphic :—

19

"The people of the country be swarte, and doth go disgisyd in theyr apparel, contrary to other nacyons; they be lyght fyngerd, and vse pyking; they haue litle maner, and euyl loggyng, & yet they be pleas(a)unt daunsers. Ther be few or none of the Egipcions that doth dwell in Egipt, for Egipt is repleted now with infydele alyons."

It may also be safely assumed that Boorde obtained his examples from *English* Gypsies, seeing that a trace of English is evident in combination with Gypsy proper. Thus in his tenth sentence occurs the expression "*a word*ey susse (tusa) = *a word* with thee. Most of Boorde's sentences have been dissected and explained in a previous portion of our work. According to Professor Miklosich, to Dr. Zupitza of Vienna, belongs the honour of having first recognized the true character of our English Doctor's examples of "Egipt speche,' which are admitted to be the oldest known specimens of the Gypsy language.

It is a curious circumstance that modern research should be indebted to two of our own countrymen for the earliest ethnographical and linguistic data which have been found relating to the Gypsy race. The first historical reference to the Gypsies occurs in the work of an Irishman, entitled "Itinerarium Symonis Simeonis et Hugonis Illuminatoris ad Terram Sanctam," primus eruit ediditque Jacobus Nasmith, A.M., S.A.S., Cantab., MDCCLXXVIII., Ex. Cod. MS., in Bibliotheca Coll. Corp. Christi Cant., No. 407. Simon Simeon vel Simeonis (Fitz Simeon, in the vernacular), 'was a Minorite of the rule of St. Francis, of a Convent established in Dublin, from which city, in company with another friar, Hugh the Illuminator, he commenced his pilgrimage on the 15th of April, 1322.' He informs the readers of his Itinerary, in somewhat Quixotic language, that having 'despised the summit of honour,' he was 'inflated with the Seraphic ardour of visiting the Holy Land.' (*Vide* "Retrospective Review," 2nd Series, vol. 11, pp. 232—254.) On their way the two friars made a short stay in the island of Crete, where, it appears, they saw the Gypsies, whom Fitz-Simeon described in a passage to which Bryant originally directed attention. M. Bataillard, of Paris, has recently pointed out that it referred to the island of Crete, and not to Cyprus, as had been previously supposed. There are some small verbal inaccuracies in Bryant's transcript of this passage, which would be scarcely worth indicating if they had not been repeated by most subsequent writers, who seem not to have verified the quotation by consulting the prime authority. The passage taken verbatim from Nasmith, the first and last editor of the "Itinerarium," (p. 17, lines 21—31,) stands thus : " Ibidem et vidimus gentem extra civitatem ritu Græcorum utentem, et de genere Chaym se esse asserentem, quæ raro vel nunquam in loco aliquo moratur ultra xxx dies, sed semper velut a deo maledicta vaga et profuga post xxxᵐ diem de campo in campum cum tentoriis parvis oblongis nigris et humilibus ad modum Arabum, *et* de caverna in cavernam discurrit; quia locus ab *eis in*habitatus post dictum terminum efficitur plenus vermibus et *aliis* immunditiis, cum quibus impossibile est *co*habitare."

Page 5, after 14th line, insert: 1874.—"The Times," July 21, 2nd col., p. 1, an announcement in Romanes of Mr. Hub. Smith's marriage to Esmeralda Lock; repeated in "The Guardian," July 22;—also, "Illustrated London News," October 31, p. 214, an announcement in Romanes of Romany Ballads, by Prof. Palmer, Mr. Leland, and Miss Tuckey.

Grammar.

NOUN.

Page 14.—After paragraph commencing "Besides," add "According to M. Vaillant, (Grammaire Rommane, Paris, 1868, p. 37,) the Roumanian Gypsy noun forms its genitive in -esko, *m.*, -eski, *f.*, and the genitives of the pronouns (40) are *sing.*, manki, tuki, leski, laki; *pl.*, amenki, tumenki, lenki; while the possessive adjectives (41,) are *sing.*, maro, tiro, lesko, amaro, tumaro, lengo; *pl.*, miri, tiri, leski, amari, tumari, lenj'i. The agreement in this respect, as otherwise, between the two dialects is remarkable."

Page 15, line 14.—*Akoro.*, *vide* Anitrakero (Anghiterra-kero), Welsh Gypsy. Also in the two insults, Ti doki hev (Lieb., dakri), and Mi booliokri.

Page 16.—*Plural.*—Sometimes the plural ends in *i*, and probably results from a softening of the final *é* sound, which is a common plural termination in the deep dialect.

Page 21.—*Nouns peculiar to the dialect.*—We have since met with several of these words in foreign Gypsy Vocabularies.

Page 22.—After *Class I.*, read, "Similar terminations forming abstract nouns are frequent in the Roumanian Gypsy dialect; *vide* Vaillant."

ADJECTIVE.

Page 23.—Rankano (fornem) and kiska (god) occur in Sundt. Latcho is inserted in our vocabulary, but we have only met with it once (*vide* Welsh Gypsies). On one occasion we heard an English Gypsy use Tatcho divvus for Kooshto or Latcho divvus. Lachi and comp. Lachittur are met with in Boorde.

VERB.

Page 35.—Av, Rov, Siv, Sov, Tov, etc.
   Av-ava, *Rov*-ava, *Siv*-ava, etc.
According to some authorities, the first *v* in these verbs really forms part of the root (*vide* Pasp., Pott, etc.) A comparison with the Sanscrit supports this view.

Page 36.—To follow 15th line. 1st pers., pl., -*ása*, -*ás*. We have met with the forms -*assa*, -*as*, -*essa*, for the 1st pers., pl., pres. and fut., e.g., *Doi mendi atchessa*, or *atchassa*. There we will stop.

Page 37.—We have met with several examples of the 1st pers., pl., of the perfect ending in *dém*, e.g., *koordém* (*koordo* + *shem*), We fought. *Chidém (chido + shem,)* We put.

Page 40.—To follow Past Participle:—

The *Passive voice* is formed, in deep Romanes, by the past participle preceded by one of two auxiliary verbs.

1st. By the verb to be, *shom, shan, see*, etc., q.v.

Examples.

Mandi shom mooklo sor kokero, I am left all alone.
Yov sas dikno, He was seen.
Yov sas anlo apré adré dova tem, He was brought up in that country.

2nd. By the verb to become, *'wel, 'vel,* etc., q.v., especially when the future is to be expressed.

Examples.

O grei te vel paulo, The horse will be pounded.
Mandi te vel kerdo, I shall (or should) be done (for).

Compare *'vel* and *'wel* with Dr. Paspati, page 80. *Uvav(a), Uves(a), Uvel(a),* etc. Dr. Paspati first pointed out the existence of the verb *Uvava,* to become, which had always been previously confounded with *Avava,* to come.

PRONOUNS.

Pages 42, 43.—The promiscuous use of dative and accusative forms for the accusative is also met with in the German Gypsy dialect (*vide* Liebich, p. 102).

The pronoun in the dative is frequently found following verbs, and then apparently often partakes of the nature of a reflective pronoun, *e.g.,*—

Besh-tooki 'lé, Sit yourself down.
Hoxter-tooki, Jump ; *Praster-tooki,* Run.
Holova-les monghi, I will eat it myself.
Ghiás-peski, He took himself off.

See Pasp., *e.g.,* p. 608, sentence 40, *kamadjáv mánghe, je m'en irai.*

Dictionary.

The following words were omitted, or have been since collected :—

Booïnóva, *v.,* I boast. See Booïno
  He booïns *his* kokero, He praises himself. Note:
   Booïnelopus, p. 61, is probably Booïnela pes
Dikomengri, ⎫
Diksomengri, ⎬ Watchers, watchmen
Dikomeskro hev, Window

Dooīeni, Second
Gaveskro (gavengro), Policeman
Jindo moosh, Scholar
Kitchemeskro, Innkeeper
Klisinomengro, Lock
Koosh, *n.* and *v.*, Lie, falsehood ; *cf.* Pasp., *kushipe*
Moskro (mooshkero), Constable
*Mump*arus, Mumper
Okki, add "(hokki); *cf.* Pasp., *akā*, ceci
    Okki, lel-les tooti, Here! take it !
    Okki, *a* rei wela 'kei, Look out, there is a gentleman
      coming here ! "
Panomeskri-gav, Watering-place
Peker, *v.*, To roast ; Pekedo, *p. part.*, Roasted
Raatenghi kova, Nitre
Roomus, Romanes
Shoonomus, } News
Shoonopén, }
Stanyamengro, Stableman
Staromeskri*es*, Prisoners
Spongo, Match
Tatchomus, Truth
Tatti-peerengri, Irish, *i.e.*, hot (blooded) tramps
Trashermengro-kova, Lightning
Tilomeskro, Pot-hook
Weshenghi-chiriklo, Wood-pigeon.

See also the following Tales.

Genuine Romany Compositions.

[Want of space prevents our giving Translations.]

THE BALL.

Né chavoli, too jassa mansa kater dova bitto welgauro
tedivvus? Mandi jinova yek koshto kair adré o bitto gav

—shorokono kair see—kei see bauro kel*in'*-kamora. Pendás
o rauni kate*r* mandi o waver divvus, te wel te yoi'*s* kair te
bosher opré o welgauro divvus, yoi dela mandi posh-kotor,
ta sor meero hoben, ta piamus, te atchova odoi sor raati, te
wel mé te komova. Too wel mandi, too lela posh so mandi
lelova. Bosherás too mansa?

Our. Jova mé toosa. Nastís mandi bosherova *sar*
koshto sar too, jinéss. Mandi kairova o feterdér tastís.

Ava-tá kon! Jaw menghi!

"Sar shan, Rauni?"

"Sar shan," hotchi yoi. "Too viás kon?"

"Our, Rauni."

"Lelessa tumendi chomoni te hol, wonka too jala opré
te kel?"

"Our, Rauni, sar koméssa, parikeráw toot."

Beshtém mendi talé 'glal o misali. Dosta hoben sas
opré lesti. Hodém ta pidém, so mendi komdás. Talla
mendi ghiém opré o pōdas. Boshadém koosi. Kanna-sig
dosta ta dosta raunia ta reiáw vién adré. Komdé men
mishto. Boshadém adré dova kamora sor raati. Yon
keldé sor o raati mishto tei, raunikana dromáw (*quadrilles,
valses, etc., not hornpipes*). Mendi kedém mishto lendi tei.
Talla mendi kedé bosher*in'* lendi, yon, ta o shorokono rei,
del'*d* mendi pansh kotoráw. Pendé te mendi. "Waver
cheerus mendi wela akei." *A* vaver besh mendi kelova
lendi *a*popli.

A PRACTICAL JOKE.

Yekera, kanna tarno tatcho rinkeno dikomusti chavo sas
mé, ghióm kater *a* rauneski loobno kair. Ridóm mi kokero
adré tarno joovel'*s* rivomus. Pandadóm meero kokero opré
tatcho, pensa rinkeno tarno joovel. Meero bal sas boot
opré mi shoro, dosta lesti, sar woose*red* pardál meeri piké.
Kaulo sas, pensa chiriklo'*s* porya*s*.

Kanna sig yek *o*' lendi pootchdás mandi, te atch opré ta
kel. "Our," hotchi yoi, "mandi jinova sor teero *folk*i
kelela mishtó."

Talla mandi atchdás opré te kerova *wi*' lendi. Kanna
yon dikté (sar) mandi ker'*d*, yon pendé kater mandi, "Kek
naneí too *a* joovel, too keressa 'jaw mishto. Kek tarno
joovel kerassa pensa too. Too see *a* moosh, tatcho dosta.
Dikova tei." Vién kater mandi. Tardadé meero choχa
ta shooba opré. Talla dikté mooshkeni rivopen opré
mandi, sor o kair *o*' lendi sadé koshto dosta te maur lenghi
kokeré.

Talla yon dela mandi sorkon kova, mol, ta tatto paani,
ta vaniso te piova, komdé mandi 'jaw boot. Yon pendé,
kekera yon dikté jafra kova kedo ajáw adré lenghi
meriben.

THE PUGILIST.

Kanna shom (shōmas) mé tarno moosh, kek na kessadóm
troostál vaniso moosh, bitto *o*' bauro. Feterdér sas o moosh,
feterdér mandi komdé lesti. Kek mandi charer*ed* o bitto
moosháw. Naneí lendi koshto dosta mandi.

Mandi jindóm koorova vaniso moosh, gaujé ta Romani-
chaláw. Mandi shōmas o feterdér bitto moosh adré [o]
Stor Temáw. Kek-komeni koorela man. Yon sor jindás,
(*or* jindé) dova.

Kanna yon diké man, yon penenna yek *to* waver, "Kova
see o feterdér bitto moosh troostál sor moosháw *so ever*
diktóm. Jaw sig si-ló adré lesko koori*n*'. Yov dela troostál
lesti wastáw, pensa o bitto grei. Kek yov kesser*ed* [*for*]
kek moosh so yov koordás. Yov koordás sor o feterdér
Romani-chaláw adré lesko temáw." Yov penela konáw, te
pooro si-lés, yov koorela vaniso pooro moosh adré Anghiterra. Lesko nav see jinlo mishto kater sorkon Romani-
chaláw. Yov penela lesko kokero, keker naneí yov koordno.
Kek moosh adré Anghiterra, kek naneí koordás lesti adré
sor leski meriben.

Yek Romano moosh koordás te lesti, chiv'*d* lesti avrí
lesti jinomus bitto koosi chairus. Yov atchdás opré popli
te koor yov, *but* kek o waver moosh wela, ta lesti [o Romano

moosh] ghiás kater Drabengro te ratcher (*bleed*) lesti, keker
o Drabengro kela 'jaw, yov koordno sas 'jaw wafedo.

WHY WESTER WON'T EAT MUTTON.

Mandi shōmas yekera adré o lileí jala (*going*) pardál o
poovyáw. Diktóm bokrengro (*or* bazengro), kooser*in'* te
yoosherela bokré. Sor sas (*or* si-lé) pardál wafedé tanáw,
sor pardál lenghi shoré, ta lenghi piké, posh hodno talé, ta
kandás pensa *a* hindo-kair. O bokrengro sas draber*in'* *o'*
lendi, te sor [*had*] koli (*rags*) chiv'*d* pardál lenghi shoré.
Yov sas draber*in'* *o'* lendi, pensa o wafedo hotchado moosh.

Talla dova mandi pendóm, kek mandi hola bokro'*s* mas
kek-komi, vonka mé jiv.

(Note to page 197, line 20.)

Gypsies everywhere evince a strong love for music, but
their talents in this respect appear to greater advantage in
foreign lands than in this country. With our English
Gypsies the favourite instruments are the tambourine and
the 'boshomengri,' or fiddle, especially the latter, and we
know several good executants on the strings. One of the
most gifted and renowned violinists among the Gypsies, in
recent times, was a man named Horsery Gray, who died
some years ago. We have been told by a Romani-chal that
when Horsery had heard a tune he could play it off straightway, putting in such " variations, grace-notes, shakes, and
runs," that none of his *confrères* could compare with him.
He played entirely by ear, and not from notes. The gaujos
sent for him from long distances to hear his hornpipes.

When an old acquaintance of ours, Charley Boswell, lost
a favourite child, he refused to be comforted, abstained
from food, becoming much emaciated in consequence, and
spent all his time for several weeks after the child's
death in playing on his fiddle. He seemed to find his only
consolation in confiding his grief to his instrument, and

touching chords which responded in sympathy with his own sad mood.

The Gypsy is always foremost among the "feast-finding minstrels" which attend our English fairs and country wakes. He is to be seen in his glory at a 'kelopen' or frolic, when the mirth grows fast and furious, as with flashing eyes and excited mien he flourishes his fiddle-bow and plays the music which keeps in time the flying feet of the dancers. The Gypsy girls are not averse to air their accomplishments on these occasions, and exhibit the same lightness of toe and natural grace which are said to distinguish their continental sisters. Highly favoured is the village swain who has a "dark ladye" from the tents for his partner in the dance.

There are no English tunes with which we are acquainted which can be said to be peculiarly Gypsy. The Abbé Listz has made an extensive collection of Gypsy airs in the Slavonic provinces of the Austrian Empire, where Gypsies abound. "The natives dwelling on the Danube —Hungarians, Moldavians, Slavonians, Wallachians, and others—owe their music to the Gypsies, . . . and many of their melodies have become the national airs of those countries. Their music has been principally developed on the hospitable soil of Hungary, and from thence it has spread all over the Danubian Principalities. The Magyars have adopted them as their national musicians, and there is hardly a village without their minstrels called Lautars." —*Vide* Preface to "Gypsy Melodies, etc.," by Charles K. Laporte (London, Augener and Co.); also, "Die Zigeuner und ihre Musik in Ungarn, von Franz Listz.

CORRIGENDA.

Page
55, for 'Bangarée' read 'Bángaree'
71, line 10, for '*-shtó*' read '*-ohtó*'
75, „ 16, for 'navel' read 'umbilical cord'
81, „ 14, add '*cf.* Lieb., *grisni*, das Gericht, das Amt'
88, „ 20, for '*jäudärdka*, shawl,' read '*jändärdka*, Frauenrock'
95, „ 6, after '*adj.*,' add 'and *pron.*'
95, lines 18, 19, 20, cancel from 'Pasp.' to 'alone,' and substitute 'Pott, ii., 107'
98, line 19, for '? Pasp., *tchárdava*' read 'Pasp., *akaráva*'
101, „ 25, for 'ládipen' read 'ladjipen'
103, „ 8, *dele* 'her'
113, „ 10, for 'it' read 'is'
114, „ 11, for 'ler' read 'les (lesti)'
124, lines 4 and 5, should be in the first margin
131, line 24, for 'road' read 'rōd'
133, „ 17, add 'ill'; line 22, for '*dísiolo*' read '*dísiola*'
134, „ 3, for 'are to us' read 'are (have) we'
137, „ 2 from foot, for 'ken sigáw' read 'kenáw sig'
141, „ 7, for '*stiéf*' read '*stief*'
147, „ 1, for 'ková' read 'kóva'; and line 8, for 'dová' read 'dóva'
151, „ 23, for '*éla*, come!' read '*aváva*, to come; *uváva*, to become'
189, „ 9, *dele* ',' after 'divvuses'
195, „ 21, for 'dsiturb' read 'disturb'
219, „ 9, for 'Doovolesko' read 'Doovelesko'
220, „ 7, for 'tootí' read 'tooti'
230, „ 5, for 'toti' read 'tooti'
235, „ 23, for 'meeripen' read 'meripen'
237, „ 2 from foot, *dele* 'a'
238, „ 16, for 'bar' read 'bor'
245, „ 19, after 'grass' add ')'

INDEX.

Watson & Hazell, Printers, London and Aylesbury.

CPSIA information can be obtained at www.ICGtesting.com
Printed in the USA
BVOW01*0313310114

343350BV00009B/478/P